Ireland and migration in the twenty-first century

MARY GILMARTIN

Manchester University Press

Published by Manchester University Press
Altrincham Street, Manchester M1 7JA

www.manchesteruniversitypress.co.uk

British Library Cataloguing-in-Publication Data
A catalogue record for this book is available from the British Library

Library of Congress Cataloging-in-Publication Data applied for

ISBN   978 0 7190 9775 1   paperback

First published 2015

Typeset in Sabon and Gill by
Servis Filmsetting Ltd, Stockport, Cheshire
Printed in Great Britain
by Bell & Bain Ltd, Glasgow

Ireland and migration in the twenty-first century

Manchester University Press

Contents

Figures and tables

Acknowledgements

I grew up in a place marked by migration, but my interest in the study of migration began when I returned to Ireland in 2003, after almost a decade of living elsewhere. This book is my attempt to make sense of the changes I have experienced since then. It is a work of slow scholarship, and it has been influenced, inspired and encouraged by many people whom I wish to acknowledge. I wrote the first draft of the book while on sabbatical in 2013. Thank you to Maynooth University and the Department of Geography for facilitating the sabbatical and to my hosts at the Max Planck Institute for the Study of Religious and Ethnic Diversity, Göttingen, Germany for providing a hospitable and stimulating work environment.

Maynooth University continues to be a supportive place to work. Thanks to present and former colleagues in the Department of Geography and National Institute of Regional and Spatial Analysis – Mark Boyle, Ronan Foley, Rob Kitchin, Ro Charlton, Sinéad Kelly, Adrian Kavanagh, Steve McCarron, Conor Murphy, Shelagh Waddington, John Sweeney, Paddy Duffy, Proinnsias Breathnach, Dennis Pringle, Rory Hearne, Jennifer Lloyd-Hughes, Conor McCaffrey, Cian O'Callaghan, Gill Scott, Bettina Stefanini, Chris van Egeraat – for creating a pleasant work environment. Particular thanks to Neasa Hogan and Rebecca Boyle for infusing workdays with good sense and laughter, and to Kylie Jarrett and Anne O'Brien for their critical friendship. I have also had the pleasure of working with outstanding postgraduate researchers on migration – Angela Armen, Elaine Burroughs, Steven Lucas, Siobhan McPhee, Zoë O'Reilly, Áine Rickard and John Watters – and I appreciate all they have taught me.

Before Maynooth, I had the good fortune of working with colleagues who have become friends and research collaborators. I am very grateful to both Bettina Migge and Allen White, with whom I have worked on a range of migration-related projects and who are always a pleasure to work with. Thanks also to Piaras Mac Éinrí, Caitríona Ní Laoire,

David Ralph, Bryan Fanning and Ronit Lentin for their commitment to collegiality in migration research. I also want to acknowledge the support of Eleonore Kofman and Parvati Raghuram (from Nottingham Trent University), and Niamh Moore, Arnold Horner, Willie Nolan, Stephen Hannon, Stephanie Halpin, Joe Brady and Anne Buttimer (from University College Dublin – UCD). My time as a migrant began at the University of Kentucky, where I learned about friendship and geography from a diverse and wonderful group of people, especially Carole Gallaher, Susan Mains, Vincent Del Casino, Stephen Hanna, Owen Dwyer, Jamie Winders, John Paul Jones, Karl Raitz, Priya Rangan and Sue Roberts. Since then, my community of supportive geographers has extended to include Lawrence Berg, Jason Dittmer, Rob Wilton, David Conradson, Soren Larsen, Michael Brown, Divya Tolia-Kelly, Ayona Datta, Deirdre Conlon, Robina Mohammad, James Sidaway and Elaine Ho, so thank you for helping this book project in a variety of ways.

Across Maynooth University, I am grateful to friends and colleagues who have shared my interest in migration or who have provided necessary distractions: Caroline Ang, Chris Brunsdon, Martin Charlton, Mary Corcoran, Úna Crowley, Oona Frawley, Sinead Kennedy, Aphra Kerr, Kay MacKeogh, Rebecca King-O'Riain, Aileen O'Carroll, Stephen O'Neill, Jeneen Naji, Stephanie Rains and Gavan Titley. Thanks to the Research Development Office, and to Bernard Mahon and Ray O'Neill, for their support for research projects that I discuss in the book, and to the Irish Research Council and the Immigrant Council of Ireland for research funding. I would also like to thank Justin Gleeson and Aoife Dowling (AIRO), Ciarán Quinn and Padraic Stack (Maynooth University Library), Michelle Dalton, Jane Nolan, and Daniel Montes (UCD Library) and David Monahan for their help in sourcing and preparing illustrations, and staff at Manchester University Press for supporting the publication of the book.

Special thanks to family and friends who have lived with the idea of this book for a long time. In particular, thanks to Eoin O'Mahony for unflagging support and encouragement and entertainment, and to Gerald Mills, Maeve O'Connell, Patrick O'Keeffe and Breege Gilmartin for friendship beyond the call of duty. I'm also grateful for the friendship of John Deignan, Paul Rouse, Gary Younge, Stephen and Ann Rigney, Claire and Kevin Hargaden, Laura Canning, Sheamus Sweeney, Dervila Layden, Nancy O'Donnell, Kieran Rankin, Charles Travis and the Kates, and for the Monday night escape provided by Paula, Eileen and Gillian. Thank you to the extended Gilmartin, Cunningham and O'Mahony families (Kathleen, Ken, Karen, Ciara, Áine, Aisling, Niall, Caoimhe, Ella, John, Neil, Brian, Angela, Felix) for providing regular reminders of life outside a book. I trust this meets Áine's instruction to write about something less boring. As with any book on migration, I am very aware of those who, in the words of poet Kevin MacNeil, are here and are not here. I hope the book does them justice.

Abbreviations

CSO	Central Statistics Office
EEA	European Economic Area
ESRI	Economic and Social Research Institute
GAA	Gaelic Athletic Association
ICI	Immigrant Council of Ireland
INIS	Irish Naturalisation and Immigration Service
IRCHSS	Irish Research Council for the Humanities and Social Sciences
MRCI	Migrant Rights Centre Ireland

I

Introduction

Ireland is a place profoundly shaped by migration. In *A Book of Migrations*, her wonderful travel account, Rebecca Solnit uses Ireland as a site to reflect on the meaning of identity and place. She describes Ireland as 'a good place to think about it all' because of its long history of migration, where 'tides of invasion, colonization, emigration, exile, nomadism and tourism' have all shaped the country (Solnit 1998: 6–7). Solnit moves around Ireland, expecting to find a 'homogenous, predictable, familiar world', but instead reaching a state of inconclusiveness (Solnit 1998: 167–8). Her encounters with Irish Travellers, a group she saw as organised 'by contemporary networks rather than historical taproots', proved most unsettling to her expectations (Solnit 1998: 158). Her book serves a similar purpose. It unsettles our sense of identity as being fixed in and to place, and shows how migration – of people, things and ideas – transforms places and identities in an ongoing way.

Solnit's account of the complex and changing relationship between migration, place and identity is at odds with other, more official attempts to fix meaning. For example, *The Gathering* was an Irish government initiative held during 2013. It brought together festivals, concerts, seminars, family reunions and a range of other events under one convenient label, and used it as part of a marketing campaign to encourage members of the Irish diaspora to visit Ireland. *The Gathering* was advocated as a celebration of global Irishness. Despite its claims to inclusiveness, though, *The Gathering* displayed a particular and limited understanding of Irishness. The activities it highlighted mostly represented a traditional understanding of Irish culture, its website had a strong emphasis on history and genealogy, and its advertising campaigns predominantly featured white people. It tapped into a romanticised view of Ireland: beautiful natural landscapes, ancestral home of far-flung families, traditional music and dance, and 'the uniquely Irish sense of fun' (The Gathering 2013). In painting this picture, however, it conveniently evaded the reality of life in contemporary Ireland. In the most recent Census, which took place in 2011, over 700,000 people – 15.5 per cent of the population – did not describe themselves as 'White Irish' (CSO 2012a). Around 12 per cent of Irish residents in 2011 had a nationality other than Irish (Gilmartin 2012), and many worked in the tourism and retail sectors, areas that were central to the success of *The Gathering*. Contemporary Ireland is multiethnic and multiracial, shaped by recent immigration as well as by emigration, and connected to the wider world in a variety of ways. Yet, *The Gathering* relied on a more limited representation, crafted around concepts of ethnic belonging that stretch in a very particular way across time and space.

The absences that were central to *The Gathering* have intrigued me ever since the idea was first unveiled. If *The Gathering* was about encouraging people to visit Ireland, then it seemed appropriate to target friends and family members of people already living in the country. Yet, the thousands of events listed as part of *The Gathering* made scant reference to many of Ireland's current residents. Instead, the website featured events such as family and school reunions, and activities based around genealogy and 'roots'. While these provided reasons for people to make trips to Ireland, their effect was not just related to enhancing a sense of belonging and community. They also served to legitimate a form of exclusion, since they relied on longevity of connection and historic ties to place. Many of the events that made use of *The Gathering* label thus had limited space for participants who may not identify as ethnic Irish, or whose time in Ireland may not be very extensive. This way of thinking prioritises identity over place: *who* you think you are is more important than *where* you are. I wondered why, at a time when Ireland has its highest ever number of residents with nationalities and ethnic identities other than Irish, this particular type of community-building event emerged. Rather than trying to create a sense of community based on shared residence, it seemed to be constructing a timeless, historic, ethnically exclusive version of community. In this, *The Gathering* is part of a broader popular discourse of Irishness, expressed clearly in the 2004 Citizenship Referendum, which unambiguously changed the basis of Irish citizenship.[1] The implications of this way of thinking about Irishness are troubling for people who have made Ireland their home.

The questions raised by *The Gathering* underpin this book, which explores the relationship between Ireland and migration in the twenty-first century. Too often, migration is discussed in unidirectional terms. The focus tends to be either on the places people move to (often developed, wealthy countries or cities) or on the places people leave (often poorer or conflict-ridden regions or countries). As a result, the relationship between migration to *and* from a particular place is rarely considered. This book considers migration in a different way. Its emphasis is on Ireland and on the twenty-first century, but it has significance for thinking about the broader relationship between migration, place and identity. This relationship, I argue, is fundamental to contemporary societies. At a time of economic chaos and crisis, developing a better understanding of this relationship takes on a new urgency.

Why migration?

Nina Glick Schiller and Noel Salazar assert that mobility 'is the norm of our species' (Glick Schiller and Salazar 2013: 185), while Stephen Castles and Mark J. Miller describe the contemporary era as 'the age of migration' (Castles and Miller 2009). Their positions are compelling. Stories of origin and meaning around the world often have mobility as a central experience: the search for a promised land inspires adventure, though often it involves sacrifice. Meanwhile, changes in transport, technology and communications mean that people appear to be migrating farther, faster and in greater numbers than ever before. Yet, the United Nations (UN) estimates that just 3.1 per cent of the world's population are international migrants (IOM 2013). While the number of people involved – around 214 million – is large, in percentage terms this is relatively low. These two positions seem incompatible. How is it possible to make these assertions about norms and ages, when numbers suggest otherwise? How might we reconcile claims about the significance of migration with raw figures that suggest that the overwhelming majority of the world's population are not migrants? The answers to these questions lie in the ways in which 'migration' and 'migrant' are defined and understood.

The UN relies on national statistics to count the number and percentage of international migrants. This measure is often called 'migrant stock': it refers to the number of migrants living in a country at a particular point in time. The classification of migrant varies: while many countries follow the UN definition of an international migrant as someone living in another country for at least a year, this is not always consistently applied. The point in time is usually when a Census is taken, so inevitably the number is out of date as soon as it is recorded. This is not the only issue with how the number of international migrants is calculated. Different countries record migrants using different criteria. Some countries focus on place of birth, and count foreign-born people as migrants. Others focus on citizenship, and record people with foreign citizenship as migrants. Both these ways of categorising migrant stock result in important omissions. Defining migrant status on the basis of place of birth fails to capture the migratory movements of people born within the borders of the state. For example, it does not include circular migrants, who migrate for shorter periods and then return periodically to their country of birth (Castles and Miller 2009: 67–70). Neither does it include return migrants, who have moved to their country of birth following an extended period living elsewhere. Defining migrant status on the basis of citizenship may also exclude return migrants, as well as people who have migrated but have taken on the citizenship of their new home. These numbers can be significant: over two million people became naturalised US citizens between 2009 and 2011 alone (Lee 2012). Using these two different criteria in one country could lead to significantly different counts of international migrants. As a result, measures of migrant stock are not always directly comparable. They also are unlikely to include irregular migrants (Jandl 2012), and as a result are inevitably underestimated.

Measures of migrant stock focus on international migration: on people who cross national borders. Sometimes this occurs not because people move, but because borders change. A recent example is the break-up of the Soviet Union, where people who would previously have been considered internal migrants were transformed into international migrants (Arel 2002). However, this also highlights the issues with discussing migration with reference to international migration only. In the case of the Soviet Union, migration from Yekaterinburg (in Russia) to Vilnius (in Lithuania) would have been considered internal migration. Following the break-up, the same movement would have been considered international migration. Yet it involves the same distance travelled, as well as separation from family and friends and the difficulties of crafting a new life in a new place. Similarly, a focus on international rather than internal migration suggests that internal migration is relatively unproblematic, and that moving within the borders of a state is a comparable experience, regardless of the state where it occurs. The example of internal migration in China suggests otherwise. There, two classes of internal migrants exist: *hukou* migrants, and *non-hukou* migrants. Each person in China has a *hukou*, or residence, in a specific area – either urban or rural. *Hukou* migrants are generally urban and privileged migrants, and are permitted to change where they live. In contrast, *non-hukou* migrants are generally recorded as resident in rural areas, even though they work in urban areas, often in low-skilled and low-paying jobs. As a consequence, they are not considered urban residents, and do not have access to urban welfare benefits (Chan 2010). While the annual flow of *hukou* migrants is believed to be between 17 and 21 million, the number of *non-hukou* migrants has increased dramatically, and was estimated at 150 million at the end of 2009 (Chan 2013). The Chinese example clearly shows that the large-scale movements of people that occur within state or national boundaries are significant. Our understanding of migration as a process, as well as its effects, is incomplete if these internal movements are not also considered.

While migrant stock records migrants – variously defined – at a particular point in time, this figure does not capture the dynamism of processes of migration. Measures of 'migrant flow' attempt to address this, but are even more inconsistent than statistics on migrant stock (de Beer et al. 2010). Some states record all people moving into their territory, while others record selectively. Some states use population registers; others use passenger surveys. Despite these inconsistencies, figures on immigration are often more comprehensive than those on emigration. In general, there is limited coherence in how states collect emigration statistics, which tend to be gathered in an even more sporadic way. As a result, we rarely have an up-to-date picture of who is moving where, and why, and of how these movements of people are changing. The consequence is that when we attempt to count migrants and quantify migration, as in the case of the UN's 3.1 per cent figure, we undercount the number of people who have direct experience of being migrants, whether in the past or in the present. If we understand migration as living in a different place to where you were born, then it is clear that an emphasis on international migrant stock will never capture the extent and the complexity of that experience.

Raw numbers fail to fully capture the importance and significance of migration in the contemporary world because of these limits to how we count. They also fail because they cannot fully demonstrate the meaning of migration, both for those who are not migrants as well as for those who move. Migration and migrants change the places they move to. For example, the material landscapes of cities, towns and rural areas are transformed as a result of migration. New businesses emerge to serve the needs of new arrivals. These may include food stores, cafes, hairdressers, bars and money transfer facilities, and they provide employment as well as necessary services. Established businesses spot new opportunities, and respond by extending their stock or services, or advertising in different languages. There are changes, too, in social and cultural activities. New churches develop, and existing churches alter in order to accommodate new members. Different festivals are celebrated; different cultural events develop. However, writers and commentators have observed how the growing presence of migrants in particular societies may lead to uncertainty, tension and often conflict. Arjun Appadurai describes this as a 'fear of small numbers' (Appadurai 2006): he speculates that the fear is linked to the relationship between 'majority' and 'minority' in the era of high globalisation. As he comments, 'majorities can always be mobilized to think that they are in danger of becoming minor ... and to fear that minorities, conversely, can easily become major' (Appadurai 2006: 83). Geographer Allan Pred suggests that migrants and minorities become symbols of other uncertainties and changes. They serve as scapegoats, he says, 'for all that is newly unfamiliar, for every thing and every relation that is newly different, newly ununderstood, or newly unappreciated' (Pred 2000: 31). States frame their attempts to deal with difference in a variety of ways: from creating structures that aim to protect minority rights to insisting on assimilation. These attempts are often concurrent and contradictory, and they co-exist with civil society initiatives that are similarly diverse in scope and intention. However, the broader argument holds: that a rapid change in the form of migration to a particular place may lead to social insecurities. The newly different, particularly when that difference is easily visible or audible, draw all kinds of attention from those who remain in place.

Places and social relationships also change because people leave. The identification of the 'global care chain' illustrates just how profound these changes can be. Hochschild describes the global care chain as the 'series of personal links between people across the globe based on the paid or unpaid work of caring' (Hochschild 2000: 131). As Yeates highlights (Yeates 2004a), this may include health care as well as domestic work, across a range of scales. What matters, though, is the way in which the work of caring is stretched across time and space. For example, grandparents or other family members or friends care for children at home, while the children's parents work elsewhere, often separated for years at a time. Geraldine Pratt writes about this in the context of Filipina migrants in Vancouver, who use a particular Canadian migration scheme – the Live-In Caregiver Program – to establish their own and later their family's rights to residency in Canada (Pratt 2012). In order to do so, they are separated from their children as they grow up. Pratt recounts the testimonies of children left behind in the Philippines, often for years at a time. As Michelle, whose mother left when she was eleven, said: 'I don't have that connection with my mom anymore. It was broken, right ... She's no more to me at that time than a drawing' (in Pratt 2012: 58). When, later, families are reunited, tensions and conflicts emerge, as children who feel abandoned and their parents – predominantly mothers – who feel unappreciated have to live together again, often in difficult circumstances. The phenomenon of the 'left behind' – including the elderly as well as children – has also garnered attention in the Caribbean and in Asia (Olwig 2012; Toyota et al.

2007). The left behind, though 'often forgotten', make up a larger group than migrants themselves (Toyota et al. 2007: 157). They are affected by migration in many, often unexpected, ways.

The emphasis in these different accounts is often on the negative impacts of migration on people and on place: on families riven by migration, or on people and places struggling to cope with often-rapid changes. But migration also changes people and places in affirming ways. The role of remittances is crucial here. Migrants support the people and places they have left in a variety of ways. They send cash, used for everyday expenses. They visit with gifts, or they invest – for example in land or property or in small businesses – in the places they left. The World Bank estimates that the value of global remittance flows in 2011 was US$501 billion (World Bank 2012). Beyond the direct impact of remittances, migration brings new activities and vibrancy to places that may have been in decline. It creates new connections between people and places that previously seemed distant and separate; and it disrupts taken-for-granted understandings of places and identities in ways that may lead to more inclusive and more tolerant communities. These new connections are alternately described as transnational or translocal, while more inclusive communities may be called multicultural or cosmopolitan, or even super-diverse. These readings offer alternative views of how migration affects people and places, suggesting that migration may have a positive and energising effect.

Migration thus has an importance and a significance way beyond the raw numbers of migrants counted by states. Those raw numbers capture some of the movement of people between states, but not the entirety and complexity of human mobility across a lifetime, both within and across national boundaries. Nor do those numbers capture the extent to which migration affects people and places: the anxieties and the excitement, the threats and the possibilities, that emerge from the decisions of one or many people to live in other places. At the heart of the process of migration are questions about what it means to be human: what it means to seek adventure, to care for others, or to respond to uncertainty and change. It is for these reasons that migration matters, way more than the figures suggest.

Why Ireland?

How is it possible, after arguing for an expansive understanding of the importance of migration, to then focus a discussion of migration on just one small state? I want to suggest that the experiences of Ireland offer a great way to think about migration more broadly. Yet, even using the term 'Ireland' comes with all kinds of assumptions that could limit how we approach the topic. The first assumption relates to the meaning of 'Ireland'. In this book, I primarily focus on the Republic of Ireland, with some brief references to Northern Ireland. A focus on the Republic of Ireland as a sovereign state emphasises migration policy: who gets admitted to Ireland, and under what conditions. This is a state-centred approach to migration, which provides useful insights into broader structural issues that facilitate or inhibit international migration. However, it is less useful for understanding the experiences of migrants or the variegated responses to the process of migration. An alternative approach is to look at the experiences of migrants living in Ireland. This frames Ireland as a bounded space that can be clearly defined and mapped and known. In its emphasis on what is contained inside, connections to other places and people are minimised or ignored. If the focus is on people rather than on a bounded space, 'Ireland' could be defined in terms of Irish nationals living both in and beyond the state. Yet what does this mean for people strongly connected to the idea of Ireland whose nationality is not Irish? All of these ways of thinking about 'Ireland' are examples of what researchers have called 'methodological nationalism': the idea that the nation or state 'is the natural social and political form of the modern world' (Wimmer and Glick Schiller 2002: 301). For Wimmer and Glick Schiller, studies of migration have been dominated, and as a consequence limited, by methodological nationalism. States clearly continue to play an important role in managing migration, but what we know about migration is so shaped by states and nations that we struggle to understand migration in any other terms.

So how can a study of Ireland and migration move beyond methodological nationalism? The work of geographer Doreen Massey is very helpful here. Massey has been writing about place for decades. While she recognises the impulse to bound places and to create borders, she wants us to think about place differently. 'Consider any real place', she writes, and administrative and political boundaries 'have little real purchase' (Massey 1991: 28). Instead, she wants us to think about places in terms of networks and connections rather than borders and boundaries; as dynamic rather than fixed; and as marked by internal conflicts rather than being homogenous and cohesive. Places, Massey writes, are always connected to the wider world in a variety of ways. If we think of 'Ireland' as just such a place, it allows us to focus on networks and connections rather than just on borders and boundaries. When Massey wants to describe her understanding of place in concrete terms, she uses the example of Kilburn High Road in London. She calls it a 'pretty ordinary place', but then describes the newspaper seller with copies of local papers from counties in Ireland, graffiti in support of the IRA, the sari shop, the advertised concerts that include Irish comedians and bands as well as Indian actors, the Heathrow-bound planes overhead and the street-level snarled-up traffic escaping out of London (Massey 1991: 28). It may be a pretty ordinary place, but this masks the way it and other ordinary places are linked together through the movements of people and things.

Thinking about Ireland in this way certainly helps to move us beyond methodological nationalism. It allows us to consider how the movements of people and things and ideas, over time, have created connections between ordinary places. I have experienced those connections in unexpected ways in different places I have visited and lived in. Travelling around Newfoundland in Canada, the accents of people transported me to the southeast of Ireland. They are markers of a movement of people that began in the seventeenth century, when people from Ireland were seasonal migrants, overwintering in Newfoundland for cod fishing. When I lived in Lexington, Kentucky in the 1990s, excavation work for a building uncovered a forgotten graveyard. The newly exposed nineteenth-century gravestones marked the short lives of immigrants from named townlands and parishes in Ireland. In Santa Cruz de la Palma, on one of the smaller Canary Islands, the main street is called after the city's first mayor, a trader from Cork called O'Daly. When I travelled in rural Tanzania in the mid 1980s, I came across a small shop with a Kerrygold butter sticker. These encounters are memorable because they appear out of place – they disrupt the tenuous certainties we hold about how places are. Yet, equally, they are not out of place. These movements are, in the words of Massey, pretty ordinary. Our challenge is to look for the ordinary in the seemingly extraordinary: to look again at how Ireland as a place is shaped and changed by migration, and how migrants are in turn affected by and alter Ireland as a place.

Accounts of the relationship between Ireland and migration often highlight the extraordinary. These narratives focus on the persistence of emigration as a way of life in Irish society. Kerby Miller wrote about this as exile: he argued that the Great Famine of the 1840s forced people to emigrate of necessity rather than by choice, and that it intensified migration from poorer and rural parts of the country (Miller 1985). By the 1880s, when Ernest Ravenstein formulated the first 'laws of migration' (Ravenstein 1885), men and women born in Ireland[2] were living all across Britain, as well as in North America and further afield. They were settling in cities like Liverpool and Glasgow and New York and Boston, but they were also moving beyond large cities, to smaller towns and rural areas. The newly uncovered graveyard in Lexington, Kentucky was

close to the part of that city still known as Irishtown, a low-lying, economically disadvantaged area at the intersection of railways that were
laid down during the nineteenth century. As people from Ireland made
new homes, they encountered obstacles that included prejudice and violence. An extensive literature has developed on the difficult experiences
of Irish people in the United States and Britain in particular. From the
powerful visual characterisation of the Irish 'race' in simian terms to
the violent acts of anti-Irish and anti-Catholic groups like the Know-
Nothings, the reactions to people from Ireland in other places were often
racist and xenophobic (Gilmartin 2013a). This is the main narrative of
post-Famine emigration from Ireland: exiles who encountered profound
challenges, but who – over time – managed to create positions of influence and power in their new homes. The insistence on uncovering the
Irish ancestry of US Presidents, regardless of how tenuous the connection, is an example of this search for migrant success stories.

There are dominant themes in the stories that are told about emigration from Ireland. The first is this emphasis on a commonality of experience: on oppression, discrimination, marginalisation and, eventually,
on prevailing over these adversities. The persistent characterisation of
emigration as exile is telling here, with the act of moving constructed as
some form of collective or individual failure. The second is an insistence
on 'exceptionalism', even though extended experiences of emigration
are not unusual across European countries. Lithuania, Italy, Greece
and Portugal, for example, have equally long and extensive histories
of emigration, and there is persistent emigration from other countries
such as Britain. Paradoxically, the third is a tendency to strip back and
smooth over the complexities of emigration: to disregard the various
reasons that underpin people's decisions to move to particular places,
and their experiences as a consequence of migration. If we are to move
beyond a bounded understanding of Ireland and its relationship with
migration, then it is important to both acknowledge and challenge these
dominant themes. For example, not all migrants from Ireland in the
post-Famine era prospered. The extent to which women from Ireland
became involved in prostitution, in cities like New York, has been
documented (Groneman 1978), but it is a story that is rarely discussed.
Others lived short lives: the gravestones in Lexington marked the deaths
of many young people in their twenties and thirties. Later successes
may well have been built on the foundations of these sacrifices. Other
migrants took different routes, becoming active participants in impe-
rial and colonial endeavours around the world. They were involved in
colonial conversion projects, whether this was the introduction of new
religious practices or the spread of capitalism or 'civilisation'. And these

contradictory tendencies persisted as migration from Ireland continued: people from Ireland were slave owners *and* indentured labourers, members of the elite *and* union activists, liberated from *and* longed for Ireland, prospered *and* suffered. These tensions marked migration both before and after Irish independence, and continue to mark migration from Ireland today.

When I teach university undergraduate students in Ireland about migration, I ask them each to construct a migration family tree. I do this so that students get a sense of the tensions and complexities of migration from Ireland, both from their own perspective and then, collectively, with their fellow students. The stories about migration that they uncover, each year, are both predictable and unpredictable. They identify collective patterns – periods when more migration happened, places that were more popular as emigrant destinations – but they also identify patterns of movement that are not easily categorised, and experiences of migration that defy simplistic explanation. The migration family trees generally focus on the period after Irish independence. They show the waning importance of the US and the ongoing importance of Britain as migration destinations, but they also show the growing draw of Australia and the wide reach of emigrants from Ireland. They also show the vast range of reasons for the initial decision to migrate and decisions to move on or to stay: from work and study, to the desire for adventure or escape, to love and other relationships and family responsibilities that either root people in place or provide imperatives to move. They also capture the extent to which people move more than once in their lifetimes, and how those moves often include a return to the place they earlier left, for either permanent or temporary periods. My own migration family tree is similarly ordinary and extraordinary. I grew up in Sligo, in the northwest of Ireland. My mother's parents spent years in New York, in the 1920s and 1930s, before returning to the place they grew up, in rural Leitrim. Eight of my parents' thirteen siblings spent most of their lives outside Ireland: six in the greater London area, and two in the US. My dad worked in Birmingham for a while, before moving to Ireland to take up a job. My brother, sister and I, between us, have lived in the US, Britain, Australia, South Africa, Indonesia, Qatar and Egypt. Our cousins are scattered across Ireland, Britain and the US: from Sligo to Dublin, from Glasgow to London, and from New York to South Dakota, Texas and California. Some think of themselves as Irish, while others have little or no affiliation to the place their parents grew up.

But these migration family trees also capture the concurrent movement of people to Ireland. My classes include first- or second-generation

migrants, whose parents brought them to Ireland from countries like
Poland. They include students whose parents come from different countries and who met while one or both were international migrants. They
include students who have chosen to move to Ireland as part of their
studies in another country. And they include students whose families
have direct or indirect experience of immigration to Ireland, stretching back over generations. These movements to Ireland may be less
numerous and less substantial than the movements of family members
from Ireland. They are, nonetheless, a very important component in
understanding the broader relationship between Ireland and migration.
Despite this, our knowledge of migration to Ireland is patchy, sporadic,
and limited. Ravenstein, in 1885, showed that people from Britain had
a substantial presence in parts of Ireland in the 1870s. At the time,
this would have been considered internal migration, since Ireland was
then part of the United Kingdom. However, even after Ireland gained
independence, people from Britain remained the largest migrant group
in the country, until 2011. Yet we rarely consider people from Britain
as migrants, in the process displaying the same problematic assumptions of belonging that returning Irish experience (Gilmartin 2013b).
Instead, our attempts to understand Ireland as simultaneously a place
of immigration have been concentrated on recent years, and on the
changing patterns of migration to Ireland that have emerged since the
late 1990s. While the growth in migration to Ireland in that period is
partly explained by returning Irish migrants – a pattern that was similar
to the early 1970s – people also started moving in larger numbers from
other places, such as Nigeria, Poland, Lithuania, China, India and the
Philippines, to live, work, or study. These movements co-existed with
others that were more established, such as migration to Ireland from
Germany, France and Italy, as well as from the US. There had been
earlier attempts to explain some of this migration as 'counter-cultural':
people, particularly from more urbanised and industrialised parts of
Europe, moving to Ireland to escape the pressures of modern life and to
establish other, more environmentally sensitive ways of living (Kockel
1991). This counter-cultural movement was enabled by rural depopula-
tion as people from rural Ireland moved to cities and towns, in Ireland
and elsewhere.

Here, too, is another gap in the ways in which the relationship
between Ireland and migration is understood. Internal migration –
movement within boundaries – also matters when we seek to understand
how places are shaped by, and in turn shape, migration. For decades,
migration – both internal and international – was a process that allowed
the continuation of particular forms of rural livelihood in Ireland. In

general, eldest sons inherited family farms or businesses, and younger sons and daughters were expected to move away and encouraged to find work, sometimes after further study. Those opportunities were to be found in cities and towns: in Ireland, particularly in Dublin. These expectations helped create a 'migration imperative'[3] in many parts of Ireland. In the 1980s, most of my classmates in a girls' convent school expected that they would leave Sligo at some point: to study, to work, or to live. I was seventeen when I first moved to Dublin, and my experience was commonplace. My brother and sister both left Sligo for Dublin when they were eighteen. Our father encouraged us, telling us to travel and experience the world when we were young and free to do so. But even if this movement of young people away from rural areas, villages and towns is expected or encouraged, it has consequences. Writer bell hooks described the journey that took her away from the place she grew up, and how it opened up a gap between her and her family that was more than the physical distance between them. 'Each movement away', she wrote, 'makes return harder' (hooks 1989: 74). Similarly, Stuart Hall says, of migrants going 'home', that there is no home to go to, because once you leave, both you and the place you leave are irrevocably changed. In Ireland, the poignant experiences of the 'left behind' are charted by Ní Laoire (2001). Their fears are represented in plays and literature, where the returning emigrant threatens to disrupt a precarious social equilibrium.[4]

Paying attention to the ways in which these different movements of people are connected matters, because it moves our understanding of the relationship between Ireland and migration beyond narrowly focused narratives. Migration to and from a place happens simultaneously, though the scale and extent of movement varies, sometimes significantly. While international migration is important, its relationship to internal migration must be explored. Accounts of migrant success co-exist with experiences that are less positive and more traumatic. Structural issues intersect with individual experiences in framing how, why and when people migrate, and what happens to them as a consequence. But these connections are also important because of how they shape place. Ireland as a place has been influenced by both the act and the meaning of migration: by the physical movement of people in, to and from Ireland, and by the symbolic implications of that movement. It is not always easy, or indeed convenient, to identify these linkages and connections. But if we are to develop our understanding of place in the progressive way suggested by Doreen Massey, then it is important to consider the relationship between migration and place in a more expansive and critical way.

Rethinking migration, place and identity

In 2010, photographer David Monahan started a project called *Leaving Dublin*, where he took photographs of people at night, before they emigrated from Ireland. His photographs, many of which are featured on his website, have been reproduced in newspapers and displayed in exhibitions around the world, from the US to Brazil, from the UK to Australia to Japan. The night shots celebrate Dublin as a city, with portraits of people posed in front of places that are significant to them: from recognisable landmarks to smaller, more intimate places of meaning. They also, in Monahan's words, are meant 'to immortalize what is being lost to our country' (Bowden 2010). Looking at the photographs, which primarily feature young, solemn men and women, I am struck by how they echo previous images and representations of emigration and departure. They are suffused with a sense of loss, heightened by the fact that they mostly feature people alone. Despite claims about how the photographs are intended to be celebratory, they are equally likely to evoke sentiments of sadness, exile and a sense of fatalism, all of which are enhanced by the darkness of the night. When Monahan, in his blog and elsewhere, discusses the people he photographs, his narratives are more nuanced. The images, though, tap into a familiar visual shorthand that continues to mark emigration from Ireland in terms of exile and loss.

The rapidity with which public discourse in Ireland responded to an increase in levels of emigration from the country was quite remarkable. Initial reports from the Central Statistics Office (CSO) suggested that 2009 was the first year since 1995 that Ireland had experienced net emigration. These figures were later revised to show 2010 as the first such year. However, commentaries on the initial 2009 figures were accompanied by declarations that this was a 'symbolic landmark' (*Irish Times* 2009) and that 'we are retracing our steps down a road we hoped we would never walk again, the way of exile and emigration' (Neligan 2009). The extent to which the level of migration acts as a signifier of Ireland as a place and of Irish identity was apparent here. Similarly, the extent of immigration to Ireland in the previous decade had also served as a signifier of Ireland and Irishness: in that instance, of an economically successful, fully globalised space. Yet, emigration from Ireland continued during those Celtic Tiger years of the 1990s and early 2000s. Some was temporary migration: people taking advantage of Working Holiday Visa programmes in English-speaking countries such as Australia, New Zealand and Canada. Some was for education and training, such as the continuation of medical migration as doctors sought experience overseas. But there was also crisis emigration from

Ireland. Small-scale studies in the UK, for example, highlighted the extent to which people moved there from Ireland to escape violence and other difficult situations (Walls 2005). Reports from migrant support and advocacy groups in the US highlighted the vulnerability of some migrants from Ireland, a status that was often exacerbated by undocumented status. And immigration to Ireland also continues, despite the excessive emphasis on emigration. While the number of immigrants has fallen, each year Irish emigrants return, and each year people move to Ireland for a variety of reasons.

These different realities are not well captured in the images that make up *Leaving Dublin*. The places represented in the images show a Dublin of monuments, rather than a place of social interaction. It would be difficult, from these images, to gather a sense of contemporary Dublin: of the various ways in which the city itself has changed and continues to change as a result of both internal and international migration. Rather, these images present Dublin as a place that is being hollowed out by emigration, rather than a place that continues to grow and change. The people pictured are overwhelmingly white and predominantly identify as Irish. Their migration decisions are often presented as forced and unwanted. One telling image represents a young woman, Claire Weir, sitting beside a hoarding inscribed with graffiti (see Figure 1.1). Its key message, in stand-out letters, is expressed in two words: shame, and regret. It takes a lot longer to see that the full wording reads 'in a world full of shame and regret, do something to be proud of' (Monahan 2010). It is the obvious words, though, that best capture the attitude to migration suggested by these images as a collection. These are regret over individual decisions, and the imputation of a sense of collective shame. Historian Kevin Whelan wrote that 'our demographic balance sheet has always been a barometer of national self-confidence' (Whelan 2006). The visual emphasis on shame and regret, and the narratives that accompany this and other images on the *Leaving Dublin* project website, certainly underscore Whelan's position. However, this position reflects a further set of problematic assumptions. The 'our' of Whelan's statement, as well as his 'nation' with its changing levels of self-confidence, are so taken for granted as to need no explanation. Yet that 'our' and that 'nation', terms also used by Monahan, are far from self-evident, but rather, are always in a process of negotiation. Migration – and its representation in simplistic terms – is central to that process.

The continuities and changes in contemporary patterns of migration to and from Ireland, and the ways in which these movements of people are put to work in the services of broader narratives about place

Original work in colour

1.1 Leaving Dublin

and identity, are what make this particular period both interesting and important to study. Traditionally, discussions of the relationship between migration, place and identity focus – as Kevin Whelan did – on nations and states as the 'natural' scale of analysis. Bounded states serve as ethnic homelands, creating the 'home' that nurtures the diaspora and that, in turn, needs to be protected and guarded from foreign influence. More recently, cities have become an alternative site for the discussion of the migration, place and identity nexus. In particular, there is a tendency to represent cities as sites of diversity, tolerance and cosmopolitanism, in stark opposition to rural places characterised as bounded, intolerant and suspicious. The relationship between the 'city' and the 'nation', in these competing characterisations, is complex. The cities characterised as diverse or cosmopolitan are often capital cities or significant cities within national boundaries. Their form and function is shaped and moulded by their position within the spatial hierarchy of the nation. Yet, there is a reluctance to see cities in terms of these broader networks – to surrounding areas, to rural areas, to broader national imaginaries. Instead, global cities are linked together, secure in their cosmopolitan superiority, replicating similarly exclusionary understandings of place and identity that serve to fix meaning rather than highlight its contingency.

The characterisation of the nation beyond its borders also fixes meaning. The ongoing battles over the St Patrick's Day parades in the US, most notably in New York and Boston, highlight the problems both with seeing cities as only cosmopolitan and with seeing nations as having an essential meaning. Since the 1990s, activists in New York have been arguing for the inclusion of a gay and lesbian presence in the city's annual St Patrick's Day parade. Their claims are repeatedly denied, because the organisers of the parade – the Ancient Order of Hibernians – say that their presence in the parade would be anathema to the Order's values. The annual clash centres on the meanings of both 'Ireland' and 'Irish', and on their expression in a public space. Here, a group of more recent immigrants – part of the movement of people out of Ireland in the 1980s and 1990s – find that their understanding is in conflict with that of an earlier group of immigrants and their descendants (Marston 2002). An event like *The Gathering* appears to target that more conservative group, whose sense of Ireland differs from that expressed in the St Patrick's Day parades in Dublin, Cork and Galway. Yet, gay and lesbian activists insist on the legitimacy of another definition of Irish, and continue to make their point on the streets of New York. This is despite the fact that their legitimate claims to be defined as Irish are resisted by their co-ethnics, and that they are denied a right to political representation by the Irish state, which restricts voting to people actually resident in Ireland on the day of an election.

How, then, might we attempt to move beyond the desire to fix, bound and separate? How might we move beyond the ethnic nationalism of *The Gathering* or the 2004 Citizenship Referendum, or beyond the strangers who shout 'go home' at migrants and visible minorities on the streets of Ireland (NCCRI 2008)? How might we resist the tendency to see the relationship between Ireland, Irishness and migration as inexorable, with migration seen primarily as emigration, but always as a challenge to national integrity? Drawing on the work of Doreen Massey, I suggest that this requires attention to the 'thrown-togetherness' of place and space (2005), and that this involves challenging two key limitations to how migration and its relationship to place and identity is understood. The first limitation that needs to be challenged is the methodological *and* epistemological nationalism that characterises so much research on migration. Certainly, as a bounded, sovereign space, the Irish state is free to define who may legally move to and live in Ireland, and under what conditions. But Ireland's membership of the EU means that its ability to restrict migration from other EU countries is limited, and its ability to discriminate against those migrants – for example in relation to access to public services – is compromised. More broadly, the existence of legal frameworks does not necessarily mean that people abide by them. Moral panics in Ireland – over human trafficking, 'welfare tourists' and 'sham marriages', for example – show the extent to which people bend, manipulate and challenge existing restrictions, or are perceived to do so. Equally, the ongoing presence of undocumented Irish migrants in the US, and the various tactics now being employed by Irish visa overstayers in Australia and New Zealand, show how sovereign laws are often and widely disregarded. As human creations, policies, laws and regulations in relation to migration are always open to challenge and change. This realisation means that while the scale of the state matters for understanding migration, it cannot fully determine either the form of migration or the experiences of migrants. So, the state or the national scale must be understood in conjunction with other scales of analysis: other spatial forms, such as cities, regions, communities, or neighbourhoods; other social forms including, but not restricted to, gender, race, sexuality and class. This also allows us to resist the spatial hierarchies that inform contemporary efforts to theorise migration. In these hierarchies, states and cities are given most prominence, with limited attention to other spatial scales. Even attempts to challenge these spatial hierarchies lead to their re-inscription, as transnationalism is shaped and determined by national borders, and the emphasis on diversity in cities diverts attention from the stark realities of urban segregation. The second limitation that needs to be challenged is the obsession with difference. This is not to deny the relevance of difference for understanding the relationship between migration, identity and place. Of course the ways in which migrants are marked as different and out of place are crucial to making sense of the experiences of migration. This issue has been extensively discussed in relation to immigration to Ireland, with particular reference to race and gender.[5] Equally, those definitions of difference also serve to re-define place. But the tendency to emphasise difference *in place* detracts from the ways in which migrants and non-migrants share experiences in particular places. It also minimises the similarities in how migration and migrants – across time and space – are characterised, managed and defined, and what this means for our understanding of places. Instead, therefore, we must also focus on networks, connections and links: to look for what is similar in the experiences of migration and migrants, and to insist on the importance of these similarities.

In order to challenge and subvert these bounded and restricted understandings of migration, place and identity, this book takes a different approach. The main focus of the book is the relationship between

Ireland and migration in the twenty-first century. This is an important period, because it is characterised by narratives of both newness and tradition. The discussions of newness focus primarily on immigration to Ireland, which changed from the late 1990s onwards. The appeal to tradition is most concerned with the patterns of emigration from Ireland in the aftermath of the Irish bank bailout and the resulting structural adjustment programme. Neither characterisation – newness or tradition – is complete. Yet, it is precisely the co-existence of such competing narratives of the relationship between migration, place and identity that makes this such an important and interesting period to study, and that allows us to use the example of Ireland – broadly defined – to rethink migration. Because of this desire, the book is organised around key linking themes that are central to migration studies. These are *work*, *social connections*, *culture* and *belonging*, and each theme is of relevance to emigration and immigration, to emigrants and immigrants, as well as to those people and places that are 'left behind'. Work is an important theme for two reasons: because of the connection between the decision to migrate and employment opportunities, and because of the experiences of migrant workers. A focus on social connections highlights the ways in which people create, maintain and extend their social networks in and through the experience of migration. Culture is an important means for discussing the impacts of migration on particular places, and on the ways in which cultural productions are used to make sense of migrant experiences. Belonging shows the formal and informal means by which migrants are included and/or excluded from the places they move to and leave. Each of these themes is discussed in an integrated way: bringing together different types of migration, linking different places and showing how migrant identities intersect with other forms of identity such as gender, race, nationality and class.[6] This approach allows us to focus on the lived experiences of migrants, and to search for similarities in migrant experiences that extend across national borders and that occur at a range of different scales. It also allows us to interrogate other structures of inclusion and exclusion, showing how migration both responds to and also serves to shape these structures, which in turn are intricately involved in the act of place making. The themes are loosely grounded in Ireland, in the process pointing to the contingent nature of Ireland as place and as identity. They are framed by Chapter 2, which provides a framework for mapping migration to and from Ireland, and the experiences of migrants and non-migrants in and beyond Ireland, in the twenty-first century. Chapter 3 focuses on work; Chapter 4 on social connections; Chapter 5 on culture; and Chapter 6 on belonging. The concluding chapter, Chapter 7, draws this book together, and moves beyond 'Ireland' in order to rethink the wider relationship between migration, identity and place.

We need to rethink this relationship in order to challenge the simplified stories that are told about ethnic homelands and bounded states and spaces. These stories are too often pressed into action to suit narrow or exclusionary political or other agendas, and in the process reify place as fixed and essential and unchanging. The complexity of migration as a process and an experience, and the thrown-togetherness of migration and place and identity, require us to be attentive to the unexpected as well as the predictable, the ordinary as well as the extraordinary. I learned this lesson on a visit to my parents from my then home in Kentucky. One afternoon, my mother and I drove to her brother's house in rural Leitrim. My uncle and his family lived where my grandparents – the one-time New York residents – had brought up their five children before seeing two of them in turn emigrate. Driving along a narrow country road, with room for just one car, my mother stopped the car to talk to an elderly man. He was wearing an overcoat and cap, his feet clad in wellington boots, with a sheepdog by his side. It was difficult to imagine him anywhere other than that rural area, where he seemed rooted and completely at ease. My mother's cousin, they exchanged pleasantries before he spotted me in the passenger seat and leaned in the window. 'Mary', he said, 'you're the one in Kentucky.' As I nodded, he continued: 'I used to work with lads from Kentucky, from Louisville, when I worked on the steamers on the Great Lakes.' In that instant, my preconceptions about this man I had known all my life were shattered. His life extended way beyond the narrow confines I had allowed him; his experiences as a migrant and a return migrant had shaped him, the places he lived and the place he returned to. That lesson has added relevance in the early twenty-first century. At this time, when migrants have come to stand in for all that is 'newly different' (Pred 2000: 31), the recognition of both the ordinariness of migration and the complexity of the relationship between migration, place and identity, demands our attention.

Notes

1 Prior to the 2004 Citizenship Referendum, anyone born in Ireland was automatically entitled to Irish citizenship. Following the referendum, birthright citizenship no longer exists, and citizenship entitlement is now based on descent and/or legal residence (White and Gilmartin 2008).
2 At this stage, Ireland referred to the entire island. This changed with the partitioning of Ireland into North and South that began in 1920. After this, patterns of migration from the island began to change. There continue to be commonalities

in the contemporary migration experiences of both Ireland and Northern Ireland, such as the importance of Britain and the broader Commonwealth as migrant destinations, the recent growth in immigration from the EU and the tendency for people from both Ireland and Northern Ireland to be seen as 'Irish' in their new homes (Devlin-Trew 2013; Ní Laoire 2002; O'Connor 2013). As Devlin-Trew points out, however, 'as well as commonality, there is difference' (2013: 6), particularly in relation to migration policies.

3 I have borrowed this evocative phrase from David Cairns, who used it to describe attitudes to migration in Ireland and Portugal during a talk at Trinity College Dublin on 7 March 2013.

4 Two representative examples are *The Field*, by John B. Keane (1976), and *That They May Face The Rising Sun*, by John McGahern (2002).

5 Of particular importance is work on immigration and racism (Fanning 2002; Lentin 2007a, 2007b; Lentin and McVeigh 2002, 2006; Ulin et al. 2013), gender (De Tona and Lentin 2011a, 2011b; Pillinger 2007) and intersectional approaches that highlight gender, race and sexuality (Luibhéid 2013).

6 In order to do this, the book draws on a wide range of primary and secondary data. The main source of primary data is a research project that I carried out with Professor Bettina Migge, University College Dublin. The project, entitled 'Towards a dynamic approach to research on migration and integration', was funded by the Irish Research Council for the Humanities and Social Sciences (IRCHSS), and ran from December 2008 to December 2010. It involved longitudinal qualitative research with sixty recent migrants to Ireland. The book also makes use of primary data from a research project that I carried out with Bettina Migge, Alice Feldman and Steven Loyal on behalf of the Immigrant Council of Ireland (see MCRI 2008 for the full report. The research is also discussed in more detail in Loyal 2011). Sources of secondary data include the CSO, the Gaelic Athletic Association (GAA) and a wide range of published reports and research that focus on migrants in Ireland and Irish migrants outside Ireland.

2

Mapping migration

When Ernest Ravenstein published his 'laws of migration' in 1885, he illustrated his findings with a series of maps (Ravenstein 1885). Most of the maps show where internal migrants in the United Kingdom lived: these included maps of 'the national element', 'the Irish element', 'the Scotch element' and 'the English element'. But one map attempts to show the movement of migrants (see Figure 2.1). It is entitled 'Currents of Migration', and at first glance it is difficult to make sense of. The map is in black and white and hand drawn, and is a jumble of arrows pointing in all kinds of different directions. I love this map, precisely because it is confusing and complicated and quite different from the other maps included with his article. It is, I think, a wonderful way of showing how difficult it is to capture the movements of people, but it also works to show the different ways in which those movements are connected. In mapping the currents of migration, Ravenstein also tried to show the 'counter-currents'. As he wrote, 'side by side with each main stream or current of migrant there runs a counter-current' (Ravenstein 1885: 187).

I keep returning to Ravenstein, because he was perhaps the first social scientist who attempted to systematise the study of migration. His works are widely cited but, as Russell King wryly comments, 'rarely read [which] sometimes leads them to be harshly criticised' (King 2012: 138). Yet, reading Ravenstein again, it is clear that he had a more nuanced understanding of migration than his critics give him credit for. In the 1885 paper, he wrote about the different kinds of migrants – local migrants, who had moved within a town or parish; short-journey migrants; people migrating in stages; long-journey migrants; and temporary migrants (Ravenstein 1885: 181–4). In a later paper, in 1889, he wrote about the difficulty in comparing statistics on migration because places used different measures to count migrants (Ravenstein 1889: 242–3). In both papers, he insisted on seeing currents of migration always in conjunction with counter-currents: he wanted to understand how movements to *and* from particular places affected each other.

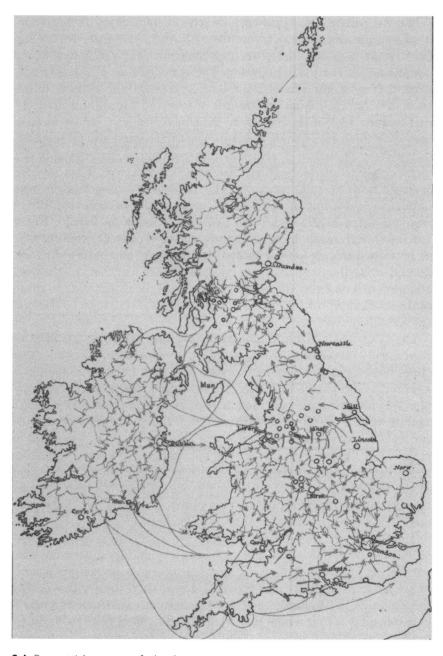

2.1 Ravenstein's currents of migration

While Ravenstein distinguished between different types of migration, he didn't prioritise one over the other. Rather, he sought to develop his laws of migration based on movement of people in general, and not just on international migration. There are, of course, aspects of his work that seem less convincing today. Ravenstein wrote about differences between the migration patterns of men and women. He observed that women were more migratory than men but, in contrast to men, they were more likely to be internal rather than international migrants (Ravenstein 1885: 196–7). Russell King praised this, describing it as a 'prescient generalization' (King 2012: 139). Of course, it ignored the evidence from Ireland, because by the 1870s and 1880s, women from Ireland were also migrating to the US in large numbers: the majority of migrants from Connacht for most of this period were female (Nolan 1989: 48). Ravenstein focused on movements of people *within* the UK, so he missed this. If he had spotted it, we might have had a different general understanding of the migration of women. Yet, in drawing attention to women as independent migrants, Ravenstein was far ahead of the scholars who followed him, who saw female migrants as dependent on male movers.

The 'Currents of Migration' map, together with the nuances of Ravenstein's discussion of migration, offer us a useful way to think about how we might map migration to and from Ireland. 'Mapping' is a term that has gained new currency across a range of academic disciplines: from genes and genomes, to 'mapping the margins' of violence against women of colour (Crenshaw 1991). Much of this work uses the concept of mapping in a figurative way. I am much more interested in mapping as a grounded practice. For me, mapping is a way of thinking about the world in spatial terms. While mapping is often understood as directed towards a particular outcome – a tangible map – I find John Agnew's description of mapping more compelling. He claims that mapping is not just about 'cartographic illustrations', but rather about understanding the relationship between processes and context (Agnew 1996: 144). Mapping migration, then, is primarily concerned with uncovering and representing the relationship between the movements of people and the places they move to, from and through. This is why the 'Currents of Migration' map is so important, because it attempts – however crudely – to show this relationship. It is in contrast to other types of maps of migration – maps that show 'immigrant ghettos', for example – that attempt to fix and bound place, rather than seek to understand its dynamic quality. Yet, the map is just one possible way of representing the underlying information. Understanding how that information is gathered is equally important for the practice of mapping. Mark Monmonier, who wrote a great account of just how maps lie, based his book on a similar guide to statistics by Darrell Huff (see Monmonier 2005 for a discussion of the links). Lying with maps, Monmonier claimed, is a special case of lying with statistics, but both serve to distort geographic realities.

In this chapter, I want to first frame migration to and from Ireland in the twenty-first century. By this, I will show how migration and migrants are defined through legislation, policy and practice, and how these definitions change in response to broader social, political and economic concerns. I next map migration to and from Ireland, sometimes described as migrant flows. In doing so, I hope to show the limits to how we might chart currents and counter-currents of migration, but also to highlight what we might learn about the 'geographical realities' of migration. I then 'map' people who are classified as 'migrants' – or 'migrant stock' – in Ireland and elsewhere, and show what can be said about their geographic realities in place. The discussion is partial and incomplete, but I show why this is the case, rather than making definitive claims about migration and migrants. In doing so, I want to translate Ravenstein's currents of migration for the twenty-first century.

Framing migration

People move, but states create international migrants. The distinction is important. When we talk about migration today, it is most often in terms of an act that crosses international borders. The nature of those borders, and the conditions under which people are free to cross them, is defined by states. A state could, if it wished, choose to open its borders and allow unlimited mobility into and out of its territory. But states no longer take this option. Instead, controlling migration and migrants has become one of the main ways in which contemporary states exert their power and control. As Kitty Calavita writes, restrictions on immigration 'can be seen as a "symbolic crusade" by states experiencing the decline of their national sovereignty and territorial integrity' (Calavita 2005: 166). The importance of immigration to the state means that it is the starting point for understanding contemporary migration.

The relationship between states and migration, particularly immigration, is framed through laws and policies. Laws define citizens and non-citizens, they codify different types of immigrants and, increasingly, they specify sanctions for those who break them. State laws also specify how people ought to be treated, and the conditions under which differential treatment of people is permitted. These laws may often be contradictory. In her account of how Italy and Spain came to terms with new patterns of immigration, Calavita suggested that they used laws *both* to construct immigrant illegality and difference *and* to foster immigrant integration (Calavita 2005: 11). There is a clear tension here, and it is a tension that plays out, in different ways, across states that receive immigrants. The desire to treat people equally and to foster social togetherness comes into conflict with the desire to protect the state and its citizens. In this conflict, it is often immigrants who lose out.

These tensions have become apparent in Ireland. They are illustrated by Table 2.1, which provides a list of Acts of the Oireachtas[1] since 1996 that relate wholly or partially to migration. Ireland became a country of net immigration in 1996, and legislation in this period, under the influence of the 'Rainbow Coalition',[2] focused on the protection and enhancement of social rights for the population as a whole and for refugees in particular. The Refugee Act (1996), which outlined the rights of asylum seekers, was described as a progressive piece of legislation (Fanning 2002: 99). However, the Refugee Act was one of the casualties of a change of government in 1997, and it was never fully implemented. Instead, the new Fianna Fáil-led government made amendments to the Act to 'reflect current realities' (O'Donoghue 1999), such as the significant increase in the annual number of asylum seekers. As politicians sought to address these new 'realities', there was a rapid increase in legislation addressing the issue of migration and a significant change in emphasis. In contrast to the progressive 1996 Refugee Act, later Acts with a specific focus on migrants are much more concerned with prohibitions and restrictions. They define migration-related offences, outline provisions for detaining and deporting migrants and provide more discretionary powers to the Minister for Justice, Equality and Law Reform. The Acts also introduce the term 'non-national' to describe migrants to Ireland. Though this is an improvement on the previously used term, 'alien', it has its own difficulties. Acts that relate partially to migration include the Nationality and Citizenship Acts. These outline the changing basis for Irish citizenship: many argue that the changes were a specific response to growing levels of migration (Lentin 2007a; White and Gilmartin 2008). Other Acts – such as the Equality Acts and the Freedom of Information Act – provide rights to migrants as part of the general population. Additionally, Equality Acts provide some protection to people on the basis of race, though not nationality. In 2007, a comprehensive Immigration, Residency and Protection Bill was introduced. By 2015, this Bill had not yet been passed by the Oireachtas.

This series of laws creates the framework that allows the Irish state to create different categories of immigrants with different sets of rights. As levels of immigration to Ireland increased, from the 1990s onwards,

Table 2.1 Acts of the Oireachtas 1996–2012 with relevance to migration

Year	Act	Details
1996	Refugee Act	Outlines a system for processing asylum applications in Ireland.
1997	Freedom of Information Act	Gives individuals the right to access information held by government departments and public bodies.
1998	Child Trafficking and Pornography Act	Introduces the offence of child trafficking.
1998	Employment Equality Act	Outlaws discrimination at work on nine grounds, including race and religious beliefs.
1999	Immigration Act	Outlines provisions for the detention and deportation of 'non-nationals'.
2000	Equal Status Act	Outlaws discrimination in the provision of goods and services.
2000	Illegal Immigrants (Trafficking) Act	Prohibits trafficking in illegal immigrants.
2001	Irish Nationality and Citizenship Act	Outlines the basis for Irish citizenship.
2003	Immigration Act	Introduces carrier liability, and makes provisions for detention and deportation.
2003	Employment Permits Act	Outlines the sanctions for 'non-nationals' who work in the state without a valid employment permit and for their employers; and outlines the powers of the Gardaí in this situation.
2004	Irish Nationality and Citizenship Act	Changes the basis for Irish citizenship, following the 2004 Referendum.
2004	Equality Act	Extends the provisions of the Equal Status Act and the Employment Equality Act.
2004	Immigration Act	Outlines the role and powers of immigration officers, the obligations of 'non-nationals' in Ireland, and amends provisions for detention and deportation.
2005	Social Welfare Consolidation Act	Defines 'habitual residence' for the purposes of accessing social welfare payments.
2006	Employment Permits Act	Introduces a new employment permits system.
2008	Criminal Law (Human Trafficking) Act	Distinguishes between different kinds of child and adult trafficking.
2009	Social Welfare and Pensions (No. 2) Act	Introduces the concept of 'right to reside' as an additional test in association with habitual residence for accessing social welfare payments.
2011	Civil Law (Miscellaneous Provisions) Act	Introduces changes to immigration and citizenship law, including requirement to produce identification if requested to do so by Gardaí, and the introduction of fees.

Sources: Joyce 2010, 2011, 2012a; Quinn 2007.

the distinctions between different classes of immigrants became more fine grained. I have suggested elsewhere that there four broad categories of immigrants to Ireland: those who are encouraged, those who are tolerated, those who are expedient and those who are discouraged. Encouraged immigrants include returning Irish nationals as well as skilled labour or business immigrants. Tolerated immigrants are those from the EU, as well as holders of working holiday or tourist visas. Expedient immigrants are those who serve a useful economic function, such as students or immigrants who move to Ireland to work, but not as skilled labour. Discouraged immigrants are primarily asylum seekers (Gilmartin 2008). In this 'hierarchy of acceptability' (McDowell 2009), it is those who are expedient and discouraged, such as students or asylum seekers or work permit holders, who endure the most surveillance, who have the least rights and who are the most likely to see the terms of their stay in Ireland altered at short notice. While laws are the foundation for the regulation of immigration and immigrants, it is important to highlight the extent to which statutory instruments, rather than Acts, are increasingly being used for immigration-related issues. Statutory instruments are usually not debated by the Oireachtas, but instead are approved by a person to whom that power has been delegated, usually a minister in the government. In 2011, for example, while there was no Act passed by the Oireachtas in relation to migration, eleven statutory instruments were introduced (Joyce 2012a). The nature and scope of these statutory instruments varied, but many involved introducing or increasing fees for immigration- or citizenship-related transactions with the state. In 2009, there were significant changes to labour migration schemes. These changes included giving labour migrants in Ireland additional time to seek a new job if made redundant as well as increasing the fees charged for visas and permits (Joyce 2010). Additional changes were made to labour migration schemes in 2010 (Joyce 2011). The immigration regime for students was changed in 2011, imposing a limit of seven years' residence in Ireland for degree-level students (Joyce 2012a: xvi–xvii). Calavita, in discussing the experiences of Italy and Spain, commented on the 'continuous starts, shifts, impasses and changes of course' that characterise the attempts of both countries to legislate for immigration (Calavita 2005: 37). She describes the situation as follows:

> In less than two decades, there were four major pieces of legislation in Italy (1986, 1990, 1998, and 2000) and three in Spain (1985, 2000, 2001), with dozens of additional policies established by administrative decrees and government circulars. In the same period, there were six legalization

programs in each country, always accompanied by statements underscoring the extraordinary circumstances justifying this by-now ordinary component of their immigration policies. (Calavita 2005: 37–8)

Ireland has had fewer and more restricted regularisation programmes than Italy or Spain. Recent programmes include the IBC/05 Scheme and the Undocumented Workers Scheme. Around 17,000 people were given leave to remain in Ireland through the IBC/05 Scheme, which gave immigrant parents of children born in Ireland before June 2004 a qualified right to remain in the country (Coakley and Healy 2012). In contrast, just 185 people applied for regularisation under the 2009 Undocumented Workers Scheme, which targeted migrants who had become undocumented 'through no fault of their own' (Joyce 2010: 22). However, though its use of regularisation programmes is less, Ireland shares with Italy and Spain a proliferation of often contradictory and constantly changing immigration legislation and regulations.

These parallels with Italy and Spain are important, because they place Ireland in its broader regional and international context. Piaras Mac Éinrí has suggested that the starting point for understanding Irish migration legislation is in fact UK legislation, because of the existence of a Common Travel Area between the two states since the 1920s. The Common Travel Area allows passport-free movement between the two countries, and was used to justify both countries' decision to remain outside the Schengen accord. In addition, neither Ireland nor the UK participates in the EU common migration policy. Instead, they decide on their involvement in a common European migration policy on a case-by-case basis, choosing to opt in to any policies they desire. In general, Ireland will only opt in to policy if it does not affect the Common Travel Area (Joyce 2012a: 9). However, even though Ireland remains outside Schengen, its experience of and response to immigration is profoundly shaped by its membership of the European Union. First, this is because it learns from other EU members in relation to immigration legislation and policy. As Gavan Titley points out, Irish officials repeatedly drew on the experiences of other EU countries in arguing for the importance of 'getting it right' in relation to immigration (Titley 2012: 821–2). Second, this is because EU nationals make up the majority of immigrants to Ireland, and they have moved to Ireland by virtue of their citizenship of an EU state. Adrian Favell tried to capture this type of movement in the phrase 'regional "free mover"', which he used to distinguish intra-EU migration by East Europeans from 'immigration' (Favell 2008a: 703). Yet, Favell overestimates the extent of the freedom offered to EU nationals. The limits to this freedom are clear in Ireland, where, following the

Social Welfare and Pensions Act (No. 2) 2009, EU nationals living in Ireland for more than three months do not have an automatic 'right to reside', but instead are required to show that they have a job or, if not, that they will not be a burden on the Irish state. People who do not have a 'right to reside', regardless of citizenship, have no entitlement to a wide range of Irish social welfare payments, and may be deported from the country.

In contrast to the ever-expanding prohibitions and restrictions placed on immigration to Ireland, there are no such restrictions on emigration from Ireland. Other countries may impose *de jure* or *de facto* restrictions. These can include requiring citizens to obtain an exit visa, requiring unmarried women to obtain permission from their father to emigrate, restricting emigration for people who have not completed national service, or having a passport cost that is too expensive for many citizens (McKenzie 2007). None of these restrictions exists for Irish citizens, whose right to immigrate is thus primarily shaped by the country they wish to move to. The main destinations for Irish emigrants – the UK, Australia, the US and Canada – frame immigration in ways that are linked but different. The Common Travel Area facilitates the immigration of Irish citizens to the UK, without restrictions. In Australia and Canada, in contrast, the early privileging of white immigrants (from Ireland and elsewhere in Europe, such as the UK) was replaced by a system that emphasised skills. While relatively small numbers of Irish people move to Australia and Canada on a permanent basis, a significant number start on a more temporary basis, using the Working Holiday programmes as an initial entry route. The US moved from a family-based to a skills-based system in the 1960s, which made it more difficult for many Irish nationals to immigrate. However, the US also directs periodic measures towards Irish nationals both in and outside the US. For example, the visa lottery system introduced by the US in 1987 awarded disproportionate numbers of US visas to Irish citizens. One particular version of the system, the AA-1 programme, was specifically opened up to undocumented Irish living in the US. Between 2002 and 2004, 40 per cent of the visas issued each year were reserved for Irish nationals (Hethmon 2003: 388–9). To give an extent of the scale of this programme, 16,344 diversity visas were issued to Irish nationals in 2004 alone (Law 2002: 23). This pattern continues today. The US introduced an Intern Work and Travel Program in October 2008 – this is a pilot programme with Ireland only, and it allows Irish citizens to work and travel in the US for up to twelve months (Embassy of the United States Dublin, Ireland n.d.). However, these efforts are directed towards Irish citizens. People who have lived in Ireland, regardless of their length of stay, are not eligible for these schemes unless they have taken out Irish citizenship. So, mobility and the right to immigrate are based on what Ayelet Schacar calls the 'birthright lottery', with Irish citizens often holding winning numbers (Schacar 2009).

The tensions in how migration is framed play out in different ways in different spatial contexts. In Ireland, there are no legal restrictions on internal migration for Irish or other citizens who have a right to reside in the country. People are free to move between urban and rural areas, for example, or within urban areas. Unlike in the US, there are no regional differences in professional certification, so once a doctor is registered to work in Ireland, he or she is in theory free to work anywhere in the country (Ellis 2012). In practice, however, there are some restrictions. For example, people who are dependent on the state for housing do not have freedom of movement without consequences, as local authorities regulate access to social housing. Equally, asylum seekers must live where they are housed, which could require them to move between direct provision accommodation centres at short notice. Work permits or student visas may be tied to specific employers or education institutions, and this also places a *de facto* restriction on internal mobility. This could have broader consequences – it could limit job opportunities or access to services, for example – but these are not formal legal restrictions. However, there are growing restrictions on immigration to Ireland, with efforts in particular directed towards people from outside the EU who do not qualify as skilled labour migrants. Meanwhile, Irish politicians continue to advocate for the rights of undocumented Irish migrants in the US, and to find routes to emigration for Irish citizens.

Laws are central to this process of framing migrants. The Irish state, in common with other countries in Europe and elsewhere, uses laws in both instrumental and symbolic ways to construct differences between citizens and non-citizens, and to create differences between non-citizens. These laws are changed frequently, as shown in Table 2.1, and the practice of legislating for immigration and immigrants is complicated further by statutory instruments that change the conditions of lives for immigrants, often at very short notice. In the past few years, changes to the cost of applying for visas and citizenship have imposed a growing financial burden on migrants to Ireland from outside the EU, while changes to the 'right to reside' have further removed EU migrants from the responsibility of the state. Yet, people continue to move to Ireland, and migrants continue to make Ireland their home. These movements of people to and from Ireland are discussed in the next section of this chapter.

Mapping migrant flows

One of the key ways in which migrant flows are presented is in terms of sources and destinations: where people move from and to. Ravenstein's 'Currents' map was an attempt to show this within the confines of the United Kingdom. The spread and scope of contemporary migration requires a more extensive map: one that takes in the world in its entirety as well as showing Ireland in more detail. The sources and destinations of international migration to and from Ireland are broadly categorised into five categories. The first is the UK, the second is the rest of the EU-15,[3] the third is the EU-12,[4] the fourth is the US and the fifth is described as 'Rest of World'.[5] According to the CSO, the Rest of World and EU-12 are the most important sources of immigrants to Ireland, while the Rest of World and the UK are the most important destinations for emigrants from Ireland. Poland and Lithuania are currently the most important source countries in the EU-12, but people move to Ireland from all of the EU-12 states. The UK remains both an important source *and* destination for migrants to and from Ireland. In Rest of World, the main destinations include Australia, the US and Canada. However, more specific information on other important destinations is not readily available in Ireland, so even though people move from Ireland to a wide range of countries, this is not shown in Irish statistics.

The CSO provides estimates of people moving to and leaving Ireland by nationality and by destination. Details of immigration to Ireland, by nationality and by source, are shown in Table 2.2. This table provides some evidence of the complexity of categorising in-migration. Clearly, some of the differences between numbers for nationality and source, such as in the case of the UK or Rest of World, stem from the return migration of Irish nationals. However, it is likely that people also move to Ireland from places other than their country or region of nationality, for example a French national who moves to Ireland from Canada or from Vietnam. These broad regional categorisations also fail to show movement within a region, for example a New Zealand national who moves to Ireland from Australia.

The lack of certainty about statistics on migration to Ireland can be explained by the way in which this information is gathered. If you arrive at Dublin airport on a flight from outside Ireland, you go through Passport Control, staffed by members of the Garda National Immigration Bureau (GNIB). Passport Control has changed its appearance over the past few years, but it is now a series of glass-fronted booths where GNIB staff sit and check people hoping to enter Ireland. There are usually separate booths to check European Economic Area (EEA) and non-EEA passport

Table 2.2 Immigration to Ireland by nationality and by source, 2006–14 ('000s)

	2006	2007	2008	2009	2010	2011	2012	2013	2014
Nationality									
Irish	18.9	30.7	23.8	23.0	17.9	19.6	20.6	15.7	11.6
UK	9.9	4.3	6.8	3.9	2.5	4.1	2.2	4.9	4.9
Rest of EU-15	12.7	11.8	9.6	11.5	6.2	7.1	7.2	7.4	8.7
EU-12/13	49.9	85.3	54.7	21.1	9.3	10.1	10.4	10.9	10.0
Rest of World	16.4	19.0	18.6	14.1	6.0	12.4	12.4	17.1	25.5
Total	107.8	151.1	113.5	73.6	41.8	53.3	52.7	55.9	60.6
Source									
UK	17.7	18.2	19.4	13.4	9.1	11.9	8.4	9.7	9.7
Rest of EU-15	13.5	20.3	14.5	18.1	7.8	9.7	10.2	10.3	11.2
EU-12/13	49.3	72.6	45.5	17.5	8.7	9.8	9.3	11.8	9.8
Australia[a]	–	–	–	–	–	–	–	5.3	3.6
Canada[a]	–	–	–	–	–	–	–	1.1	1.2
US	4.0	5.3	5.0	3.0	1.7	3.3	4.9	3.6	2.6
Rest of World	23.3	34.7	29.1	21.6	14.5	18.6	19.9	14.1	22.4
Total	107.8	151.1	113.5	73.6	41.8	53.3	52.7	55.9	60.6

Sources: CSO 2012b, 2013, 2014.
Note: [a] Statistics for Australia and Canada were included in Rest of World before 2013.

holders, but if it is busy, this is often not strictly enforced. However, there is a difference in how EEA and non-EEA passport holders are processed. If you have an EEA passport, the GNIB staff member usually glances at it and at you, and waves you through quickly. There is no record kept of the passport, or of your movement into the country. For an EEA citizen, there are few restrictions on entering Ireland. If you are a non-EEA passport holder, it is more difficult. There are eighty-five countries whose citizens do not need a visa to enter Ireland. If you come from any other country, you need a visa, and you must apply for it in advance of your travel. As a non-EEA citizen, you have to fill out a landing card, and you can be refused permission to enter the country. In 2012, 2,239 people were refused permission to enter Ireland (Shatter 2013a). Dublin airport is just one of the routes that people can enter Ireland. There are international flights to other public airports, such as Shannon, Cork, Knock, Waterford, Kerry and Donegal. There is a network of smaller airports that accept private international flights. There are international ferry services to Dublin, Rosslare and Cork, and a range of smaller ports and harbours. It is also possibly for people to enter the Republic of Ireland across the land border with Northern Ireland/United Kingdom. Many of these entry points do not have a permanent GNIB presence.

The limited recording of people at the point of entry to Ireland means that there is no formal, systematic account of the numbers of people immigrating to the country. Instead, attempts to understand the numbers of people moving as immigrants to Ireland rely on a range of sources, all of which give a partial account of this movement. For example, people from outside the EEA who plan on staying in Ireland for more than three months are required to register with the GNIB, but there is no such requirement for people from the EEA. Anyone can register for a PPS number,[6] but there is no requirement to do so. The Quarterly National Household Survey (QNHS) – the basis for estimates of migrant flows – asks when people last moved to Ireland. If this was within the last twelve months, people are asked if they intend to stay in Ireland for more than a year.[7] Recently, other sources of information, such as asylum applications and work visas issued, have also been consulted. However, the dynamic nature of immigration to Ireland, combined with the limitations in data collection, mean that figures for immigration are always estimates and, it seems, always partial.

When you leave Ireland, there is even less official attention paid to your departure. At airports, airline staff will check identification, but there is no formal passport check by the GNIB. While there are counts of passengers arriving and leaving Ireland by air and sea through the main airports and ports,[8] these passengers are not differentiated as migrants or as tourists. The movement is counted, but there is less attention paid to its meaning. The lack of attention to recording people at the point of departure means that there are even more limitations to estimates of migration flow from Ireland. Again, the QNHS is the basis for these estimates: it asks if a person who was previously interviewed but no longer lives at the address still lives in Ireland. If not, the survey asks what country he or she now lives in. So, the person who provides details about emigration from Ireland is not the emigrant, but someone 'left behind'. Table 2.3 shows the CSO estimates for emigration from Ireland by nationality and destination, and suggests that the UK and Rest of World are important destinations for Irish emigrants.

While Table 2.3 offers some broad patterns, it provides little definitive information about migrant flows from Ireland. The level of information collected by the Irish state on people leaving the country is limited. The CSO relies on information from other states, such as UK National Insurance numbers or Australian visas issued to Irish people, to provide a better sense of the level of emigration of Irish nationals to these countries. However, this provides limited information about the range of countries Irish nationals move to. It also fails to capture the movement of people who live in Ireland but do not have Irish nationality, so it is difficult to chart more complex patterns of movement, such as onward migration to another country rather than return migration to a country of origin. While newspaper headlines offer certainty in their accounts of emigration from Ireland, the reality is that figures are more tentative.

The UK is consistently the most important destination for emigration from Ireland. However, as in Ireland, UK records of immigration and emigration are limited. The best proxy to show movement from Ireland to the UK is the record of National Insurance numbers issued to Irish nationals. Table 2.4 shows this information for the period from 2002 to 2013. However, these numbers are not an accurate guide to immigration, since they may be issued to people who then leave the UK soon afterwards, and since they do not show circular migrants (people who previously lived in the UK and received a National Insurance number then). Instead, they suggest a change in patterns of movement, without providing very robust evidence for this. The 2011 Census gives more detailed information. It suggests that of the 407,357 people living in England and Wales but born in Ireland, 32,945 (7.9 per cent of the total) arrived between 2007 and 2011. Of those, 14,793 were recorded as living in London (NOMIS 2013).

In contrast, information on emigration from Ireland to Australia, a destination of considerable importance, is more comprehensive, at least in relation to place of birth. Information on the immigration

Table 2.3 Emigration from Ireland by nationality and by destination, 2006–14 ('000s)

	2006	2007	2008	2009	2010	2011	2012	2013	2014
Nationality									
Irish	15.3	12.9	13.1	19.2	28.9	42.0	46.5	50.9	40.7
UK	2.2	3.7	3.7	3.9	3.0	4.6	3.5	3.9	2.7
Rest of EU-15	5.1	8.9	6.0	7.4	9.0	10.2	11.2	9.9	14.0
EU-12/13	7.2	12.6	17.2	30.5	19.0	13.9	14.8	14.0	10.1
Rest of World	6.2	8.2	9.0	11.0	9.3	9.9	11.1	10.3	14.4
Total	36.0	46.3	49.0	72.0	69.2	80.6	87.1	89.0	81.9
Destination									
UK	8.8	11.1	7.6	13.2	15.3	20.0	19.0	21.9	17.9
Rest of EU-15	5.7	3.5	7.8	7.4	11.9	13.9	14.4	11.5	16.2
EU-12/13	2.3	7.7	10.1	25.2	14.6	10.4	9.6	14.2	8.7
Australia[a]								15.4	10.0
Canada[a]								5.3	4.7
US	3.3	3.1	2.4	4.1	2.9	4.7	8.6	6.2	6.9
Rest of World	15.8	20.8	21.3	22.2	24.5	31.7	35.6	14.4	17.5
Total	36.0	46.3	49.2	72.0	69.2	80.6	87.1	89.0	81.9

Sources: CSO 2012b, 2013, 2014.
Note: [a] Statistics for Australia and Canada were included in Rest of World before 2013.

Table 2.4 National Insurance numbers issued to Irish nationals, 2002–13

Year	Male	Female	Total
2002	3,949	4,135	8,084
2003	4,529	4,639	9,168
2004	4,580	4,689	9,269
2005	5,089	5,140	10,229
2006	4,751	4,770	9,521
2007	5,580	4,986	10,566
2008	6,016	4,534	10,550
2009	5,848	5,213	11,061
2010	7,360	6,542	13,902
2011	9,445	7,613	17,058
2012	7,986	6,728	14,714
2013	9,297	8,111	17,408

Sources: Department for Work & Pensions 2013, 2014.

to Australia of people who were Irish born is available from its Department of Immigration and Citizenship, which reported 135,931 arrivals in Australia by people born in Ireland during the financial year 2011–12, and 139,092 in 2012–13. Details of these arrivals are shown in Table 2.5. It is important to distinguish between the different categories. A settler is someone who intends to live in Australia permanently. In contrast, a long-term visitor is someone who plans to live in Australia for at least 12 months, but not permanently – this includes people travelling on the Working Holiday Visa programme. A short-term visitor is someone who intends to spend less than 12 months in Australia (this category includes tourists and holiday makers). So, of the 135,931 arrivals in Australia in 2011–12, just 2,239, or 1.6 per cent of the total, were people who planned to move to Australia on a permanent basis. By 2012–13, that percentage had dropped to 1.2 per cent. In both years, the majority planned to settle in Western Australia and New South Wales. Though smaller again, 507 of the departures of Irish-born from Australia in 2011–12 and 547 in 2012–13 were Australian residents planning to leave the country permanently. Of these, 674 had lived in Australia for over five years. Most current migration from Ireland to Australia is long term but not permanent, and occurs through the Working Holiday Visa scheme. On 31 December 2013, there were 10,104 Irish Working Holiday Visa holders in Australia, a drop from the 15,005 recorded in 2012 and the 15,874 recorded in 2011 (Australian Government Department of Immigration and Citizenship 2012a, 2013b).

Table 2.5 Arrivals and departures by Irish-born in Australia, 2011–13

	Arrivals			Departures		
Category	2011–12	2012–13	Category	2011–12	2012–13
Settler arrival	2,239	1,662	Permanent departure	507	547
Long-term resident return	829	713	Long-term resident departure	262	265
Long-term visitor arrival	15,451	16,847	Long-term visitor departure	5,887	8,503
Short-term resident return	40,406	42,285	Short-term resident departure	40,726	44,775
Short-term visitor arrival	77,006	77,585	Short-term visitor departure	77,262	80,338
Total arrivals	135,931	139,092	Total departures	124,644	134,428

Sources: Australian Government Department of Immigration and Citizenship 2013a, 2014.

The limitations to how migrant flow is measured in Ireland were made very clear when the CSO published its 'Population and Migration Estimates' in September 2012 (CSO 2012b). This is an annual publication that shows estimates of international migration to and from Ireland, as well as estimates of overall population change. The 2012 release significantly altered previous estimates, with a background note suggesting that 'the QNHS may have underestimated the level of both immigration and emigration' in the period from 2007 to 2011 (CSO 2012b: 11). The underestimates were significant. Total immigration to Ireland between 2007 and 2011 was recalculated at just over 433,000, an increase of 33 per cent from the original estimate of around 323,000 (Gilmartin 2013c). Despite the significant revision to the estimates, media reports focused on emigration rather than immigration. An *Irish Times* report is representative, with its opening line commenting that 'emigration from the Republic continued to increase' (Kenny 2012a). There is no mention in the report of the revision to immigration figures, or of the people now living in Ireland who were not included in previous estimates. There were also revisions to the figure for total emigration to Ireland, which – at just over 317,000 – was 7.8 per cent higher than the original estimate. The revisions are also symbolically important because they show 2010, rather than 2009, as the first year of net emigration from Ireland since 1995. The first suggestion that 2009 marked this turning point was met with soul-searching by commentators. 'The export of our children makes a return' was the evocative headline over one *Irish Times* commentary (O'Brien 2010). When this was later revised to 2010, there was silence.

Even less attention is paid to migration within Ireland. Again, the QNHS gathers details about where people who participate in the survey have moved from – with a focus on county-level detail – and the places previous participants have moved to. The information is gathered in the same way as details about international migration, but it is not made publicly available in the same way. Instead, data gathered is used for population projections, but not to chart internal migration more generally. As a result, there are no annual records of internal migration within Ireland. The only publicly available count of internal migration in Ireland occurs through the Census, which generally takes place every five years. The Census asks where people were born, and where they lived a year ago, which goes some way to getting a sense of movement of people within Ireland. From the 2011 Census, we can see that just 1.4 per cent of the population of Ireland was living in a different county to a year previously (CSO 2012d, Table CD129). This percentage was relatively consistent across all counties, ranging from a low of 0.74 per cent in Donegal to a high of 2.49 per cent in Roscommon. However, when we compare county of birth to county of current residence, we see that just 62.4 per cent of people in Ireland live in the county where they were born. For counties without a maternity hospital, this percentage is even lower. Just 38.8 per cent of the people living in Kildare, 41 per cent of the people living in Wicklow, and 49.4 per cent of the people living in Leitrim were born in that county (CSO 2012d, Table CD139). Censuses also provide some indication of migration between Ireland and Northern Ireland. In 2011, 37,900 people living in Northern Ireland (2.1 per cent of the total population) were born in Ireland, while 58,500 people born in Northern Ireland (1.3 per cent of the population) were living in Ireland (CSO and NISRA 2014: 38). 2,094 people living in Ireland in 2011 had lived in Northern Ireland a year previously (CSO 2012e, Table CD604). Close to 15,000 people regularly commute between Ireland and Northern Ireland for the purposes of work or study (CSO and NISRA 2014: 60). On balance, though, statistics on internal migration within Ireland are limited and, despite its clear limitations, data on international migration is more comprehensive.

The statistics gathered by the Irish state and by other states provide some basic insights into the characteristics of immigrants and emigrants, including descriptive information on age and gender. In relation to gender, in Ireland as elsewhere, migration is predominantly the preserve of younger people. Each year from 2008 to 2014, between 81 and 92 per cent of people who emigrated from Ireland were aged between 15 and 44. In the same period, between 74 and 87 per cent of the people who immigrated to Ireland were also aged between 15 and 44 (CSO 2013, 2014). In terms of gender, over a longer period the distribution of men and women in flows of migration to and from Ireland remains relatively similar. However, as Table 2.6 shows, on a year-by-year basis there are differences in the proportion of women migrating within each of the nationality groupings. In this, 2008 marks an important turning point, since it represents the start of the recession in Ireland and the collapse of the construction sector, where employment was heavily male- and immigrant-dominated. The proportion of male immigrants dropped in 2008, as did the proportion of female emigrants. Writing in 2008, Bronwen Walter pointed out that the levels of emigration of Irish males were linked to periods of economic downturn. As she commented, 'at times of *maximum* outflow from Ireland, men outnumber women' (Walter 2008a: 185). This pattern appears to be repeated in the current recession in Ireland, at least for Irish nationals. The pattern is quite different for other national groups, with shifts and reversals from year to year in the gender balance of migrant flows. Overall, immigrant flows to

Table 2.6 Migration to and from Ireland by nationality and percentage of females, 2006–14

	2006	2007	2008	2009	2010	2011	2012	2013	2014
Immigration	% F	% F	% F	% F	% F	% F	% F	% F	% F
Irish	49.7	48.9	50.4	43.5	49.7	49.5	42.7	40.1	52.6
UK	42.4	44.2	39.7	43.6	44.0	46.3	50.0	51.0	59.2
Rest of EU-15	48.8	60.2	59.4	68.7	58.1	52.1	66.7	63.5	49.4
EU-12/13	38.5	44.3	54.7	48.8	49.5	54.5	52.9	51.4	52.0
Rest of World	51.8	49.5	49.5	50.4	53.3	52.4	61.3	50.3	54.5
Total	44.1	47.1	52.4	49.9	51.2	51.0	52.8	49.5	53.4
Emigration	% F	% F	% F	% F	% F	% F	% F	% F	% F
Irish	47.7	52.7	45.8	35.9	42.2	41.7	44.3	46.8	44.2
UK	27.3	37.8	35.1	38.5	46.7	60.9	42.9	48.7	40.7
Rest of EU-15	51.0	51.7	66.7	74.3	55.6	64.7	55.4	72.7	59.3
EU-12/13	47.2	34.1	27.9	31.1	32.6	51.1	43.2	50.0	39.6
Rest of World	54.8	43.9	38.9	60.9	41.9	48.5	32.4	39.8	59.0
Total	48.1	44.5	39.8	41.8	41.5	48.1	43.9	49.4	48.7

Sources: CSO 2012b, 2013, 2014.

Ireland have become more feminised since the recession began, though there is more variation in the gender breakdown of emigrant flows from Ireland in this period. Ravenstein drew attention to the gender dimension of migration in 1885, suggesting that there were differences in the likelihood of migration and in the distance migrated between men and women. Table 2.6 suggests that gender differences remain, well over 100 years later.

Despite some insights, information about migrant flows to and from Ireland is limited. There are some claims that can be made with a degree of authority, such as the age profile of migrants, the broad sources and destinations of migrants and an apparent relationship between broader economic conditions and how migration is gendered. In general, though, the information gathered is both general and incomplete. That it is possible to keep more comprehensive data about immigration to Ireland is clear from other sets of statistics. For example, the Office of the Refugee Applications Commissioner (ORAC) gathers information on asylum seekers in Ireland, and publishes this on a monthly basis. The reports show in detail the numbers of claims for asylum, and the outcomes from claims that have been processed (ORAC 2013). Equally, the Irish Naturalisation and Immigration Service (INIS) publishes all records of visa applications received and their status on its website, on a weekly basis. Their record for the week from 10 to 16 June 2014 showed 95 applications refused and 145 approved, mostly for short-term visits (INIS 2014). The Department of Jobs, Enterprise and Innovation (DJEI) publishes a monthly list of work permits issued, which gives information by nationality, employer, county and sector. For example, of the 4,007 work permits issued in 2012, a significant majority (2,293, or 57.2 per cent) were issued to employers in Dublin. Indian nationals received 1,389 permits (34.7 per cent of the total), while US nationals received 527 (13.1 per cent). The employers who received most work permits included some in the technology (e.g. Facebook and Google), health (e.g. Health Services Executive) and food processing (e.g. Anglo Beef Processors) sectors (DJEI 2013). In addition, there are regular audits of the population of students from outside the EU. This information is gathered about the immigrants in Ireland who, in general, have fewest rights. There is significantly less information gathered or made publicly available about more privileged immigrants, such as those from the UK, or from other EU countries, or people who qualify for 'Green Card' work permits. Equally, the lack of attention to emigration – in comparison, for example, to data collection in Australia – allows all kinds of claims to be made about flows of people from the country, again with limited basis in fact. In reality, the only claim we can make with any kind of certainty about migration flows to and from Ireland is that statistics are partial and incomplete, that they fail to capture the complexity of contemporary migration and that they provide only a blurry snapshot of who migrates.

Mapping migrant stock

In general, records of migrant stock are more comprehensive than records of migrant flows. The term 'migrant stock' describes people living in a country who have previously lived elsewhere. There is no general agreement on how exactly migrant stock should be defined, but there is some consensus that it should refer to people who have lived elsewhere for at least a year. In most countries, the key marker is being born elsewhere. This is particularly important in countries that offer birthright citizenship, such as the US. There, the term 'foreign born' is used to distinguish immigrants from US natives. In other countries, like Ireland, nationality is more often used as a marker of immigrant status. This is because many people born outside Ireland have Irish nationality, and so identify as Irish regardless of where they were born.

In Ireland, the Census offers three possible identifiers of migrancy. These are nationality, place of birth and living outside Ireland for at least a year. All three provide the opportunity for write-in answers, so nationality, place of birth and where a person has lived are all self-recorded rather than a box that is ticked. Table 2.7 shows these indicators of migrant stock for each of the last three Censuses in Ireland. Of these three measures, the most accurate indicator of being or having been a migrant is the first, 'lived outside Ireland'. This specifically indicates people who have lived in another country for at least a year, and includes Irish nationals and people with other nationalities. In 2011, the proportion of the population that had lived outside Ireland was 19.4 per cent, the highest of all three indicators. Almost half of these had most recently lived in the UK (Gilmartin 2013c). In 2011, almost 17 per cent of the population was born outside Ireland, and 13.2 per cent had

Table 2.7 Indicators of migrant stock, 2002, 2006, 2011

Indicator	2002 % of population	2006 % of population	2011 % of population
Lived outside Ireland	16.9	18.9	19.4
Born outside Ireland	10.4	14.7	16.9
Nationality other than Irish	7.1	11.2	13.2

Source: Gilmartin 2013c.

Table 2.8 Ten largest national groups in Ireland by population, 2002, 2006, 2011

Rank	2002	2006	2011
1	UK (101,257)	UK (112,548)	Poland (122,585)
2	US (11,135)	Poland (63,276)	UK (112,259)
3	Nigeria (8,650)	Lithuania (24,628)	Lithuania (36,683)
4	Germany (7,033)	Nigeria (16,300)	Latvia (20,593)
5	France (6,231)	Latvia (13,319)	Nigeria (17,642)
6	China (5,766)	US (12,475)	Romania (17,304)
7	Romania (4,910)	China (11,161)	India (16,986)
8	Spain (4,347)	Germany (10,289)	Philippines (12,791)
9	South Africa (4,113)	Philippines (9,548)	Germany (11,305)
10	Philippines (3,742)	France (9,064)	US (11,015)

Source: Gilmartin 2013c.

a nationality other than Irish. There have been significant increases in both of these percentages, as well as in the numbers of people who fall into these categories, since 2002. The number of people with a nationality other than Irish has increased by 143 per cent in this nine-year period, from 224,261 in 2002 to 544,357 in 2011 (CSO 2012e).

Public reports by the CSO distinguish migrants on the basis of nationality rather than on the other two indicators of migrant stock. They write about 'non-Irish nationals', a change from the earlier identification of people as 'non-nationals' and, in their report on migration and diversity, highlighted that there were 199 different non-Irish nationalities living in Ireland in 2011. Of course, there were significant differences in the numbers of different nationalities: 153 countries had 1,000 or fewer nationals living in Ireland, 34 countries had between 1,001 and 10,000 nationals in Ireland, and the 12 countries with over 10,000 nationals in Ireland made up 74.4 per cent of all non-Irish nationals in the country. Table 2.8, which shows the ten largest nationality groups in Ireland for the last three Censuses, gives a good overview. In 2011, the other two countries with over 10,000 nationals in Ireland were China and Slovakia (CSO 2012e).

The level of detail collected by the Census means that we know a lot about the living conditions of immigrants in Ireland. Even if we take nationality as a marker, we can show where people live and who they live with, we can identify where they work and the kinds of jobs they have, and we can get information about other personal characteristics and practices such as age, level of education, religious beliefs and language proficiency. The CSO report on 'Migration and Diversity' provides an overview of this information, paying particular attention to where and how people live, and what they do (CSO 2012e). Most of this information is provided by individual nationality (e.g. Polish) or by nationality grouping (e.g. Asian or African). So, the report tells us that the largest increase in the previous five years was in the number of Polish nationals, that they mostly live with other Poles, and that there is a higher than average proportion of Poles who cannot speak English well. In highlighting these specific aspects of Polish nationals in Ireland, the cumulative effect is to present a picture of a group that is relatively segregated from the general population (CSO 2012e: 7, 17, 28). The selective ways in which the characteristics of other national groups are highlighted serve to paint similar pictures. For example, one piece of information is highlighted in relation to Bangladeshis in Ireland, which is that they record the highest proportion of women aged over fifteen looking after the home (CSO 2012e: 22). For Somalis, two pieces of information are highlighted: that they have the highest proportion of one-person households, and the highest percentage of people who cannot speak English well (CSO 2012e: 16, 28). In highlighting differences that may, in turn, be constructed as problematic, reports such as this help to create or reinforce broader national stereotypes in Ireland.

The summary report, which is written in an informal, chatty style, opens with a discussion of where non-Irish nationals live in Ireland. It includes a dot map of towns where over 20 per cent of the population has a nationality other than Irish, and maps of Dublin showing raw numbers of EU16–27, Other European, African and Asian national residents (CSO 2012e: 11–12). The focus on where people live is not unusual: as states try to make sense of migrant or diverse populations, they often begin by looking at places of residence. Yet, highlighting and representing where people live in this particular way causes problems. The dot map marks places as different, based on the proportion of non-Irish nationals living there, but gives no sense of the diversity of this population, or of the processes that led to this particular concentration. The maps of raw numbers, which use the colour orange to highlight areas where more than 1,000 of the particular group live, follow in a long tradition of visual representations of migrants as different (and, sometimes, as dangerous). Again, these maps of raw numbers give no sense of context: of how these numbers relate to the broader population of that area, or of the processes – for example, the location of a large accommodation centre for asylum seekers – that may have resulted in this particular pattern. Yet these are powerful and memorable images, and their complex meaning and construction is hidden in the apparent simplicity of their message.

I want to use the information gathered in the Census to provide three very different snapshots of migrant stock in Ireland. First, I want to show how using other measures to represent where people live gives us a very different sense of residential patterns. Second, I want to focus briefly on how people live, and suggest that the residential patterns we see may be connected to broader structural processes that have not been sufficiently examined. Third, I want to look at people's employment, and highlight emerging patterns of sectoral concentration for immigrants in Ireland, which have implications for where and how people live. I use nationality as the basis for my discussion, though I recognise the problems with this measure. However, the patterns I discuss show stark differences between national groupings that are important to consider.

While the CSO maps raw numbers of non-Irish nationals, I have used a statistical measure called Location Quotient. Gerald Mills and I calculated this for UK, Polish and Lithuanian nationals in 2006, and found that UK nationals had a very different residential pattern to Poles or Lithuanians (Gilmartin and Mills 2008). When I repeated this calculation in 2011, with the help of Justin Gleeson, these differences remained. To explain, Location Quotient compares the proportion of a particular group living in a specific area to the proportion of that group living in the area as a whole (in this case, for example, the proportion of UK nationals living in an electoral division to the proportion of UK nationals living in the Republic of Ireland). If people were equally distributed across the country, we would end up with a map with no colour variation. Because people are not equally distributed, though, our map is variegated, with the darkest shade showing more than twice the national average in a particular area, and the lightest shade showing less than the national average. Figure 2.2 shows the 2011 map for Polish nationals in Ireland, and Figure 2.3 the 2011 map for UK nationals. As you can see, they show very different patterns of residence. UK nationals are more likely to live in the wealthier suburbs of Dublin, and in rural areas along the west coast. In contrast, Polish nationals are more likely to live in the newer suburbs of Dublin, and in towns and villages across Ireland.

I could use these maps to tell stories about the residential clustering of Polish nationals in Ireland in a way that conjures up images of 'ghettos' or 'enclaves'. Equally, I could use these maps as a starting point for broader questions about why these patterns have emerged. Another piece of information from the Census, on housing tenure, offers a starting point for answering this question. Housing tenure refers to the claim that people have on the place where they live: for example, is it owned or rented? Table 2.9 shows housing tenure by nationality, as recorded by the 2011 Census. In pointing out the differences in housing tenure on the basis of nationality group, Table 2.9 provides an insight into why

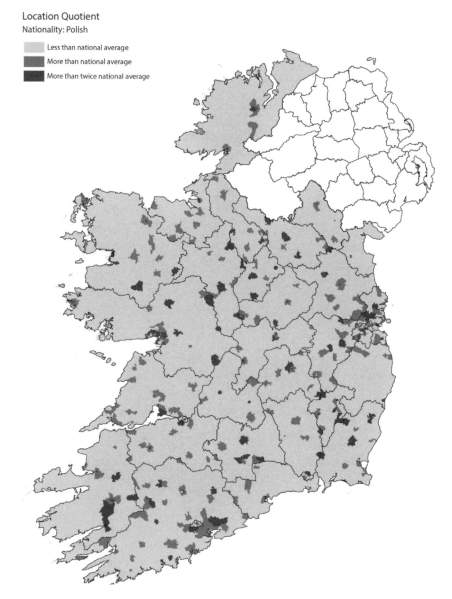

Location Quotient
Nationality: Polish

- Less than national average
- More than national average
- More than twice national average

2.2 Residential distribution of Polish nationals by electoral division, 2011

the patterns of residence shown in Figures 2.2 and 2.3 have developed. In particular, the concentration of EU-12 nationals in private rental accommodation, much of which is to be found in the outer suburbs of Dublin or in towns across the country, following the Celtic Tiger

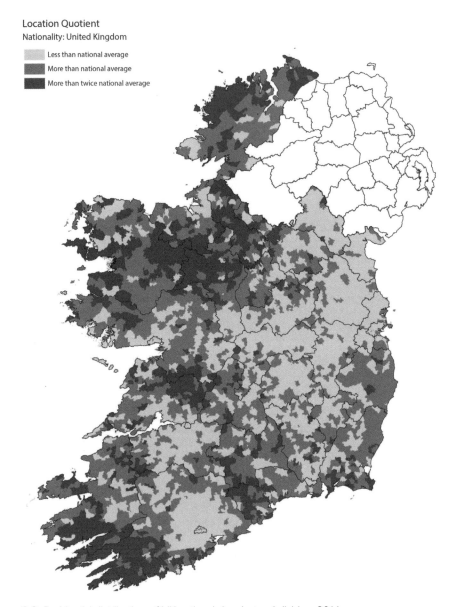

Location Quotient
Nationality: United Kingdom

- Less than national average
- More than national average
- More than twice national average

2.3 Residential distribution of UK nationals by electoral division, 2011

property boom, explains some of the residential distribution of Polish nationals (see also Smith 2014). This type of residential concentration is not necessarily a problem, as others have pointed out (Phillips 2006; Simpson 2007). Where it may be a problem is if it is associated with

Table 2.9 Housing tenure by nationality, 2011

Tenure	Total %	Irish %	UK %	Rest of EU-15 %	EU-12 %	Rest of World %
Owner-occupier with mortgage	35.4	38.3	34.1	18.3	5.7	15.6
Owner-occupier, no mortgage	34.4	38.1	28.4	10.1	0.4	3.2
Rented from private landlord	18.5	12.0	25.5	64.2	84.4	66.6
Rented from local authority	7.8	7.9	8.6	3.3	5.9	8.5
Rented from voluntary body	0.9	0.9	1.0	0.9	1.2	1.7
Occupied free of rent	1.5	1.6	1.7	1.4	0.6	1.8

Source: Gilmartin 2013c.

'poor educational, housing and employment conditions' (Simpson 2007: 423) in the medium to longer term.

This is why it is important to consider broader patterns of employment in Ireland. Table 2.10 shows a selection of the main sectors of employment in Ireland in 2011, and the percentage employed in these sectors by broad nationality group. There are clear differences in where different national groupings are employed. In general, the patterns of employment for Irish and UK nationals are quite similar. However, there are notable differences for other national groupings. For example, over half the EU-12 nationals in Ireland are employed in just three sectors: wholesale and retail, manufacturing, and accommodation and food services. Almost 20 per cent of Rest of World nationals are employed in health and social work, while another 23 per cent are employed in wholesale and retail, and accommodation and food services. There are gender differences also. For example, 93 per cent of the Polish nationals employed in construction are male, while 61 per cent of those employed in accommodation and food services are female. These types of sectoral concentrations are not unusual for immigrants across a range of contexts. Michael Samers has suggested that there are some common trends in the economies of wealthier countries that influence where immigrants work, such as the dominance of service-related employment, a demand for workers in 'welfare' activities such as health care, a proliferation of flexible and more precarious jobs and demand for some types of 'skilled' workers, such as IT specialists (Samers 2010: 144–5). These global patterns are repeated in the Irish context. In Ireland, though, it is equally important to note the sectors where immigrants are less likely to be employed, such as education and public administration and defence. These are more stable and less precarious sectors of employment, and not having access to these sectors, while being concentrated in other

Table 2.10 Employment by nationality and sector, 2011

Sector	Total	Overall %	Irish %	UK %	Rest of EU-15 %	EU-12 %	Rest of World %
Wholesale and retail	260,257	14.6	14.3	15.6	9.3	22.7	10.5
Health and social work	194,916	11.0	11.2	12.3	5.5	4.1	19.3
Manufacturing industries	181,486	10.2	9.9	10.0	12.7	16.0	6.4
Education	163,675	9.2	10.1	8.9	7.7	1.7	4.7
Public administration and defence	111,533	6.3	7.2	3.4	1.2	0.4	1.6
Accommodation and food	102,533	5.8	4.2	6.0	10.9	18.1	12.9
Construction	85,982	4.8	5.1	4.6	1.3	4.5	1.9

Source: Gilmartin 2013c.

sectors, may restrict people's ability to access more secure housing tenure.

There are difficulties with taking a national lens to investigate the experiences of immigrants, in Ireland and elsewhere. This is because a national lens has the capacity to overstate 'both the *exclusion* of all foreigners, and the *inclusion* of all citizens' (Calavita 2005: 159). Yet, this perspective points out patterns that may show a tendency towards exclusion on the basis of nationality, and may be useful in understanding particular difficulties faced by people because of their status as migrants or as members of a specific group. This was the argument in the UK, where activists argued for years for a separate Irish ethnic category. This finally happened in 2001 (Walter 1998; Howard 2006), and the results highlighted the social polarisation of the self-identified Irish community in Britain. Analysis of the Census in England showed polarisation in terms of education, health, work and housing (FIS 2007). In particular, it showed that a high proportion of older Irish had no formal qualifications, while a high proportion of younger Irish had the highest level of qualification; and that white Irish people were more likely than white British people to indicate that they were not in good health. There was a relatively high level of Irish employed in managerial professions, but also in routine jobs: there was sectoral concentration of Irish men in construction, and of Irish women in health and social care (20 per cent and 27 per cent, respectively). In 2001, over 26 per cent of Irish owned their own home outright, while 21 per cent lived in social housing (FIS 2007). While there were some efforts to explain these differences as directly connected to age, this is a simplistic interpretation of the complexity of the Irish presence in Britain. As Walter (2008a) points out, social exclusion in contemporary Ireland – whether this relates to violence, social or economic marginalisation – remains an important explanatory factor for ongoing migration to Britain, and marginalisation must be attributed not only to an aging population of post-war migrants. This takes on a new urgency in the current moment. 'Generation Emigration' in the *Irish Times* offers the opinion that:

> It has become a cliché at this stage to refer to the new Irish migrants to London as educated, career-driven and ambitious professionals. Even if builders, apprentice tradesmen and shop assistants are usually too jaded after a day's work to write and counter this image, it is probably largely true. (Dwyer 2012)

This repetition of the trope of 'new wave' emigration belies the ongoing complexity of Irish migration to Britain, as well as the diverse experiences of the Irish living in Britain: if the patterns of previous migration streams are repeated, arriving as a professional may not necessarily lead to upward mobility (Hickman 2011).

Returning to Ravenstein

I opened this chapter with a discussion of Ravenstein's map of currents and counter-currents of migration. This map, with its jumble of cross-cutting arrows, is a useful metaphor for mapping contemporary migration to and from Ireland. At first glance, it seems so confused as to be meaningless. Look again, though, and smaller patterns emerge. They suggest relationships between particular places – some strong, some not so strong – that are dynamic and flexible, and that change in response to structural, group and individual preoccupations and concerns. We see this at work in the dynamics of migration to, from and within Ireland. When we use state-gathered data on migration, we can identify broad patterns of migration flow and broad information on migrant stock. Those broad patterns of movement show similarities and changes in how men and women move within Ireland, how they circulate between Ireland and other countries, and how they move from other countries to Ireland. Broad information on migrant stock provides insights into the experiences of migrants in and beyond Ireland. On its own, though, this data is not enough. If we are to better understand the relationship between migration, place and identity, we need to use other sources of information and ask other kinds of questions. One way in which we can deepen our understanding of migration is by exploring the wider context for contemporary migration to and from Ireland. That context is a legal and policy framework that is clearly influenced by Ireland's membership of both the Common Travel Area with Britain and the European Union. So, even though Ireland retains some sovereignty over immigration laws and policy, this is shaped by what Britain does, and moulded by the priorities that emerge at the EU level.

Statistics on migration tell a powerful story about the movement of people, while legal and policy frameworks provide a context for that movement. Problems arise, though, when these are seen as complete rather than as partial accounts of migration. *Emigré*, a comprehensive research project on the contemporary emigration of Irish nationals, acknowledges this, stating that 'national level aggregate data ... only provide part of the story' (Glynn et al. 2013: 29). To address this, the *Emigré* project used a mixed-methods approach, including cluster analysis, household surveys, online and face-to-face surveys, and interviews. Its findings, which are restricted to the emigration of Irish nationals from Ireland, highlight the complex motivations and experiences of migrants and the spatially differentiated effects of migration. Its work uses state-gathered migration statistics as a starting point for a more thorough and nuanced investigation of emigration at a particular point in time. It shows both the uses and the limitations of state-gathered statistics, and the importance of paying attention to what these statistics both do and do not show. In developing his laws of migration, Ravenstein was also keenly aware of the limits of the data he used. He described the data as incomplete, pointed out its shortcomings and highlighted possible misconceptions (Ravenstein 1885). His qualifications are important, because they point to an ongoing issue with the use of official statistics on migration. In contemporary Ireland, the limited official information about emigration creates the space for all kinds of claims about migrant flows to be made with seeming authority. The proliferation of those claims detracts attention from the experiences of immigrants living in Ireland, who are often represented in limited and partial ways. The chapter has shown how Censuses may be used, in Ireland and elsewhere, to highlight situations where people's experiences and opportunities may be restricted or limited because of their status as immigrants. Though this too is a partial representation, it challenges more prominent stories that, through recirculation, get repeated as fact. State-gathered data, as Ravenstein showed only too clearly, has an important role to play in understanding the complexity of migration. On its own, though, it is best for helping us to uncover patterns. For understanding migration as a process and as an experience, we need other, additional sources of information.

In the chapters that follow, I also move beyond the formal mapping of migration that is provided by national-level data. I focus on different aspects of migrants' lives, such as work, social connections, culture and belonging, in ways that highlight lived experiences that are shaped, but not determined, by broader structures. In doing so, these chapters challenge the homogenising tendencies of state-gathered data. For example, while statistics such as those in Table 2.10 can highlight the ways in which different kinds of migrants are channelled to work in particular roles or sectors, Chapter 3 shows in more detail both the mechanisms by which that occurs and the consequences for migrant lives and experiences. Chapter 4 discusses the ways in which migrants forge social connections. In some instances, those social connections are enabled by a shared nationality, as in the national groups shown in Table 2.8. However, that is just one possible point of connection, and nationality can be exclusive as well as inclusive, an issue that is discussed in more detail in Chapter 6. Meanwhile, Chapter 5 shows the different roles culture plays in the lives of migrants and in the places they move to and from: issues that cannot be easily quantified, but that are nonetheless important for developing our understanding of migration. These chapters point to the limits of and difficulties with the classification of migration. They emphasise the complexity and, at times, contradictory nature of migration and migrant experiences, and they show the importance of connecting migrant experiences – Ravenstein's currents and counter-currents – across place and time.

Notes

1 The Oireachtas refers to the Irish Parliament, which includes a lower house (Dáil) and an upper house (Seanad).
2 The 'Rainbow Coalition' included left-wing parties (Labour, Democratic Left) and a right-wing party (Fine Gael).
3 These are: Austria, Belgium, Denmark, Finland, France, Germany, Greece, Italy, Luxembourg, Netherlands, Portugal, Spain, Sweden. Ireland and the UK are the other EU-15 members.
4 These are: Cyprus, Czech Republic, Estonia, Hungary, Latvia, Lithuania, Malta, Poland, Slovakia, Slovenia (who joined the EU on 1 May 2004), along with Bulgaria and Romania (who joined on 1 January 2007). This changed to EU-13 from 2014 onwards, to reflect Croatia joining the EU on 1 July 2013.
5 In 2013, the CSO started to identify Australia and Canada separately from Rest of World in relation to some migration statistics.
6 A PPS number is a Personal Public Services number. It is required for interactions with the Irish State (e.g. for accessing social welfare payments or for paying tax).
7 The use of '12 months' is consistent with the broad definition of migrant in Ireland, which relates to someone who plans to or who has spent at least 12 months living in another country.
8 There were over 12 million arrivals and over 12 million departures in 2010 (CSO 2012c).

3

Work

When the *Emigré* research project team published its final report on contemporary Irish emigration, it noted a surprising finding. 'Contrary to what many people might expect', it wrote, '47% of today's emigrants were in fact employed in full-time jobs before they left' (Glynn et al. 2013: II). This finding ran counter to common beliefs in Ireland about the relationship between migration and employment, which framed migration both *to* and *from* Ireland as a job-seeking strategy. This belief is not restricted to the Irish context: academic research, policy formulation and media representations in Ireland and elsewhere help to shape a 'common-sense' understanding that people move primarily for the purposes of work. This understanding frames migrants – either as individuals or as part of a household – as profit-maximising work seekers. It emphasises the economic dimension to migration, with work as a crucial component in enabling economic profit or gain.

The emphasis on a close relationship between migration decisions and work has resulted in a wide range of research on the topic. In his overview of the relationship between labour and migration, Kelly highlights a number of conceptual issues of particular relevance to both international and internal migration studies: elite labour migration, temporary (and vulnerable) migrant labour, racialisation and gendered divisions of labour (Kelly 2012). These are interlinked, because they are all concerned with how the intersection of migration and work creates hierarchies: of mobility, of belonging and of access and opportunity. One of the clear ways in which these hierarchies can been seen is through the creation of a global category: that of the 'skilled migrant' (Samers 2010: 164–7). Different countries have different ways of defining this term, but it broadly refers to people with specialist training that is in demand in particular places. Canada and Australia pioneered the creation of the skilled migrant category, as they sought to give particular privileges to migrants with specific training and skills. This is a pattern that has now been replicated elsewhere, such as in the US, the Middle East and across the EU. There are often overlaps between the skills that are in demand, so much so that Richard Florida has suggested that there is now a global marketplace for skilled migrants (Florida 2007). Borders are more porous for skilled migrants, and also for 'business migrants', who often receive residence or citizenship rights in return for a specific investment in a country. This is not to deny the difficulties that some privileged migrants experience. David Ley writes about business migrants in Canada who, despite being asset rich, struggled to develop businesses or infiltrate the business culture in their new home (Ley 2010). However, privileged migrants have greater formal recognition of their skills and experience, and easier access to a more long-term and less precarious status than many other migrants.

The contrast between the treatment and experiences of skilled and business migrants and other migrants provides another clear example of hierarchies at work. Many people who migrate and seek work do so under difficult conditions. Academic researchers have described their experiences in terms of 'sectoral concentration', '3D' jobs, 'precarity' and 'deskilling'. Sectoral concentration refers to the tendency of particular migrants – distinguished, for example, on the basis of nationality, race, ethnicity or gender – to cluster in particular types of employment, sometimes described as 'dirty, dangerous, or demeaning' (the 3Ds).[1] Examples of 3D work include meat or poultry processing, security or cleaning. This work often is physically demanding, carries a high risk of injury and involves unsocial working hours, generally for low pay. These types of jobs may also be precarious, with short-term contracts, variable hours of employment and few or no social benefits. Precarity in employment has become more common and more widespread, and is certainly not just restricted to migrants. However, migrants often have fewer employment opportunities, so their likelihood of remaining in precarious employment may be higher. This, in turn, may be linked to deskilling, which refers to the consequences of people not working in areas where they have formal training or extensive experience. Over time, their formal qualifications may no longer be valid, their experience may be dated or irrelevant and they may lose confidence in their ability to perform specific jobs. In this context, the category of skilled migrant is problematic. It implies that other migrants are unskilled, rather than acknowledging that their skills are not in specific demand in a particular place.

In this chapter, I look at the relationship between migration, work and Ireland, paying attention to the hierarchies that emerge when migrants experience work. There is now a wide-ranging academic literature on migrants at work in Ireland, which investigates issues such as labour market characteristics, impacts, earnings, discrimination and deskilling, both before and during the economic crisis, and often from a quantitative perspective (see Barrett et al. 2006; Barrett and Kelly 2012; Barrett et al. 2008; Loyal 2011). There is also a broad body of literature produced by civil society groups that, while smaller in scope, provides first-hand accounts of the experiences of less privileged workers in contemporary Ireland, and some insights into the gendered division of labour (see, for example, MCRI 2008; MRCI 2006, 2007a, 2008, 2012; Pillinger 2007). However, there is less attention to the experiences of contemporary Irish emigrants as workers, though there are historical accounts that focus on sectoral employment, such as construction work or nursing (Cowley 2001; Ryan 2007a, 2007b; Walter 2001). In order to address these imbalances, and to show the connections between the experiences of migrants in different contexts, I expand the discussion of migration, work and Ireland by focusing on three interconnected topics. First, I examine a specific employment sector, health care, which is often classified as skilled migration. By considering health care migration more broadly, it is possible to show how skilled and unskilled migration intersect, and how both are connected to complex patterns of both internal and international migration. Second, I look at inadvertent migrant workers: people whose main motivation for migration is not necessarily work, but who become part of the labour force in their new homes for a variety of reasons. This includes students and migrants on working holiday visas who, as migrant workers in different contexts, share similar experiences of precarity and marginalisation. Third, I consider the relationship between migration and work in place, paying particular attention to the similar patterns of inclusion and exclusion that different migrants experience in the workplace. This section pays most attention to the experiences of migrants in Ireland, but draws clear links between these experiences and those of migrants in other spatial contexts. These different ways of considering the relationship between migration, work and Ireland highlight the similarities in how migrants experience work across a range of contexts, the links between different currents of migration and the impacts of the differentiation of migrants and migration for the experiences of people in place.

Migration and health care

My aunt was one of many Irish women who moved to the UK and trained and worked as a nurse (Ryan 2007a). She moved in the 1950s, but the consequences of that migration flow were still apparent in the 2001 Census in the UK, which found that 27 per cent of Irish women worked in health and social care (FIS 2007). This figure includes other health and social care workers, such as doctors, social workers, nurses' aides and care assistants. Yet, in the UK the association of nursing with Irish women remains strong, and is being reconstituted again. The ongoing public sector recruitment ban in Ireland means that many newly trained nurses now move to the UK in order to access work and gain experience.

Just as Irish-trained nurses continue to migrate to the UK and elsewhere for work, nurses trained elsewhere continue to work in Irish hospitals. A combination of increased investment in the Irish health care system, population growth, changing training and work practices meant that, from the late twentieth century onwards, Irish hospitals began to experience a shortage of nurses. In response, hospitals started to recruit nurses directly in other countries, particularly the Philippines and, later, India. The export of nurses from the Philippines was a long-established practice, facilitated by the state as a form of economic development. Ireland became the latest in a long list of countries happy to recruit Filipina/o nurses (Yeates 2004b). Nurses trained in the Philippines were attractive to Irish hospitals for a variety of reasons. Many Irish hospitals had been set up by Catholic religious orders, and the hospitals retain a Catholic ethos. The predominance of Catholicism, combined with the standard of English-language proficiency, meant that nurses from the Philippines were seen as culturally compatible. Later, Irish hospitals started to recruit nurses from Kerala, in India, for similar reasons. Between 2000 and 2008, 40 per cent of newly registered nurses in Ireland came from outside the EU, and 87 per cent of these came from either the Philippines or India (Humphries et al. 2009a). Many of the nurses recruited during this period still live and work in Ireland, often in the larger cities. Internal migration is important for understanding this particular pattern of employment. While many Irish-trained nurses gain their early work experience in urban hospitals, they often move from larger urban areas to smaller cities and towns or to rural areas. Their internal migration, to other parts of Ireland, leaves vacancies in the biggest and busiest hospitals in the state, and these vacancies are generally filled by international migrants. This is a lovely example of Ravenstein's currents and counter-currents of migration that, in turn, has further implications for the Philippines and Kerala and Ireland.

Nursing is just one aspect of health care work. Another, equally important aspect relates to doctors. International migration by doctors is widespread. Migration often starts during the initial phase of training. Students move to other countries to train as doctors, for a combination of reasons: cost, time, access and, occasionally, a belief that it will give them a superior standard of training. Medical schools in Ireland have benefited from this. In 2003, for example, 62 per cent of all medical students came from outside the EU: these students contribute significantly higher fee income to their college or university than EU nationals (Medical Council 2004: 17). The Royal College of Surgeons in Ireland also runs medical degree programmes in Bahrain and Malaysia. But migration continues when trained doctors graduate. The international migration of doctors is sometimes described as the 'medical carousel', as doctors move to other countries to expand their expertise and training and to make more money, and in turn are replaced by migrant doctors from elsewhere.

The Irish Medical Organisation (IMO), in a campaign against cuts to doctors' salaries, claimed that cuts would result in mass emigration of doctors from Ireland (IMO 2013). This claim understated the extent to which emigration is already a key aspect of the working lives of doctors, in Ireland and elsewhere. In her unpublished study of medical migration in the context of Ireland, Angela Armen comments that Irish doctors tended to emigrate, irrespective of broader patterns in the general population (Armen 2008:108). For example, 71 per cent of the doctors trained in Irish medical schools between 1950 and 1966 had gone abroad, mostly to the UK and also the US (Armen 2008:109). When Armen conducted a randomised survey of people employed as doctors in Irish public hospitals in February 2006, she found that over 90 per cent of Irish-trained consultants had trained abroad, with 70 per cent spending at least three years overseas (Armen 2008: 164–5). The most common destination was the UK, followed by the US, Australia and Canada. In the survey and in later interviews, people gave different reasons for this. Some spoke of inadequate training in Ireland or the need to obtain specialised training elsewhere; others saw overseas work as providing additional and valued experience; while a significantly smaller number highlighted lifestyle, adventure and personal development. For junior doctors trained and still working in Ireland, Armen's research suggests that they saw working abroad as part of a longer-term career strategy that would eventually secure them a position as a consultant in an Irish hospital. She observes that a significant number of survey respondents believed 'a fellowship abroad is almost mandatory for a consultant post in Ireland' (Armen 2008: 162).

Equally important is the extent to which the vacancies created in the Irish health care system by the emigration of doctors from Ireland were filled by immigrant doctors. Armen also charts this in her study, and shows that doctors from outside the EU were concentrated in particular regions of Ireland and in particular types of positions. By

Table 3.1   Non-Irish SHO and registrar population by Health Service Executive (HSE)
region, 2006

Employing authority	% Non-Irish registrars	% Non-Irish SHOs
HSE Hospitals – Dublin South	64	61
HSE Hospitals – Dublin Midlands	88	68
HSE Hospitals – Dublin N/E	76	100
HSE Hospitals – Mid West	77	62
HSE Hospitals – North East	94	77
HSE Hospitals – South East	85	74
HSE Hospitals – South	66	59
HSE Hospitals – West/North West	88	54
Voluntary Hospitals	67	43

Source: Adapted from Armen 2008: 133.

2006, 54 per cent of non-consultant hospital doctors (NCHDs) had a
nationality other than Irish. This included 76 per cent of registrars, 57
per cent of senior house officers (SHOs), 29 per cent of interns and 20
per cent of senior/specialist registrar (SpR) posts (Armen 2008:132).
The differences are important. SpR posts are connected to recognised
and structured training schemes and are competitive and coveted. In
2006, 80 per cent of these posts were held by Irish nationals. In contrast, registrar posts are rarely associated with training schemes, and
are often perceived as 'dead end jobs' (Armen 2008:106). In 2006, 24
per cent of these posts were held by Irish nationals. In addition, there
are differences in where people work on the basis of nationality (Table
3.1). Irish national registrars and SHOs are more likely to work in
urban and voluntary hospitals, while non-Irish registrars and SHOs are
predominantly employed in smaller hospitals (for example, in the North
East, Midlands and West/North West). The situation was described by
one of Armen's interviewees in this way. He explained how the work
demands in Irish hospitals for all NCHDs, regardless of nationality,
created exploitative working conditions. As he outlined, 'Irish graduates
got fed up and moved away because they were facing two things, very
difficult circumstances in which to work … and secondly if they stayed
in the system their careers would actually stop'. When Irish graduates
left, 'the slots which were left by them were taken over by doctors from
India, Pakistan and Middle East and Africa … [T]hey felt exploited at
the hands of the system because training was fragmented, there were
no formalised training programmes' (in Armen 2008: 198). As Armen's
research shows, Irish doctors were more likely to get access to special-

ist training programmes, and less likely to fill the registrar posts that are more common across the full range of Irish hospitals. Her findings are supported by more recent qualitative research with non-EU doctors working in Ireland, who described their employment as service work that gave little or no opportunity for training or career progression (Humphries et al. 2013). The social and spatial hierarchies of medical employment in Ireland were reinforced by migration, which created an *us* and *them* across hospitals, in specialised training appointments and in areas of expertise. In Ireland, as in the UK, migrant doctors were more likely to find work in less prestigious positions such as gerontology, and less likely to work in more prestigious (and lucrative) posts, such as cardiology (Bornat et al. 2011).

A focus on hospital staff is just one aspect of health care. Care also takes place in other contexts, such as nursing homes and private homes. In Ireland, as elsewhere, people who are trained to carry out particular jobs are not always successful in migrating on the basis of that qualification. As Geraldine Pratt shows in Canada, many of the migrant women employed through the Live-In Caregiver Program are qualified nurses who work in private homes, taking care of children or elderly people (Pratt 2012). In Ireland, qualified migrant nurses work as nurses' aides, or provide live-in care for older people who are unable to care for themselves (MRCI 2012). It is expensive to register as a nurse in Ireland, and migrants do not always have access to the necessary funds or knowledge to do this. Working in a related, if less lucrative, field offers an alternative, if less privileged, route to migration. However, it restricts the possibilities for social mobility, for first-generation migrants in particular. Pratt wrote about the contrast between the circumscribed lives that migrant women led in Canada and the lives of material privilege this enabled for their children in the Philippines. In Ireland, a documentary film called *Promise and Unrest* showed this in a very poignant way. The film featured Noemi Barrado, a Filipina woman who worked as a care assistant in Dublin. When she eventually saved enough money to bring her daughter Gracelle to live with her in Ireland, the two of them shared a one-roomed apartment with Noemi's friend. Their living conditions in Ireland were contrasted with the Philippines, and the comfortable, well-equipped house that was Gracelle's home before she moved to Ireland with her mother (Grossman and O'Brien 2010).

Migrant workers provide health care in a variety of ways. In Ireland, migrant nurses – from the Philippines, India and elsewhere – tend to fill vacancies in large urban hospitals, with Irish-trained nurses often preferring to work in smaller hospitals and in more rural locations. Migrant workers also provide care in other contexts, such as private houses and nursing homes, but often with inferior pay and conditions. Medical students from outside the EU who train in Ireland help to subsidise Irish medical schools, while experiencing restricted access to specialised training posts in Ireland when they qualify. Doctors who have been trained elsewhere – for example North Africa, Asia and the Middle East – move to Ireland and work in the less prestigious hospitals and posts, often moving between hospitals and jobs every three or six months. They replace Irish-trained doctors who migrate to gain experience and prestige, but who assume that they will eventually return to Ireland to take up a position as a consultant. The 'medical carousel' is thus both internal and international; and affects staff with a variety of skills and expertise, and across a range of specialisms.

Inadvertent workers

Student migration is big business. The US and the UK are the two main destinations for international students: in 2009, over one million international students were recorded in these two countries alone. However, other countries have also been traditionally important destinations, such as Australia, France, Germany and Canada. Beyond this, many countries have recorded a significant increase in international student migration, with two- and threefold increases common over a short period (King and Raghuram 2013: 127–8). People move to study for a variety of reasons, which include the attractiveness or availability of a particular course or place of study; the desire for new social and cultural, in addition to academic, experiences; or longer-term plans for immigration. Yet, the individual reasons for student mobility cannot be separated from the higher education institutions that recruit them (Samers 2010: 79–80). As universities in many Western countries seek to cope with reduced state funding of education, they feel compelled to seek out new sources of income. International students are often seen as a convenient way of plugging that gap. In many instances, international students are charged significantly higher fees than their local counterparts. In Ireland, for example, the distinction is between EU and non-EU students, with students from outside the EU paying fees that could be three or more times higher than EU students. A similar distinction exists in the UK. Meanwhile, countries outside the EU, such as Australia, the US and Canada, also operate fee policies that distinguish between students on the basis of residence and/or nationality. Some international students come from privileged backgrounds and have family or independent wealth to support their studies, and there is a belief that 'students who move generally belong to the middle and upper classes' (King and Raghuram 2013: 131). Others receive scholarships that allow them to study and live in another country. For many international students, however, studying abroad would not be possible without some form of locally based employment. Places that attempt to attract international students recognise this, and often have specific policies around employment for students.

In Ireland, an audit of students from outside the EU was held in March 2009. At that stage, it was estimated that there were just over 34,000 non-EU students living in Ireland: 39 per cent in universities, 26 per cent in further education colleges and 30 per cent in recognised language schools (Department of Justice and Equality 2009). Global spatial hierarchies are clear here: while Chinese nationals appear in all categories, students in universities come from countries like the US, India, Malaysia and Canada, while students in language schools come from countries such as Brazil, Mauritius, Korea and Mongolia. In Ireland, students taking recognised courses – the universities, further education colleges and language schools included in the 2009 audit – are permitted to work: up to twenty hours a week during term time, and up to forty hours a week outside term. The courses and colleges are generally in larger urban areas, such as Dublin, Cork, Limerick and Galway. While there is often work available in these cities, the types of employment available to students tend to be limited, casual and flexible. We interviewed international students in Ireland who worked in a variety of casual jobs, which included retail, restaurants and low-paid jobs in universities, for example as research assistants.[2] One young woman from the US, who was registered as a postgraduate student in a Dublin university, described her job as an *au pair* for an Irish family (2007US01). She lived in their house so that she would not have to pay rent, and in return for a place to live and €115, she worked for at least thirty hours a week. She made breakfast for the three children each morning, took the two older students to school and looked after the youngest child, aged two, some mornings. She did laundry, ironed and tidied, and cooked some meals, and stayed with the older children from when they came home from school until they went to bed. She also worked every Saturday morning, and occasionally for full days at weekends, and was expected to develop special activities for the oldest child, who had a disability. Despite this, on the basis of stories she had heard from other *au pairs* working in her neighbourhood, she thought that perhaps she got preferential treatment because English was her first language. She would have preferred to live independently, but felt that was not possible, given the cost of living in Ireland and the kinds of other jobs that were available to her as a student. As a postgraduate research student, she thought she could only legally work twenty hours a week, and that that would not give her sufficient income for rent and other living expenses. When I was a postgraduate student in Kentucky, I experienced similar restrictions. My scholarships were usually for a nine-month period, and, while they covered my living expenses during that time, they were not sufficient to fund me for the other three months of the year. During those summer months, I was legally permitted to work only on campus, so I spent my time working in campus offices for hourly pay, spending hot and humid summer days photocopying, and answering telephones to people who struggled to understand my Irish accent. I accepted this as a short-term survival strategy, as did many of the people we interviewed who had moved to Ireland to study.

In a world that distinguishes between skilled and unskilled migrants, students occupy a liminal position. King and Raghuram suggest that students are seen as desirable 'because of the skills they bring and then subsequently develop in the countries into which they move' (King and Raghuram 2013: 127). However, it seems that in Ireland, students are also valued for their economic contribution: specifically the fees they pay, and the work they do. While higher education institutions in Ireland vaunt their desire for internationalisation, and set targets for the number and proportion of international students they hope to attract, the definition of 'international' generally relates to high fee-paying students from outside the EU. As an example, when I asked a university International Office for help with interpreting a degree transcript from a Polish university, I was told that the office did not deal with or support EU students. The relational nature of 'international' (King and Raghuram 2013: 132) was made very clear in that exchange. Recent changes to legislation mean that people who graduate with a postgraduate degree from an Irish higher education institute have a year to find work in the country. Prior to those changes, a recent graduate from outside the EU was required to leave the country on graduation if he or she had not secured a work permit. Apart from this, time spent in Ireland as a student does not count towards residence requirements when a person is applying for Irish citizenship. Time as a student is time apart, offering partial access to Irish society, but in exchange for significant economic investment. The work that students do is a crucial aspect of their contribution and their experience, but it is subjugated to their status as students.

Students represent one category of inadvertent migrant workers. Ireland's relationship with student migration is primarily as a destination for students, whether as a place to learn English or as a place to study for particular degrees, such as medicine. People are less likely

Table 3.2 Australian Working Holiday Visas issued to Irish nationals, 2002–13

Year (to end of June)	Number of visas issued
2002	11,000 (est.)
2003	11,500 (est.)
2004	12,260
2005	12,585
2006	12,554
2007	13,554
2008	17,133
2009	22,759
2010	14,790
2011	21,753
2012	25,827
2013	19,117

Sources: Australian Government Department of Immigration and Citizenship 2012b: 12 (Table 1.05), 2013c: 18 (Table 2.05).

to migrate as students from Ireland, with low levels of participation in student mobility schemes such as Erasmus in Irish higher education institutions (Vossensteyn et al. 2010). As Cairns points out, the majority of young people in Ireland do not consider transnational mobility for educational purposes (Cairns 2014: 238). Instead, people from Ireland are more likely to become inadvertent migrant workers through their participation in a working holiday programme. Reciprocal working holiday programmes exist between a small range of wealthy countries. They began as an arrangement between Australia and the UK in 1975, which allowed people from the UK aged between eighteen and twenty-six to holiday and work in Australia for up to twelve months (Clarke 2005: 309). Since then, the upper age limit has been increased, and the range of countries extended. For example, Australia now has working holiday arrangements with twenty-eight countries. Ireland has working holiday arrangements with Argentina, Australia, Canada, Hong Kong, Japan, New Zealand and the Republic of Korea (South). Of these, the working holiday programme in Australia is the most popular. Table 3.2 shows the number of Australian working holiday visas issued to Irish nationals between 2002 and 2013. Working holiday programmes account for a significant proportion of international migration from Ireland. As Table 3.2 shows, the temporary move to Australia was well established before the economic crisis began in Ireland. During the peak years of the Celtic Tiger, at least 11,000 visas were issued annually to Irish nationals. Though the programmes are designed for a twelve-month stay, many programme participants find ways of extending their stay beyond a year. For example, people who sign up to work for a short period in rural Australia are permitted to stay in the country for an additional year.

Research in Australia on working holiday makers tends to focus on spatial and social aspects of the experience. In a range of published articles, two particular themes emerge (Allon 2004; Allon and Anderson 2010; Allon et al. 2008; Clarke 2005; Peel and Steen 2007). The first is the creation of 'backpacker' enclaves: exclusionary places that are populated and maintained by working holiday makers and other backpackers, and that often lead to tensions with local communities. The second is the local, risky behaviour of backpackers. This research emphasises the 'holiday' component of the working holiday programme. In contrast, there is little discussion of work experiences: again, work is seen as incidental to the broader social aspects of the programme. Yet, when there are references to work, they highlight the ways in which people in Australia on the working holiday programme have become a crucial component of the country's casual or short-term labour market. Backpackers have been described as central to seasonal agricultural harvesting, and important to the hospitality industry (Peel and Steen 2007: 1065). These are employment sectors characterised by temporariness and a need for flexibility. People working in these and other areas sometimes report 'exploitation, dangerous and unsafe working conditions, and physical and verbal abuse' (Allon and Anderson 2010: 19). Yet, the apparently temporary nature of their stay in the country, and the emphasis on their stay as facilitating a process of personal development, means that these experiences are often side-lined. Instead, the focus is primarily on social and anti-social activities. This limited understanding of migrants and their role in the labour market – whether as working holiday makers or as students – means that they remain as inadvertent workers, while at the same time underpinning significant types of economic activities.

Migrants and work

Inadvertent workers, whether students or working holiday makers, are vulnerable to exploitation at work. They join a wide range of labour and other migrants who are also vulnerable. In Ireland, the Migrant Rights Centre Ireland (MRCI), over many years, has been drawing attention to the difficult conditions faced by many migrant workers. In a series of reports, focusing on different sectors of employment, it points out forms of exploitation and abuse. Its research has paid most attention to people in more vulnerable employment positions, such as agricultural workers, domestic workers and people employed in service industries like restaurants and hotels (see, for example, MRCI 2006, 2007a, 2008, 2012). In its work, it lobbies policy makers, advocates on behalf of individual workers and engages in direct action with employers and other interest groups.

The MRCI and other civil society groups, such as the Immigrant Council of Ireland (ICI), have consistently highlighted the inequities of Irish labour-migration policy (ICI 2003; MCRI 2008). Their initial attention was directed towards a labour-migration policy that distinguished between EU citizens, working visa/work authorisation holders and work permit holders. EU citizens had unrestricted access to the Irish labour market, and working visa/work authorisation holders had privileged access in their area of expertise (health, construction or IT). In contrast, work permits were tied to specific employers, provided limited protection to workers, carried few or no family reunification rights and gave restricted access to long-term residency or citizenship. Activist groups described the work permit system as a form of indentured labour, which created the conditions for abuse of workers by unscrupulous employers. The work permit system assumed that permit holders were single, with no family responsibilities, and that they were economic opportunists who would leave Ireland when it was no longer in their interests to remain. It was, in effect, a version of the guest-worker programmes in other countries that had attempted to plug labour shortages with temporary migrants. As places like Germany found out, assumptions of temporariness rarely translate as expected in practice (Castles 1986). People develop attachments to their new homes, or experience alienation or distancing from their places of origin. They remain as temporary migrants, and the initial conditions of their engagement with their new homes shape their later experiences. This also has consequences for their children – the second-generation – who are both at home and not at home in the places their parents have moved to.

Lobbying against the work permit system in Ireland resulted in a change to Irish labour-migration policy in 2007. However, the reformed system – an integrated work permit system – further intensified the contrast between skilled and unskilled workers. This distinguished between migrants on the basis of skills *and* salary. Anyone earning over €60,000 a year qualifies for a Green Card, which gives privileged access to long-term residency in Ireland. In general, anyone earning less than €30,000 is not admitted to work in Ireland – the unstated assumption is that these types of lower-paid jobs will be filled by migrants from within the EU. In general, work permits are limited to those who will earn over €30,000 a year. If they have certain skills – again, in health care or IT – they might qualify for a Green Card even if their salary was between €30,000 and €60,000 per annum. There is no clear indication of how these salary levels were determined. Despite significant cuts in salaries since 2007, particularly in the public sector, where the majority of health professionals are employed, the salary levels have not been revised. This new Green Card system makes a crude association between desirability and salary levels. In this way, it addresses a more general hostility to so-called economic migrants who might become a drain on the resources of Irish society – the salary levels, which are significantly higher than the average industrial wage, suggest people with access to both financial and social capital. However, it also reinforces the limited understanding of skilled migration: skilled, in this meaning, refers to skills that attract higher salaries because the entry point is high, rather than necessarily skills that are in demand for a fairer or better functioning of society. If, as Bridget Anderson suggests, the term migrant has come to signify the global poor (Anderson 2013), then these types of skilled migration policies are a way of keeping them both poor and outside.

Ireland's restrictive migration policy makes it difficult for most people from outside the EU to move to and work in Ireland. For the small number who do move, many have been able to work in areas where they have training and experience. Once people receive formal permission to work, their experiences of working in Ireland are often favourable. For example, we interviewed a woman from Kerala who had been recruited to work as a nurse in a large Dublin hospital. She told us about the support she received from her employer in making the move to Ireland, and about the different training opportunities she had received. For this woman, working in Ireland had been a positive experience: she said 'the professional growth I had after coming here is tremendous ... lots of opportunities for training' (2004IN01). An Australian woman, working as a skilled health professional in a large Irish town, was similarly positive. She had been recruited in Australia, and she told us 'I absolutely love the job now', commenting in a later interview that 'I have had a lot of opportunities for training ... over here that I might not necessarily have got or had at home' (2007OZ01). Elsewhere, research with people working in a variety of skilled employment positions suggested similarly positive experiences (Boyle 2006; Krings et al. 2009, 2013a, 2013b; Loyal 2011). When people are recruited specifically for their skills, and when employers are directly involved in that recruitment process, people often spoke about working in Ireland in positive terms. If they had complaints, these were related to more general work practices that affected people regardless of nationality – such as the public-sector pay cuts that began in 2009 and the reduction in the professional development funding – rather than specifically related to their individual migrant experiences. The experiences of skilled labour migrants from outside the EU contrast sharply with those of another group of migrants – asylum seekers. The main source countries for asylum seekers in Ireland, since 2009, are Nigeria, Pakistan, China, Democratic Republic of Congo, Afghanistan and Zimbabwe (ORAC 2010, 2012, 2013). The annual number of applicants for asylum has dropped from a high of 11,634 in 2002 to a low of 946 in 2013 (Gilmartin 2013c; ORAC 2013), and the success rate for asylum applications in Ireland remains very low by European standards. However, the treatment of asylum seekers in relation to work has longer-term consequences. The system of direct provision introduced in April 2000 means that asylum seekers are provided with accommodation and meals, and a small weekly allowance (€19.10 for adults; €9.60 for children). In return, they are not permitted to work or, as adults, engage in full-time study (Breen 2008). The asylum process in Ireland is notoriously slow, with people waiting years for a determination on their application. Those years of enforced idleness take a toll. People lose skills, abilities and confidence and, if they are eventually successful in their claim for asylum, have to overcome the effects of years of unemployment. Asylum seekers in Ireland are, in effect, long-term unemployed. Their chances of re-entering the labour market in an appropriate way are undermined by each successive year spent in the asylum process.

Of course, an emphasis on work visas and work permits occludes the fact that most migrants in Ireland need no special permission to work in the country. The majority of immigrants to Ireland over the period from 2000–13 were citizens of an EU country, and so were mostly free to live and work in Ireland without restriction.[3] People from the EU-10,[4] particularly Poland, Lithuania and Latvia, had started moving to Ireland prior to 2004, using the work permit system to gain access to the Irish labour market. After 1 May 2004, these migration flows continued, and in some instances increased in size, but no longer as formal labour migration. Instead, migrants from newer EU countries were quickly integrated into the Irish labour market, filling vacancies in specific sectors such as construction, agriculture, retail, tourism and manufacturing. In Northern Ireland, there were similar patterns of migration from EU-10 countries in the period, particularly Poland, Lithuania and Slovakia (CSO and NISRA 2014). Statistics from the 2006 and 2011 Censuses in Ireland, shown in Table 3.3, illustrate the extent of this sectoral concentration. Table 3.3 shows two significant points. The first is the extent to which nationals of the newest EU countries who live and work in Ireland are concentrated in sectors with more precarious and flexible

Table 3.3 Sectoral concentration of EU-10/12 nationals in Ireland, 2006 and 2011

	2006		2011	
	% Overall	% EU-10	% Overall	% EU-12
Construction	11.1	18.9	4.8	4.5
Manufacturing	12.6	19.5	10.2	16.0
Wholesale and retail	13.4	15.1	14.6	22.7
Accommodation and food services[a]	5.2	15.1	5.8	18.1
Public administration and defence	5.3	0.2	6.3	0.4
Education	6.6	0.5	9.2	1.7
Health and social work	10.0	2.2	11.0	4.1

Sources: CSO 2007: 118–20 (Tables 30A, 30B, 30C), CSO 2012f: 78 (Table 14A).
Note: [a] This was classified as 'Hotels and restaurants' in 2006.

employment, such as wholesale and retail, and accommodation and food services. This also appears to be the case in Northern Ireland, with evidence of migrant sectoral concentration in construction, hospitality and manual/casual labour (Irwin et al. 2014: 16–20). The second is the extent to which EU-12 nationals are *not* employed in more secure, skilled employment, such as in education, health and social work, and public administration and defence. While there have been some changes, for example a large percentage increase in the numbers employed in education, these areas of employment remain effectively closed off to most EU-12 migrants. This is in sharp contrast to UK nationals, for example, whose employment patterns are quite similar to those of Irish nationals. It suggests a particular form of protectionism in relation to jobs that represent the interface between the Irish state and its citizens. Education and public administration, for example, embody the state in very particular ways. Education is one of the ways in which a specific Irish identity is constructed. This is principally the case at primary school level, where, in general, teachers are required to be proficient in the Irish language. This is exclusionary, since proficiency requires long-term exposure to the language. People who have trained as teachers elsewhere are unlikely to be fluent in Irish, and thus are unlikely to receive employment in Irish primary schools. Many positions in public administration also require Irish-language proficiency, thus making them less accessible to people from places other than Ireland.

In Ireland, as elsewhere, sectoral concentration can be identified on the basis of broad nationality groupings. It can also be identified on the basis of gender, with particular concentrations of men and women in different types of employment. For example, EU-10/12 men are predominantly concentrated in construction, while women from the EU-10/12 are disproportionately employed in wholesale and retail. This mirrors similar patterns in Britain, which, like Ireland, provided unrestricted access to labour markets for EU-10 nationals from 1 May 2004 onwards. In particular, the 'Polish builder' quickly became an object of media and academic attention in Britain, with a wide range of studies focusing on the experiences of Polish men as construction workers (Datta and Brickell 2009; Parutis 2014). This had previously been a focus for researchers of Irish migration to Britain (Cowley 2001). As late as 2001, 20 per cent of Irish men in Britain were employed in construction-related activities (FIS 2007). The film *Kings*, adapted from the play *The Kings of the Kilburn High Road*, presented one version of this type of gendered sectoral concentration, together with its associated personal and emotional tolls. The film showed men living together, working together, socialising together and experiencing alcoholism, violence and poverty. However, Irish women in Britain were also concentrated in particular types of employment, such as the 27 per cent of Irish women employed in health and social-care activities in 2001 (FIS 2007). These types of sectoral concentrations, whether by gender or by nationality, impose limits on migrant experiences of work. They create expectations and stereotypes that are difficult to avoid or escape – the Irish navvy, the Polish plumber, the Filipina nurse – and their persistence affects the place of migrants in a national labour force.

Sectoral concentration also has a longer-term consequence, in that it may result in deskilling. Many studies of migrants at work in Ireland highlight this phenomenon, showing how some people struggle to find employment commensurate with their level of education and experience (Barrett et al. 2006; Gilmartin and Migge 2011; MCRI 2008; O'Connell and McGinnity 2008). In our research, we interviewed a Polish teacher who worked as an administrator in a construction company, a Polish marine biologist educated to postgraduate level who worked as a hotel porter, a Polish pharmacist who worked for a retail company and a Slovak architect who, following a long period of unemployment, was doing casual work for a former employer. But deskilling was not confined to EU-12 nationals. We also interviewed a highly qualified childcare worker from Italy who was compelled to retrain in order to find work, an Italian engineer who worked as a technician and an Italian archivist who was unable to find any paid employment and who worked as an unpaid volunteer in a charity shop. When we first met, many viewed their employment position as temporary, and had hopes of improving their situation over time. However, as the recession took hold, people felt trapped in jobs that did not use their training or skills, and could see no way out. In this way, deskilling became permanent. Without experience or ongoing professional development, hard-won qualifications became increasingly irrelevant, and people settled for any type of employment because, as a young German woman told us, 'it is risky to stay out of a job and you never know how long it will take' (2007GER02b). Yet, we also found that people were often willing to accept difficult working conditions if other areas of their lives were good or improving. This was especially true when people were happy in their romantic relationships: it was as if this mitigated against deteriorations in work life (Gilmartin and Migge 2013). Our study was short – we talked to people over a two-year period. It is difficult to know if this level of individual accommodation for inadequate experiences at work will persist over a longer time frame.

For the small number of people classified as skilled migrants, who move freely between countries and whose qualifications and skills are recognised in a variety of national contexts, the relationship between migration and experiences of work are positive. For many migrants, however, moving and working can be fraught. Sectoral concentration makes it difficult for people to have unimpeded access to a national labour market, and exclusionary employment practices further enhance the sense that certain jobs are meant or preserved for certain people. It can be difficult to get recognition for education or experience from other places, and people sometimes internalise these structural barriers as personal failings (Gilmartin and Migge 2011). At times of economic crisis, such as the ongoing recession in Ireland, migrants are also more likely to lose their jobs than are the native population, a situation exacerbated by the concentration of migrant workers in more precarious employment (Barrett and Kelly 2012; Goodwin-White 2013). One strategy for dealing with this, which has been identified across a range of cities and countries, is for migrants to become involved in entrepreneurial activities. We interviewed a number of people who, in the face of difficult employment experiences, were hoping to set up their own businesses. These included one woman starting a cookery school, a second using her skills as a graphic designer to produce educational material for children and a third retraining as a gardener. Across a range of cities, the private taxi industry has become a means to self-employment for migrant men in particular. Entry costs to the industry are generally low, regulation of hours worked is often lax and the work offers upfront and often cash payments. Yet, migrant and ethnic minority men who work as taxi drivers in Ireland may experience hostility, discrimination and abuse: in Dublin, I have heard stories about taxi ranks where they are not welcome and customers who refuse to get into their taxis. Other taxi drivers festoon their cars with markers of Irish identity: Irish flags, Irish colours and stickers or signs that say 'Irish taxi driver'. On one level, these might be seen as expressions of banal nationalism. However, in a barely regulated industry where drivers struggle to make a living, these markers of belonging simultaneously work to exclude. This is further perpetuated by the myths about migrant and ethnic minority taxi drivers that circulate in general conversation. These include the story that one black man sits all the knowledge tests for potential black taxi drivers, with intimations of inadequate knowledge; as well as the stories that link migrant taxi drivers to various forms of criminality, including sexual assault and rape. Recent studies in Galway and in Drogheda reach similar conclusions about the processes of exclusion in the taxi industries in those cities (Jaichand 2010; Maguire and Murphy 2012, 2013). In urban Ireland and elsewhere, international migrants keep cities moving, but only because those cities in turn place limits on their ability to participate and belong.

The work of migrants

'When do the differences between migrants and natives matter?' Bridget Anderson asked this question at the Dublin launch of her recent book,[5] and it is an important question for thinking about the work of migrants. The first difference that matters relates to access to work. It matters when migrants are restricted – whether implicitly or explicitly – from working in particular sectors, or encouraged to work in others. We see this in the context of Ireland and Northern Ireland, where sectoral concentration means that migrants from the EU-12 are channelled to work in construction, in manufacturing, in service industries and in agriculture, regardless of their skills, qualifications and experience. While this may be acceptable to migrants in the short term, in the longer term it leads to deskilling and underemployment, and it makes it more difficult for migrants to work in other sectors. The longer-term impacts of sectoral concentration are apparent in the experiences of Irish migrants in Britain, who continue to be employed in construction (for men) and in health care (for women), with implications for integration and for social and economic mobility. The second difference that matters is treatment at work. As this chapter shows, migrant workers are often vulnerable employees. This may be because their permission to be in a country is linked to their employment, or because they do not have the means to defend themselves against discrimination or exploitation, or because they are seen or see themselves as working on a temporary basis with fewer rights to protection. Migrants who work in low-paid and precarious jobs and sectors are clearly susceptible to exploitation. For example, research in Ireland and Northern Ireland on mushroom workers highlights the social isolation, lack of regulation, underpayment and fear that characterises the experiences of workers in the sector, which is concentrated in the border region (MRCI 2006; Potter and Hamilton 2014). But skilled migrants, like doctors, also face difficulties at work. For all migrants, differential treatment at work may be intensified along other axes of discrimination such as race or ethnicity or gender (McGinnity and Lunn 2011; O'Connell and McGinnity 2008). If migrants have more difficult working conditions or if they are paid less than their native counterparts, this has longer-term consequences for social cohesion. The third difference is the tendency to define people who migrate primarily in terms of their relationship with work. The term 'labour migrant' sums up this problem: the term is rarely used to describe internal migrants, who are characterised in much more complex ways. Yet, when people tell stories about why they chose to migrate, work is often just one of a number of factors that they mention. Other reasons for migration include relationships, such as love or family; study; experience or adventure. Sometimes people talk about migration as a way of improving their own or their family's quality of life and opportunities, which may be only partially connected to work. This seemed to be the case for the business migrants David Ley wrote about, many of whom highlighted the importance of different educational or other opportunities for their children. The messiness of people's reasons for migration cannot be easily reduced to a simple explanation: that economic differentials determine migration. Equally, the fact that people do not prioritise work in their narratives of migration does not mean that they do not have experience of work in their new homes. Understanding this complex relationship between people's reasons for migration, their narratives of migration and their experiences of being migrants requires that we think about work in place.

Highlighting significant differences does not take away from the important similarities between migrants and natives in relation to work. The first is the way in which the flexibility demanded from migrant workers – a category that includes inadvertent workers such as students and working holiday makers – is increasingly the norm for native workers. The second is the creation of hierarchies of workers. The distinction between skilled and unskilled migrant workers is a clear example of this, where rights and privileges are predicated on a perception of usefulness, but it is also translated to native workers. The third is the need to see migrant workers and native workers as part of an integrated and interdependent local and global labour market. As a member of the staff of the Council of Sydney pointed out, backpackers supply 'labour for a whole stack of activities that are needed in the City for its global status' (in Allon and Anderson 2010: 17). In Ireland, migrant workers sustain key sectors of the economy, such as tourism or IT. The attempts to showcase Ireland as a digital hub are enabled by the migrant workers who work in jobs that are provided by mobile multinational capital. The commuter train that I take to work each morning also brings workers to Intel and HP in north Kildare. We travel together, people speaking many languages and from many different countries, all affected by the economic crisis that undermines the broader quality of life in Ireland. Understanding what we share as well as how we differ is crucial for a deeper appreciation of the relationship between work, migration and place.

Notes

1 While 'dirty' and 'dangerous' are generally accepted as two of the Ds, there is no consensus on the third: demeaning, difficult, degrading and dull are frequently used.

2 Quotes from participants in the IRCHSS-funded project 'Towards a dynamic approach to research on migration and integration' are identified throughout the book by year of arrival (either 2004 or 2007), nationality (e.g. POL for Poland) and a numeric identifier.

3 This was the case from 1 May 2004 for EU-10 nationals, and from 20 July 2012 for nationals of Bulgaria and Romania.

4 The EU-10 became the EU-12 on 1 January 2007. Statistics from this point onwards are labelled as EU-12, even though Bulgarian and Romanian nationals were not given immediate access to the Irish labour market.

5 Notes from a talk by Bridget Anderson at Trinity College Dublin on 27 April 2013.

4

Social connections

This chapter focuses on social connections: on the ways in which people create, maintain and extend their social connections through the experience of migration. Migration is a social experience. When academics and others attempt to make sense of migration, they often frame it in social terms. Phrases that are regularly used in the context of migration include social group, social identity, social cohesion, social capital, social networks, social bonds, social bridges, social exclusion, social inequality and social change. Each of these ways of thinking about migration has its own extensive literature.[1] As a result, 'social' has a broad range of meanings in the study of migration. The breadth of ways in which social is understood creates its own difficulties, in part because it results in people creating boundaries around the term and the groups it signifies. As a result, discussions about the impact of migration on particular places may imply that there is a fixed, almost unchanging society that immigrants enter, or that migrants create social groups in place that may be easily defined and assessed.

In this chapter, I consider three different ways of thinking about social connections: language, family and community. These are just three of the ways in which migration as a social phenomenon is discussed: I have chosen them because they show the relationship between migration and (social) identities, a key focus of this book. In the discussion of language, family and community, my emphasis is on how new social identities are formed, on how existing social identities change and on the ways in which social identities are reconstructed in connection with or as a result of migration. The first section focuses on language. When language is discussed in relation to migration, it is often considered as an expression of culture, with the focus on how migrants maintain their mother tongue and transmit it to second and later generations (Carnevale 2013). But language is also social. It is one of the main ways in which people create social connections, but it can also create barriers and distance between people if they struggle to communicate in a shared language.

In Chapter 3, we saw the way in which proficiency in the language of the host country can facilitate skilled migration, as in the case of nurse migration from the Philippines and India to Ireland. Equally, though, limited proficiency can lead to restricted opportunities for employment. However, language is not just of relevance for migrants at work. It also shapes the possibilities for meaningful social encounters with others in a variety of contexts, whether formally through interactions with state bodies and institutions, or informally in social settings. It can contribute to a sense of belonging, as well as to a sense of being apart. The first section thus shows ways in which the relationship between language and migration might be reconsidered from a social perspective. The second section discusses family. As Cooke points out, 'nearly all migration could be defined as family migration' (Cooke 2008: 260), whether this refers to immediate members of a family migrating together, or to one member of a family migrating as part of a family survival strategy, or to the effects of the migration of individuals on families. The act of migration thus changes families, stretching them across space and time, and often resulting in new family formations. These changes are not just the outcome of individual or family decisions, but are shaped by broader structures. For example, one of the ways in which states attempt to regulate migration is by working with a very narrow definition of the family, such as husband, wife and children. As this chapter shows, official definitions of family often clash with people's lived experiences of family, creating additional hardships for migrants in place. This section focuses on the changing meaning of family for migrants living in Ireland and for migrants from Ireland living elsewhere, and shows the ways in which family changes across space and time. The final section of the chapter is concerned with community. In migration studies, the term community often refers to migrants with a shared nationality, such as the Irish community in Australia or the Polish community in Ireland. This section shows the difficulties with this approach to community, and the alternative – and at times contradictory – ways in which migrants define the term. Rather than assuming that migrants in Ireland and Irish people living away from Ireland are part of a migrant community, this section interrogates the ways in which discourses of migrant communities attempt to fix migrant identities in place. It offers a broader understanding of community for migrants, one that may include but that also moves beyond national identification. Together, the three topics – language, family and community – offer new insights into the social connections that are created, maintained and extended by migration. These insights are local, national and transnational, showing the complex networks of migrant social connections, and their impact on both places and identities.

Language

The only statement on integration as yet produced by the Irish government, *Migration Nation*, treats language as a key aspect of integration. Language acquisition is described as a 'basic integration skill', and developing a 'national English language training policy' is seen as a strategic area for integration policy in Ireland (Office of the Minister for Integration 2008: 18, 63). Furthermore, it is suggested that citizenship and permanent residency be linked to proficiency in 'the spoken language of the country' (Office of the Minister for Integration 2008: 9). Though Ireland is officially bilingual, all but one reference in the document is to the English language, which suggests that the emphasis and expectation relates to English rather than Irish.

Six years later, and there is no national English-language training policy in Ireland. The private consultants hired by the Minister for Integration in 2008 concluded that 'there is a robust case for the development of a formalised English Language system and framework for legally resident immigrants in Ireland', commenting that it has significant longer-term positive impacts for immigrants and their children (Horwath Consulting Ireland et al. 2008: 6). The consultants advocated for a publicly funded system of English-language training to ensure that all immigrants had basic skills.[2] They also suggested that 5,000 additional publicly funded places be made available each year to immigrants, and that language training should involve a mixture of formal classroom instruction and less-formal learning environments, such as conversation groups in libraries. Their recommendations have not been implemented. Instead, the website for the new Office for the Promotion of Migrant Integration, in a section on 'Learning English', first suggests attending private language schools, and then state-funded Vocational Educational Committee (VEC) classes. Not all local areas have VEC classes, and many that do place restrictions on who can participate. The website also provides information on a range of voluntary bodies that provide assistance, though not necessarily formal qualifications. If none of these works, the website has a range of other suggestions, including libraries, radio, buying a dictionary and using the BBC website (Office for the Promotion of Migrant Integration 2013).

The shift from the insistence on the important of a national language training policy to a laissez-faire and individualised approach has taken place against the backdrop of the recession in Ireland. The assumption of temporariness that underpinned attitudes to recent immigration in Ireland has played out in relation to integration, with the Minister for Integration replaced by the Office for the Promotion of Migrant

Integration, a downgrading of status. Language strategy has been one of the casualties of this downgrading, though other strategies – for example in relation to intercultural education, health care and policing – remain in place. However, the lack of attention to language training for immigrants has been highlighted as a problem in the Irish context. The Migrant Integration Policy Index, which measures integration policies across the EU and a range of other countries, suggests that Ireland has not developed basic policies for immigrants, including language training. In particular, it says the closure of the Integrate Ireland Language and Training centres in 2008 had an adverse effect on language training for immigrants (MIPEX 2010). The Irish-based Integration Centre, in its 2012 report on integration in Ireland, provided evidence of a further deterioration in language training in Ireland (Integration Centre 2012). The report highlighted two areas: language training for adults and language education in schools. In relation to adults, the report found that language training was restrictive, often expensive (and could result in the loss of social welfare payments), provided little support for advanced learners and operated without a standard curriculum. In relation to schools, the report highlighted reduced language support, in particular a significant cut in the number of English as an Additional Language (EAL) teachers in schools, and the lack of appropriate training for many of the remaining EAL teachers (Integration Centre 2012: 18–20). In 2010, MIPEX commented that 'Ireland is among the least prepared to help newcomers with specific needs to do just as well in school' (MIPEX 2010). The decreasing provision of English-language support in Irish schools gives this statement even more weight.

Of course, the emphasis on the English language is of particular interest in Ireland, which is officially bilingual, with Irish as the official first language. However, despite being the official first language, Irish is a minority language. While 1.775 million people self-reported as Irish speakers in the 2011 Census, just 77,185 said they speak Irish daily *outside* the education system, with almost 520,000 people saying they speak Irish daily within the education system only (CSO 2012g: CD936). This means that just under 2 per cent of the population of Ireland speak Irish on a daily basis by choice. In contrast, just over 514,000 people speak a language other than Irish or English at home (CSO 2012e: CD641). Of these, the most-spoken languages are Polish, French, Lithuanian, German, Russian, Spanish and Romanian (all with over 20,000 speakers). In total, thirteen languages are spoken at home by at least 5,000 speakers. Yet, schools emphasise Irish and English, and attitudes to other languages, particularly at primary level, are not consistent. In her study of schools in a large urban centre, Nowlan suggests that 'bilingual students were perceived as peripheral and problematic' (Nowlan 2008: 262). Meanwhile, Allen White's research with children in an Irish asylum centre contrasts the insistence on speaking in the English and Irish languages in schools with the acceptance and encouragement of multilingualism and code-switching at an after-school club. As one of the children he worked with told him:

> Today I was so angry because today I don't want to go to school ... everyday the teacher shout at you English! Irish! I don't like that ... every Wednesday [the day the after-school club is on] I am happy. (White 2012: 321)

Even though most schools continue to prioritise English and Irish, the proliferation of languages spoken informally in schools is seen as a cause for concern by some parents. Newspaper and other reports suggest growing numbers of Irish parents are sending their children to Gaelscoileanna (Irish-language schools) to avoid contact with immigrant children (Carey 2008; Flynn 2012; Horan 2007). While there is limited other evidence of the reasons why children do or do not attend these Gaelscoileanna, there is evidence that proportionately fewer immigrant children attend them than attend English-medium schools (Byrne et al. 2010: 282).

These broader concerns about language use and proficiency among immigrants in Ireland rest on an assumption that how English is spoken in Ireland is generally unproblematic. For migrants in Ireland, this is not always the case. A Scottish man I interviewed in Cork City was quite scathing when I asked him his views on how English is spoken in Ireland:

> They just speak so fast and they jumble all their words together and to tell you the truth I think they have a very limited vocabulary. (2007UK03)

Asking about language use was new for me, but my colleague Bettina Migge, who is a socio-linguist, insisted on the question. She and other colleagues have been developing a body of work both on Irish English and on how immigrants in Ireland speak English (Migge and Ní Chiosáin 2012), and our research gave her an opportunity to expand this work. In particular, it allowed her to talk to people from different backgrounds, with different levels of competency in English, who had arrived in Ireland at roughly the same time. While other research focused on people who did not have English as a first language, such as migrants from Poland, our study also included native English speakers who had quite different perspectives on language. Native English speakers from North America and Australia were likely to display positive attitudes to

Irish English, but those from the UK were more ambivalent. As Bettina suggests, many UK migrants to Ireland seemed to feel that 'their adoption of Irish English features would undermine their national belonging' (Migge 2012: 325). Others went further, like the Scottish man I quoted at the start of this section who saw the English spoken in Ireland as low status and inferior.

In many ways, negative perceptions of Irish English expressed by some migrants in Ireland are consistent with similar perceptions in Britain. Audible differences serve as the main marker of Irish identity in Britain, and researchers have paid attention to the broader meanings attached to Irish accents in Britain and to the ways in which people with Irish accents negotiate those meanings. As Bronwen Walter has pointed out, long-established stereotypes of the Irish in Britain 'rely heavily on language, including grammar and vocabulary, presenting "substandard English" as "evidence of stupidity"' (Walter 2008b: 174). This persists: social workers reported that many of their clients feel that they are perceived differently because of their Irish accent, and that they are treated 'as if they are stupid' (in Garrett 2005: 1366). Having an Irish accent in Britain could also have class-based associations, as sectoral employment concentration meant that Irish men were often assumed to be labourers (Walter 2008b: 176). However, the IRA bombing campaigns between the 1970s and early 1990s meant that sounding Irish became associated with the threat of danger and violence. Walter reports that many people 'kept quiet in public places so their accent could not be identified' (Walter 2008b: 177–8). As a visitor to London during the late 1980s, I vividly remember that feeling, and was always happy for the release of leaving. However, people who lived there had to deal with hostile attitudes to their accents on an ongoing basis. Walter outlines a number of strategies that people used, including trying to change or lose their Irish accents (2008b: 177–8).

For second-generation Irish in Britain, accents became a marker of difference in another way. As Marc Scully points out, 'claiming Irishness in an English accent is fraught with difficulty and possible rejection, as the two identities tend to be seen as incompatible' (Scully 2009: 126). Second-generation Irish in Britain, who spoke with local accents, did not encounter the same sort of hostility as their parents (Walter 2008b: 178–80). However, their claims to Irish identity were often discounted, both by British people and also by recent Irish immigrants, who used the derogatory term 'plastic paddy' to describe them. There are class connotations to this term, which first became popular during the 1980s. It was used by elite Irish migrants to create a distance between themselves and second-generation Irish in Britain by claiming a more authentic Irish identity, of which accent was a key part (Campbell 1999; Scully 2009). While 'plastic paddy' was used in Britain, second-generation Irish also remarked on the way their accent was used as a marker of difference in Ireland. One man who participated in a discussion group in Manchester said that the worst racism he had experienced was in Ireland, 'with Irish people having a go at [him] about being English' (in Walter 2008b: 179). Bettina and I interviewed a man who grew up in Liverpool, with an Irish mother. He spoke about changing his accent depending on where he was and who he was talking to, and about not wanting to draw attention to himself in public places in Ireland (2004UK02).

In contexts where Irish accents are less problematic, Irish migrants often actively sought to retain their accent, seeing it as a marker of cultural identity. For example, many of the Irish migrants interviewed by Patricia O'Connor in Melbourne, Australia took pride in the fact that they still sounded Irish. 'I hate being told "you have a bit of an [Australian] accent" when I'm in Ireland', one man told her, while others spoke about actively resisting developing such an accent (O'Connor 2013: 154). Similarly, some of the professional elite return migrants from the US whom Mary Corcoran interviewed in the 1990s mentioned their Irish accent as a positive marker of difference. One man described his Irish accent 'as an asset especially when trying to meet women', while another spoke of accent and turn of phrase as a resource for succeeding in the US (Corcoran 2003). On return to Ireland, though, accent changes – however slight – became a marker of difference that was mocked. Fintan, who lived in the US for seventeen years before returning to rural Ireland, described it in this way:

> if you said one word in an American accent, it was, 'Alright, come back, but don't you dare say one word in an American accent'. So you're meant to just leave all that behind you and fit in exactly with the way things are here. (Quoted in Ralph 2012: 454–5)

For many returning Irish migrants, therefore, even barely perceptible changes to their accent may become a source of mockery, even when those accents in other contexts provide access to individual social and cultural capital.

In contrast, language can also become a positive symbol of identity and community among first- and later-generation migrants. For example, Thomas Sullivan has researched learners of the Irish language in North America (Sullivan 2012). When he asked why they were learning Irish, they had many different reasons, but most centred on the Irish language as a sign of Irish identity (Sullivan 2012: 430). Yet, in his description of a range of Irish-language immersion events taking place across North

America, Sullivan notes that only a small number of participants were first-generation Irish (Sullivan 2012: 432). The majority of participants were third- or fourth-generation, who saw their efforts to learn the Irish language as the authentic marker of their ethnic identities. This set them apart from the people they disparagingly referred to the 'Shamrock Brigade' – those Americans who claimed to be Irish on St Patrick's Day, but had no knowledge of Irish culture or the Irish language (Sullivan 2012: 436). Similar sentiments are expressed by some first-generation migrants in Ireland, who have put considerable effort into ensuring that their children learn their parents' first language. For example, a network of Polish weekend schools has been established in Ireland. The five schools are seen as serving a dual role: helping Polish nationals to maintain their language skills and sense of history, as well as 'preparing Polish families for possible re-entry into Polish society and employment' (O'Brien and Long 2012: 135). The schools are run at weekends entirely in Polish, and employ Polish teachers, school-books and curriculum. Polish Saturday schools have also been established in Northern Ireland (McDermott 2012: 197). Similarly, Lithuanian migrants in Ireland have established Saturday schools to provide students with instruction in Lithuanian language and culture (Gilmartin et al. 2008: 55). Yet, other migrants to Ireland prefer their children to learn English. As a result, children often end up being more fluent and proficient in English than their parents are. The case of Ola, a sixteen-year-old female who had moved from Poland to Ireland with her parents and brother, shows the difficulties this can create. Ola and her brother often had to translate for their mother, and this was a frustration for Ola, who said 'I think she *thinks* she doesn't have to [learn English] because she can always ask me for something, my brother as well' (Nestor and Regan 2011: 44).

Recent migrants to Ireland have a complicated relationship with the English language in particular. Our research found a range of levels of proficiency and comfort, and a range of linguistic practices, from native English speakers from the US, the UK and Australia who mostly presented themselves as monolingual, to people who were actively multilingual and switched easily between English, their first language and other languages. Many people who did not have English as a first language thought, before moving to Ireland, that they had good skills. However, they struggled with accents and an unfamiliar vocabulary, as in the case of this Polish woman who said: 'it was really a small disaster, my ears were really big for a good few weeks' (2004POL04). While most felt they had reached an acceptable level of fluency in English, many continued to struggle in certain settings, such as with a group of Irish colleagues, or with accents from particular parts of Ireland. We interviewed people mostly through English, so these were people who already felt confident in their ability to communicate in English. Yet even they described a range of situations where they did not feel fully at ease, which included work, social settings and accessing services such as health care (Migge and Gilmartin 2011). There is some evidence of adaptation to this increased diversity of linguistic practice, with growing amounts of plurilingual signage in shops, banks and a range of public places, though not necessarily in policy-driven signage (Kallen 2010). However, the patchy response to linguistic diversity in Ireland means that migrants who are not fluent in English experience a range of barriers to participation in Irish society, and that these barriers are perceived as individual deficiencies rather than structural failings. The perceptive words of a Polish man illustrate this very well. Commenting on how he struggles to understand people from the North of Ireland, he observed:

> even the Irish people in my office don't understand them sometimes. But when they don't understand it means that there is something wrong with the person but when I don't understand there is something wrong with my English, so that is a little bit frustrating. (2007POL01)

Language is the basis for social interaction, but the individualisation of responsibility shown here and in the failure to develop a national language-training policy creates difficulties for migrants in Ireland. Limited language proficiency has longer-term implications: for access to work, public and other services; for developing friendships; and for family relationships. It also has implications for economic status, with suggestions that limited English-language proficiency may lead to an earnings disadvantage in Ireland (Barrett et al. 2008). Language thus serves as a marker of difference, leading to the creation of audible minorities. While this can sometimes enhance people's ability to develop social connections, as in the case of the Irish man in the US trying to meet women, it can also serve as a way of keeping people at a distance and thus limit their possibilities for meaningful social encounters.

Family

The family is important in Ireland. It is, according to the Irish Constitution, 'the natural primary and fundamental unit group of Society' and 'a moral institution possessing inalienable and imprescriptible rights' that is 'founded on marriage' (Article 41). However, the Constitution does not define 'family', and so this has been interpreted by the Irish courts in different ways at different times. O'Sullivan suggests that the key difference is between 'marital' and 'non-marital' families, with marital families – which include separated couples – enjoying more protection than non-marital families, including cohabiting and civil partners (O'Sullivan 2012). With the increase in levels of migration to Ireland, the family assumed a new importance. This is because the privileged status of the family, as outlined by the Constitution, was used to argue against deportations. This happened in quite specific circumstances. Up until 2004, anyone born on the island of Ireland was automatically an Irish citizen. Parents (and sometimes siblings) of Irish citizen children, who were not themselves legally resident in Ireland, argued that their Irish children had a right to family life. This argument was initially accepted by the Irish Supreme Court in 1990, in a case known as *Fajujonu* v *Minister for Justice*. The judgment in that case said that a citizen child had 'a constitutional right to the company, care and parentage of their parents in a family unit'. As a consequence, between 1990 and 2002, it was practice to allow residency to the parents and families of Irish-citizen children (White and Gilmartin 2008: 391). However, this practice ended with another Supreme Court ruling in 2003, in the L & O case. Here, a majority judgment that upheld the deportations of parents of Irish children argued that the Constitution did not give children a right to enjoy the company of their parents *in Ireland* (White and Gilmartin 2008: 392). Since that judgment, parents and their children – including children who are Irish citizens – have been deported from Ireland (Mullally 2011: 49). So, on the one hand, the Irish Constitution valorises and privileges the marital family unit. On the other hand, interpretations of the Constitution challenge the existence of this family unit, by insisting that legal status is more important than the family. The implications of these interpretations for (some) Irish citizens are discussed in Chapter 6, but here the important issue is the family. Migration has changed the legal meaning and definition of the family in Ireland, and this matters for thinking more broadly about the family as a site of social interaction.

Just as the 2003 Supreme Court ruling made clear distinctions between family units on the basis of nationality, so too does the Irish state in its immigration policy, particularly in relation to family migration. Eleonore Kofman has shown how family migration makes up two-thirds of migration to the US, and between a third and a quarter in Canada and Australia (Kofman 2004: 244). In 2004, though, she observed that family migration was given a much lower priority in European countries, and was based on a limited definition of the family that generally included only spouses and dependent children (Kofman 2004: 245). Since then, despite efforts to harmonise EU policy on family migration, there has been 'an increasing fragmentation and differentiation of the rights to family reunification' (Kofman et al. 2013: 25). While this comment relates to Europe as a whole, it is possible to make a similar charge in the context of Ireland. An ICI report points out that in Ireland there is no explicit right to family reunification. Just a small number of migrant categories have a statutory right to family reunification, and there is no harmonisation of the admission criteria for family reunification. In fact, many of the decisions about family reunification are made at ministerial level, on a case-by-case basis. Ireland has opted out of some European directives on family reunification, such as that relating to third-country nationals, and opted in to more restricted directives, such as that relating to scientific researchers. As a result, while labour migrants and scientific researchers are generally allowed to avail themselves of family reunification, this varies depending on their specific status, and family members usually just have the right to live, but not to work, in Ireland. Generally, family reunification is not permitted for students (ICI 2012: 12–16). And, interestingly, Irish nationals have no entitlement to family reunification, even though their family members are usually allowed to enter Ireland (ICI 2012: 24–5). More recently, the issue of 'sham marriages' or 'marriages of convenience' has raised even more concerns about potential 'misuse' of family reunification in the Irish context. This has resulted in Gardaí (Irish police) objecting to and actively preventing marriage ceremonies taking place (Joyce 2012b: 17–18, 22).

The contradictions, ambiguities and uncertainties of family reunification policy in Ireland have consequences for migrants living in the country. Research with migrant nurses – skilled labour migrants in Ireland – clearly shows the strains of family separation (Humphries et al. 2009b). Nurses from the Philippines and India spoke about the difficulties they faced in bringing their spouses and children to Ireland, and the uncertainty over their own and their children's long-term future in Ireland. While their spouses were eventually given the right to work in Ireland following a successfully lobbying campaign by migrant nurses and the Irish Nurses Organisation (Humphries et al. 2008), their children were in a much more difficult position. Each member of the family has to apply separately for residency/citizenship, but time spent by children at school in Ireland does not count. As a result, children of migrant nurses 'reach the end of their second-level education without any entitlement to apply for either long-term residency or citizenship' (Humphries et al. 2009b). This has implications also for further study in Ireland, since as non-EU nationals they are not entitled to avail themselves of subsidised fees. The nurses who participated in the study were frustrated that they were not considered 'as a *family unit*' for the purposes of long-term residency or citizenship, and some spoke about moving to other countries – such as Canada or Australia – where families were given greater priority (Humphries et al. 2009b). In our research, we encountered other difficulties. The first related to a US national who was married to an Irish national who had recently died. She was unsure about what this would mean for her immigration status. While she thought she might still quality for citizenship, she said 'I am a bit concerned about it especially when it comes to a death' (2007US03b). She also did not know if she would receive any social welfare entitlements, such as a widow's pension. The uncertainty she faced, at a time of grief and loss, was difficult for her to cope with. The second also related to a US national, who was in a same-sex relationship with an Irish national (2007US11). He moved to Ireland to be with his partner, and described all the different ways he tried to develop a more permanent, and initially independent, immigration status. He moved to Ireland first on a holiday visa, and then applied for a student visa – this should have allowed him to work part time but, because of difficulties with the college where he was registered to study, permission to work was never granted. So, in order to earn money, he would leave Ireland for short periods to work elsewhere, for example in Central America or in Germany, and then return to Ireland for three months at a time. However, moving in and out of the country placed a strain on their relationship, an outcome that was also noted more generally by the ICI (ICI 2012: 61). When two close members of his partner's family died in quick succession, he decided to return to Ireland. 'I just came and figure, what will we do?' With the help of an immigrant support group, he applied for permission to stay in Ireland with his partner, and his application was assessed on an individual basis by the Minister. He described the period of waiting to hear the outcome in a very poignant way:

> the stress of the relationship is really becoming very difficult, you don't know what is going to happen, for [my partner] it was very difficult after losing his [family members] and then losing me again he would be devastated so he didn't want to consider that option, he was actually getting to the point of being ill and the doctor put him on disability or medical leave which really didn't help because I wasn't working, I wasn't doing anything except waiting and waiting day after day. It put a lot of pressure on us. (2007US11)

In the end, and to the surprise of many people, he was granted long-term residency in Ireland. Though his position in Ireland is now regularised, it has come at a great cost – financially, professionally and emotionally. As he attempted to build his new family with an Irish national, he encountered the limits to how family is imagined in the Irish context.

Same-sex partners, civil partners, new partners, children, siblings, grandparents – all people who may or may not fall outside the official definition of family within Ireland as applied to migrants. Yet, they are important to how people, individually, define family (Watters 2011). We noticed that migrants with children often spoke about their relationship with their own parents in different ways to migrants without children. Those without children were more likely to talk about having a sense of obligation to their own parents, while those with children, or who were thinking about having children, spoke about wanting to make sure their children had a relationship with their grandparents. Often, having children made people feel the distance from their parents more acutely, as in the case of a woman from the US with a young child who said:

> And of course I miss my family, I have a large family and I would have a lot of support whereas [my husband] is an only child and his grandparents are all dead and most of his extended family live on the other side of Ireland, so it is just him and his parents who live in [the city]. (2007US04)

Here, as elsewhere, missing one's parents was tied into missing the support they – especially mothers – could give. Louise Ryan has written about this experience for Irish women in Britain, many of whom described feeling 'lonely and isolated' and 'missed having their own families close at hand' when they had young children. She also describes her own personal sense of isolation as a mother in Britain, and of being 'unreasonably resentful' of parents who had grandparents living nearby who were willing to offer help with childcare (Ryan 2008: 304). Having children often acts as a powerful impetus for people to become return migrants. A woman from Northern Ireland who returned to Ireland after years of living elsewhere described how the move had improved her children's relationship with their grandparents:

> Yeah, I think it changed for the better here. I would say the step change in the relationship was definitely moving here when they both could come down to us on the bus, even pensioners, which was just the greatest thing as opposed to a flight. So we saw quite a lot of them here and the grandparents obviously loved that too, seeing more, I think they liked that sense when it was just, oh granny is coming down for a day or two as opposed to the, granny is coming to stay. And it was a big deal and she was here for a week and we were all sick of the sight of each other all the time. So it is a much better healthier relationship I would say. (2007IR01)

This is in contrast to a Dutch woman living in Ireland, who described the quality time her parents spent with her children during their annual two-week trip to Ireland (2004NL01).

Studies of return migration to Ireland often comment on how children and/or childcare are used as an important justification for the decision to move 'home' (Farrell et al. 2012; Ní Laoire 2007, 2008; Ralph 2009).[3] In Ireland, extended families play an important role in providing childcare. Unpaid family members – often grandparents – provide both regular and sporadic childcare. This is particularly important in the Irish context, where there are insufficient local and affordable childcare places, despite a significant increase in the demand for such places (Share and Kerrins 2009). As Share and Kerrins point out, 'grandparents fill the gaps in childcare provision' (2009: 39). There is some evidence of the growing phenomenon of 'flying grandmothers' in Ireland as in the UK (Kilkey et al. 2014: 186; Ní Laoire et al. 2011: 76), with grandmothers travelling to Ireland for a short period to provide childcare, particularly during periods where there is a short-term care requirement. A Polish woman we met, who had recently given birth, described her plans for returning to work. Commenting on the standard and cost of private childcare in Ireland, she said 'it starts over €1,050 for a month full time … [and] I know the stories about Irish childcare because a lot of Polish girls work there and they always say never, ever give the child there' (2004POL06b). Because of the cost and her concerns over the quality of care and hygiene, she said 'I will try to bring my mother for a while and then maybe somebody else' (2004POL06b). Yet, this is often not an option for migrants living in Ireland, who face obstacles in getting permission for their parents to travel to the country for an extended period. The situation faced by an Irish woman whose mother lives in China is not uncommon. She would like her mother to be able to visit Ireland for extended stays, particularly so she can help with childcare, develop her relationship with her grandchildren, and so they can speak Chinese with her. However, despite assurances that the Irish woman and her husband can financially support her mother, the maximum length of visa she has received is three months (ICI 2012: 90). Yet, as debates about migration from Ireland grow and develop again, a key focus is on precisely the ways in which migration pulls 'Irish' families apart. The features in 'Generation Emigration' generally focus on people who have moved from or returned to Ireland, many of whom mention how much they miss family and how they use technology to stay in touch (for a discussion, see Gray 2013a: 27–30). Just a small number give the perspective of those 'left behind', such as Elaine Hartigan's account of her son's new life in New Zealand. She poignantly describes looking at photographs of him to prepare a card for his thirtieth birthday, and keeping 'polling cards that arrive here in the post, to use as marking pages in recipe books that remind me of him when they fall out' (Hartigan 2012). A few months earlier, an article in the *Irish Times* suggested that both parents and children hide the pain of separation in order to protect each other (Kenny 2012b).

Families are changed through migration. They are stretched in new directions and re-formed in new ways, and that process is both exciting and painful. In our research we found that as people developed new relationships and established new families in Ireland, this often led to them expressing more contentment even if other aspects of their lives in Ireland had deteriorated (Gilmartin and Migge 2013; Migge and Gilmartin 2013). However, in contemporary discussions of migration from Ireland, the emphasis is often on the painful effects of migration on families, with descriptions of a 'lost generation' of young people, and their grieving parents left behind. The ways in which the Irish state creates obstacles to family reunification for migrants living in Ireland – with 'the least favourable family reunion policies in Europe and North America' (MIPEX 2010) – are rarely considered. While the changes that migration brings to families are sometimes voluntary and positive, the changes imposed on families by state-level laws and policies that keep them separate and apart are often the most difficult to endure.

Community

Maggie O'Neill suggests that there are three basic meanings of the term 'community': relating first to place; second to a group of people living in a place; and third to 'togetherness' (O'Neill 2010: 64). She pays most attention to this third definition, suggesting that, with technological change, place has become less important. However, she also recognises the role that place plays in mediating different forms of 'togetherness', particularly when it comes to understanding the relationship between migrants and more established residents (O'Neill 2010: 65–7). While 'togetherness' captures the contingent nature of community, it is perhaps less useful in thinking about how the concept is used to enforce or underline relations of power. When it comes to migration, migrants are often defined as belonging to a narrowly defined community in the places they move to: they become particular *groups in place*. Yet, how migrants live is often more complex, with relationships of togetherness that extend beyond ethnically or nationally delineated boundaries. We encountered this difficulty when working on a project for the ICI. The ICI commissioned a study of the experiences of integration of four migrant communities in Ireland, defined by nationality. When we wrote the final report for this project, we acknowledged the difficulties with this approach, saying that 'we were reluctant to use the term "community" because it implies a level of similarity and unity that may not exist' (MCRI 2008: 3). We raised this issue again in the report, saying that 'it is often assumed that national "communities" are a reality because of the existence of "community" organisations that target specific national groups. ... [However,] many migrants ... may prefer to engage in contexts that are not specific to their national group' (MCRI 2008: 17). Yet, despite this, we repeatedly use the term 'community' in the report, in exactly the way we said we were opposed to. When we asked if there were specific national communities in Ireland, such as Nigerian or Lithuanian, we received quite different responses. These ranged from around half of Lithuanians to over 80 per cent of Nigerians surveyed who believed there was a national community, but interestingly, many fewer people thought they belonged to it (MCRI 2008: 155–6). And people had very different understandings of community. For example, some individuals spoke about an 'Indian community' or a 'black community', whereas others thought community referred to associations (MCRI 2008: 115, 155). Others again saw 'community' as networks of friends (MCRI 2008: 155–6). In her research with Latin American migrants in Ireland, Helen Marrow found that people identified with co-nationals, with people of similar class or educational backgrounds, or within the general category of 'Latin', which they felt was more neutral than in other contexts of reception, such as the US or Spain (Marrow 2013), while Lentin and Moreo highlighted communities of interest through activism (Lentin and Moreo 2012).

There is a clear tension between self-identifying as part of a particular community and being ascribed to membership of that community by others. This tension repeatedly emerged in the conversations Bettina Migge and I had with recent migrants to Ireland. Some people spoke in quite disparaging ways about co-nationals – people who shared their nationality but, they felt, little else. This was particularly marked among some Polish nationals, who were at pains to distinguish themselves from other Poles. For example, one professional woman suggested to us that 'I don't think Polish people have a good reputation here at all'. When we asked why this might be the case, she was at first tentative, saying 'I don't know, maybe because most of them wouldn't be able to speak English, most of them were in construction'. As we continued to press her on this issue, she became more animated:

I just can't understand people who have been living in a country for a number of years and can't say a word of English, they must be really stubborn. How could you not pick up or know some words? (2004POL01)

Another woman was more forthright. She was disparaging of Poles – particularly Polish men – in Ireland, saying:

The experience of Polish people I had here was always bad, it is weird, and I have been treated bad by Polish men for example, talked about bad by Polish men. So at this stage when I walk in the street and I hear Polish language I don't speak Polish language, I just keep my mouth shut. (2004POL07)

As we continued to talk, it became clear that – despite staying clear of Polish men – she would have liked there to be some sense of a Polish community in Ireland. She compared Poles to other migrant groups such as Chinese or Italian, whom she felt had a strong sense of connection and were more willing to help each other out. 'Polish people cannot make a community here and help one another', she asserted. By the next time we met, though, she seemed to have developed a stronger sense of a Polish community, in part through adversity. She talked about different experiences of discrimination at work, which included overt actions directed both at her and at other Polish people and also covert acts by Irish colleagues. These experiences seemed to confirm her sense of being Polish and of having more in common with other Poles living in Ireland. When we asked her about her views on Poles in Ireland, she talked this time about different communities of Polish people that coalesced around particular practices: attending Mass celebrated by a Polish priest; a circle that had developed around a Polish newspaper; and a group that organised cultural events (2004POL07b). She also spoke about wanting to travel in and learn more about Poland, a contrast from the first time we met when she seemed reluctant to spend time there.

In research on the experiences of migrants from Ireland living outside the country, similar tensions surface. There is a global network of Irish cultural associations and activities, from Irish pubs and Irish centres to music, dancing and language classes. There is also, in places, a strong historic association between Irishness and Catholicism. For example, county associations in New York have existed since the 1840s. Though membership has fallen in recent years, they remain active in promoting a specific version of Irish identity. Though county associations were less prominent in Britain, there are Irish centres across England in particular. I used to visit the Nottingham Irish Centre when I lived in that city, to watch Gaelic Athletic Association (GAA) matches during the summer.

The centre had a slightly run-down feel, and most of the people there at the times I visited were older men. Beyond watching Sligo play, I had no other involvement with the centre. Yet it, and centres across Britain, actively work on behalf of Irish citizens, whether through providing places for cultural activities, services and support for more vulnerable migrants, or advocacy on behalf of the Irish community more broadly. County associations and other Irish groups in the US provide similar support. Yet, in parallel, there are also many Irish migrants who avoid participation in 'community' activities and events. As one of the 'global cosmopolites' interviewed by Mary Corcoran described it:

> I eschewed a ghetto Irish association and looked down on people in Irish ghettos in Queens and other parts of New York. I avoided Irish bars, however, I did have Irish friends, but I was keen not to move in a mob ... there was a certain amount of snobbishness in terms of looking down on the Tayto-eating, Harp-swilling Irish emigrant. (In Corcoran 2003)

Corcoran describes this as a 'disavowal of collective ethnic identity', a pattern that is also highlighted in research on Irish migrants in Australia (O'Connor 2013), the UK (Gray 2004; Ryan 2007b) and Europe (Favell 2008b). 'Among the Irish [here] there's fairly strong "paddyish" club, lots of people. I'm not part of that', a man living in Amsterdam commented (Favell 2008b: 10). There is a class dimension here, with a distancing by middle-class people from class-based national stereotypes, and attempts to construct other, perhaps more cosmopolitan, identities. However, this is not only class based. Irish Protestant migrants in Melbourne avoided overtly nationalistic Irish organisations (O'Connor 2013: 156), while broader studies suggest that migrants from Northern Ireland, regardless of religious beliefs, often struggle to gain acceptance into Irish diasporic networks (Devlin-Trew 2010, 2013). In Britain, Marc Scully suggests that some recent Irish migrants are more likely to use a county rather than a national identity (Scully 2013). Some migrants actively seek to change existing organisations, such as the campaigners against the exclusionary St Patrick's Day parade in New York – both those who have been attempting to march in the traditional parade since 1990 and those who have organised an alternative parade in Queens since 2000 (Marston 2002; Mulligan 2008). The St Pats for All parade in Queens, as well as welcoming LGBT marchers and organisations, also actively encourages a broader and more inclusive sense of Irish identity. The first parade included representatives from the Choctaw nation, Korean drummers and Chilean folk musicians, and later parades have been even more inclusive of a wide range of groups who feel in some way Irish (Mulligan 2008). This inclusiveness was not universally celebrated. Annual protests against the St Pats for All parade accuse it of 'misappropriate[ing] the good name of the Irish American community … in the advancement of its alien ideologies' (in Mulligan 2008: 162). Many of these differences get glossed over in contemporary efforts to rejuvenate the idea of the Irish diaspora as a form of transnational community. O'Neill suggests that the concept of diaspora allows for a critical reflection on the meaning of community (O'Neill 2010: 71–2), but it is difficult to see this at play in contemporary Ireland. Instead, as others point out, the Irish diaspora is now being viewed 'as a resource to be harnessed to … rescue a country that is quite literally bankrupt' (Boyle et al. 2013: 86).

Defining community in national terms is fraught with difficulties. These difficulties are even more stark for migrants, who have to deal with the tensions between ascribed identities and their own sense of self. A national community may provide an anchor at a time of change and unfamiliarity, but it may equally place limits on a person's ability to settle in their new home. However, the migrant national community often becomes powerful as a perceived 'official' representative body, despite rarely being organised in this way. As a consequence, narrow versions of national community may develop, yet also become incorporated into broader discussions and negotiations with the host society. In this way, migrant national communities may become even more alienating for people who, by virtue of citizenship, are assumed to belong. From a range of research projects, it was notable that recent migrants to Ireland often thought about community quite differently. For example, they defined community in terms of friendship networks, or work colleagues, or neighbours – people they had more frequent interactions with or felt they had a relationship with. A retired couple who lived in rural Ireland spoke about feeling part of a community because of their regular Mass attendance:

> I think going to Mass and getting to know the local community that way has been a huge difference. You just see people that you recognise as you are out that you might never have had a long conversation with but say hi or whatever. (2004UK06)

This sense of belonging was reinforced in many ways. They spoke about how neighbours had helped them during cold weather when they were reluctant to drive on icy roads, and how they had helped the wife organise a surprise party for the husband's birthday. They also spoke about ways they contributed to the local area, like helping out an older man who lived near them and was bedridden, saying that reciprocity was important in building relationships with the broader community.

Even though they lived in a rural and relatively isolated area, they felt safe there because of these relationships. As the husband said, 'I have got some security, if I need some help somebody will come and help us' (2004UK06). A woman from the UK, who had moved to Ireland with her family because of her husband's job, described the 'ex-pat community' she was part of and her efforts to develop relationships within that community. For example, she had helped to set up a support group for parents at the international school her children attended, saying:

> as soon as we see that somebody is new we sort of take them under our wing and try and invite them and include them and help them and share information with them. (2007UK02)

The second time we met, the effort of running the support group was taking its toll. She described how people had come to rely on her too much, and were asking her for help that she could not provide. Yet, she continued with the support group because she felt it was needed. As she described the situation:

> you help each other with the kids and you help each other out in emergencies because we are all in the same boat. You are sort of cast adrift with no security around you (2007UK02b)

Laavanya Kathiravelu has described the relationships that develop between migrants in urban centres as 'communities of convenience' (Kathiravelu 2013). This evocative phrase has resonance for migrants more generally, as the example of the retired couple in rural Ireland shows. It may, at times, be convenient for people to make use of a national community as a way of easing their move to a new place. However, other communities are also important, such as the togetherness that emerges from shared lives or shared interests. Those everyday and regular and routine encounters are as important to developing and maintaining communities as are the public expressions of identity on days of ritualised celebration.

Migrants and social connections

The social connections that migrants develop in the places that they move to and that they maintain with their places of origin are of ongoing interest to scholars of migration, to policy makers and to the general public. Currently, that interest is channelled in two main directions. The first is migrants in place, whether this takes the form of assimilation, integration, segregation, diversity, cosmopolitanism or exclusion. The second is migrants across space, with particular attention to transnationalism and/or translocalism. While both of these approaches are present in the book, my main aim in this chapter is to think about the different factors that enable or inhibit social connections for migrants in the Irish context. The three key sections of the chapter – language, family and community – have all highlighted the ways in which broader structures intersect with personal experiences, with varying effects. Language, as a structure of communication, underpins social connections. It can be a facilitator of expanded social connections, both through language proficiency and through accent, but unquestioned assumptions about language may create or reinforce social hierarchies. The 'moral and social order' (Kofman et al. 2013: 36) of the family was explored in the second section, paying attention to the contradictions between how 'family' is morally constructed and socially and legally enacted both in and beyond Ireland. Meanwhile, the third section showed how community – particularly at the national scale – is an ambivalent, and at times problematic, construction for some migrants. It also suggested that alternative understandings of community – particularly those that are practice based – give deeper insights into migrant lives. This chapter has shown the complicated social connections that migrants develop: with other migrants, with neighbours and colleagues; with new and older friends and family members. It has also pointed to the ways in which social connections change because of migrants, whether this is through the increasing presence of different languages or the need to question or challenge limited understandings of 'community'. These connections and changes are further explored in Chapter 5, which focuses on culture and shows the further emergence of 'communities of convenience' in cultural landscapes, cultural practices and, also, in cultural representations of migration and Ireland.

Notes

1 For examples of this literature, see Faist et al. (2013), Cheong et al. (2007) and Castles (2010).

2 The consultants were in favour of training to the level of A2, described as follows: 'can understand sentences and frequently used expressions related to areas of most immediate relevance .... Can communicate in simple and routine tasks .... Can describe in simple terms aspects of his/her background, immediate environment and matters of immediate need' (in Horwath Consulting Ireland et al., 2008: 10).

3 This differs from earlier periods of migration, where it was more likely that

families based in Britain would send children 'home' to Ireland for the summer (Walter 2013a). Changing patterns of employment, specifically fewer farming families and the feminisation of the labour force in Ireland, have made this less likely.

5

Culture

Culture, Raymond Williams famously said, is one of the most complicated words in the English language. Trying to make sense of the term,
Williams suggested that it has two broad meanings. The first refers to a
structure of feeling; the second refers to a set of productions that reflect
on and attempt to shape and mould that structure of feeling (Williams
1985). It is easier to grasp what Williams means by a set of productions:
these include material and symbolic things and practices such as literature, art, music, food, clothes and building styles. Defining a structure
of feeling is more difficult, other than that it seems to refer to a shared
or common sense of what matters in a particular society at a particular
time. Of course, how culture is understood and practised – whether
as a set of productions or as a structure of feeling – is frequently contested and always negotiated. This highlights the relationship between
culture and power, which was the focus of attention for Italian theorist
Antonio Gramsci. For Gramsci, the idea of 'culture' is used to maintain
the power and privilege of (numerically) minority groups within society
(Gramsci 1971).

The idea of culture takes on particular meanings in the context of
migration. Migrants change the cultural structures and productions
of particular places, and these changes may be welcomed to an extent,
particularly in aspiring or already global cities. In these cities, the presence of migrants and the existence of 'superdiversity' are favoured as
markers of creativity and cosmopolitanism (Florida 2007; Vertovec
2007). At the same time, however, culture often becomes the site where
anxieties about migration get played out in the most immediate way.
Across Europe, this is evident in contemporary debates over multiculturalism, which is portrayed as directly associated with migrants. In
countries as varied as the Netherlands, Sweden, Denmark and the UK,
the existence or promotion of multiculturalism is seen as undermining
national identity through a dilution of national culture (Lentin and
Titley 2011). The particular object of concern in contemporary Europe

is Muslim migrants, whose beliefs and practices are portrayed as antithetical to European cultural values (Esposito and Kalin 2011). In the US, migrants from Latin America are seen as posing similar threats to national identity (Chavez 2013). The (multi)cultural practices of migrants thus co-exist in tension with the perceived threat migrants pose to national culture in receiving countries. For sending countries, there may be a different concern, which is that migrants will abandon cultural practices in their new homes. While these ways of framing the relationship between migration and culture may appear significantly different, they have one thing in common. They all illustrate the process by which migrant culture is defined by others, whether selectively championed or constructed as a threat. Through this process, migrant cultural practices are marked as different.

This chapter focuses on the complex relationship between culture and migration in the context of Ireland. Rather than focusing on culture as difference, I instead focus on culture as a set of productions that serve to connect migrant experiences in Ireland to those outside Ireland. While Williams defined set of productions broadly, I want to discuss just three in more detail in this chapter. The first is the cultural landscapes of migration. Cultural landscapes offer an insight into the relationship between migration, place and identity that is both material and symbolic. They provide tangible evidence of the influence of migrants on specific places, while also showing the ways in which migrants construct identities that are local and transnational. The challenge, though, is to identify both visible and less visible cultural landscapes of migration, because each gives important insights into the relationship between culture and migration. The second is sport. As a cultural practice, sport can help to construct a shared identity at a range of scales, but it can also be exclusionary. The particular focus of this section is the GAA, a sporting body that was established in Ireland in 1884 but that is now organised internationally. The GAA provides a means to investigate the ways in which sport as a cultural production links place and identity with both internal and international migration. The third focus is cultural representations, specifically music and fiction. Migration results in new forms of musical expression and new fictional representations of place and identity. However, the contrast between music and fiction as forms of cultural representation of Irish migration is highlighted in this discussion. While the main focus of the chapter is on different sets of productions, such as cultural landscapes, sport, music and fiction, each of these ways of considering culture has broader implications for understanding culture as a structure of feeling.

Cultural landscapes of migration

Moore Street, in the heart of Dublin, is one of the city's most iconic streets. It is certainly one of its most photographed and filmed streets, because it has been home to a large, colourful, open-air market since the nineteenth century. The centre of the pedestrianised street is full of stalls selling fruit, vegetables, flowers and fish. On a regular weekday the street is thronged and lively, and the air filled with witty exchanges between the sellers and their customers. Dublin City Council has tried to close the market and move the sellers on a number of occasions through-out the years, citing concerns about hygiene and, later, about the safety of the stall-holders. Their efforts have failed, and the market remains.

But the stalls in the centre of Moore Street are just one part of the contemporary street landscape. The street is also lined with small shops that sell a vast array of goods and services. Some of the shops, such an established butcher, have a long presence in the street. Others are more recent. They include grocery stores, hairdressers, mobile-phone unlocking services and temporary churches. The shops change hands quite often: plans to redevelop Moore Street mean that long-term leases are difficult to get, and so there is a significant turnover of businesses. Despite this, Moore Street shops remain a good starting point for fresh mangoes in season, or for spices imported from the UK, or for hair extensions. At the north end of the street, a recent property development anchored by a hotel also includes street-level and basement retail prem-ises. The basement includes a Polish bookshop and café, a store in the Lituanica chain that has opened up premises across Ireland and a food court with a range of Asian food. The food court is where I first became aware of the growing number of Mauritians in Ireland, when a stall called Coin du Mire opened. It serves as a central point for Mauritians, advertising social events and parties, as well as the services of immigra-tion lawyers and information on Canadian visas. Moore Street inter-sects with Parnell Street, which has been called both 'Little Africa' and 'Chinatown' in the ten years I have been observing and studying migra-tion in Ireland. The earlier Nigerian-run bar, called the Forum, has been replaced by an off-licence, and many of the shops and restaurants are now Chinese and Korean. A report to Dublin City Council suggested that Parnell Street be designated an 'ethnic enclave', thus attempting to replicate Chinatowns that have developed in cities around the world (Dublin Civic Trust 2011).

The example of Dublin is important, in part because of where these changes are taking place. Moore Street and Parnell Street are next to O'Connell Street, the main street of the capital city. O'Connell Street is symbolically important to Irish identity for a variety of reasons. It is named after Daniel O'Connell, who led a nineteenth-century social movement against the oppression of Catholics in Ireland. It is home to the GPO (General Post Office), the headquarters of the armed rebellion in 1916 that eventually resulted in Irish independence from the UK. Now, most official state commemorations as well as most protest marches involve O'Connell Street: it gives symbolic weight to expressions of Irish identity. In contrast to neighbouring streets, however, O'Connell Street carries few material indications of contemporary migration to Ireland. Indeed, for some migrants to and/or residents of Ireland, O'Connell Street is a symbol of practices of exclusion, most notably through the street's prominent taxi rank where black taxi drivers rarely, if ever, wait to pick up a fare. For a short time, black teenagers congregated on O'Connell Street, beside the GPO, every Saturday afternoon. A mixture of boys and girls, often with suburban Dublin accents, they were sometimes joined by smaller numbers of white teenagers, and they talked and laughed and jostled playfully in the main street of the capital city. This no longer happens. Instead, mobility is represented through mobile capital, through the shop fronts of transnational enterprises such as McDonalds and Burger King or clothing stores from the UK. It is embodied in the people who work on O'Connell Street, but there is little to mark their presence in a more permanent or noticeable way.

The changing landscapes of religion associated with migration to Ireland provide another example that straddles the divide between visible and less visible landscapes. Catholicism remains the dominant religion in Ireland, with 84 per cent of the population identifying as Catholic in the 2011 Census (CSO 2012h). The drop in the number of Irish nationals identifying as Catholic has been offset by the large number of Catholic immigrants to Ireland: for example, from Poland, Lithuania, the Philippines, India and Brazil. On one level, then, recent immigration to Ireland perpetuates the already existing dominance of Catholicism. However, it has also resulted in a growing diversity of religious beliefs and practices. There has long been a Muslim presence in Ireland, but the number of people who identify as Muslim has grown significantly in recent years, particularly in cities (Scharbrodt 2012). There has also been an increase in Christian denominations, such as Evangelical and Pentecostal religions (Ugba 2009), and in the numbers of people who describe themselves as atheist or as having no faith. Meanwhile, the proportions identifying as Jewish or as Church of Ireland continue to decrease.

In cities and towns in particular, there are some visible traces of these new landscapes of religions. These are rarely in the urban centres, but instead are more likely to be found in suburbs. The first mosque in Dublin was established in a converted Christian church in the south inner city, while a more recent development, the Islamic Cultural Centre, is in the southern suburbs, in a residential area close to Dublin's largest university. African Christian churches often began as prayer meetings in private living rooms, but as the churches expanded, sought more public and permanent accommodation. Today, signs of these churches are visible in less-affluent parts of Dublin city centre, in the suburbs and in industrial estates. In contrast, it is more difficult to identify visible traces of immigrant Catholics. This is because immigrant Catholics are more likely to use the existing material infrastructure of the Irish Catholic Church. Sometimes, this means attending regular services in English, offered by the local parish priest. As numbers grew, however, chaplaincies developed around specific communities. By 2011, there were around seventy Catholic chaplaincies in Ireland, serving communities from Poland, Lithuania, Latvia, the Philippines, Brazil, France, Nigeria and elsewhere (Gray 2013b: 65). These chaplaincies generally made use of existing churches, so they did not involve an obvious material transformation of the landscape. Yet they became important symbolically, as they became sites of community formation for new migrants to Ireland. A young Polish woman suggested that the Polish church in Dublin, which operates in a building donated by the diocese of Dublin, was often used primarily for social support. She posited that the people who attended

> might be people who would need help in a way, hoping that the church will help them in a way, sort things out for them and all that. Because many of them have ads and notices on the notice boards ... but it is in Polish and I think that the people who are not comfortable using English and communicating in English would go there for the same reason and for the religious reasons as well, hopefully. (2004POL07)

She, in contrast, preferred to attend an English-language Mass, saying she didn't like the Polish priest, finding him too political and too conservative.

The (partial) incorporation of migrant Catholics into the already existing religious landscape of Ireland is in contrast to the experiences of earlier generations of migrant Catholics. Establishing a formal and material Catholic presence mattered, in cities like New York and Boston, where different migrant groups – Irish, Italian, German, Polish and so on – competed to fund and build the most elaborate church buildings. These traces remain in the St Patrick's cathedrals of cities like New York and Melbourne, grand and imposing buildings with strong symbolic connections to Ireland. The contemporary development of mosques in Dublin, most notably in the form of the Islamic Cultural Centre, reflects a similar process at work. But this is not to deny the important social role played by religion then, as well as now. As Sterne observed of Catholics in the US, no institution could match the Catholic parish as 'a source of service and sociability, relief and recreation' (Sterne 2004: 113). The Islamic Cultural Centre in Dublin operates in a similar way, offering a wide range of services and support to a multicultural Muslim community in Dublin. Yet, because the social role of religion is less visible to those who are not part of the community, it is often side-lined. When religion is discussed in relation to migration, it often centres on disputes that emerge over the micro-scale assertion of religious beliefs, such as locating a mosque or a temple in a predominantly Christian or secular Western national context (see, for example, Dunn 2005). When the religious beliefs or practices of migrants come into conflict with those of the non-migrant population, the results can be devastating. Anti-Catholic sentiment in the UK and the US meant that Catholic migrants from Ireland, for example, experienced discrimination and violence. The influence of the Catholic Church over the provision of education and health services in contemporary Ireland means that migrants who are not Catholic may often experience exclusion or marginalisation. Equally, when a particular religion becomes synonymous with a migrant group, such as the Catholic Church for Poles in Ireland, it can also lead to internal exclusion. For example, we interviewed eleven Polish people who had moved to Ireland, and just a small number talked about the importance of religion and of Catholicism in their lives. As many again didn't mention religion, or did so in a distancing way. Yet, the association of Polish migrants in Ireland with Catholicism may create difficulties for those who do not identify as Catholic. One young man, whose parents had different religious beliefs, told us 'I don't want to stay on any of those sides, I would like just to be just new to Ireland and not keep any of those sides, just Christian' (2007POL02). The act of migration may offer a way of disengaging from inherited religious beliefs and practices. Equally, it may result in an intensification of religious belief, as religious communities offer material and symbolic landscapes of belonging in a new home.

Irish pubs offer another important cultural landscape of migration. Defining an Irish pub is difficult: Connolly et al. suggested that an Irish pub 'served Irish beer on tap and had an Irish name ... or a visible statement that the venue was an Irish pub' (Connolly et al. 2008: 601), but this definition is more relevant to pubs outside Ireland than to those actually located in the country. It demonstrates, however, the contemporary global reach of the Irish theme pub. Connolly et al.'s study focused on Irish pubs in fifteen different countries, including the US, Armenia, Poland and Lebanon. Writing earlier, Mark McGovern suggested that over 1,600 Irish pubs had been opened worldwide in the 1990s. Companies export Irish pub designs and kits: themes include 'country cottage', the 'Irish pub shop' and the 'Gaelic pub' (McGovern 2003: 89–90). During the 1990s, these newly opened Irish pubs were important for migrants from Ireland: they offered places to work, as bar staff or as musicians, for example, and they also offered places to meet with other Irish migrants as well as local people. When I lived in Lexington, Kentucky, an Irish pub called McCarthy's was opened in 1996. It was owned by Irish people, and mostly staffed by Irish migrants, both recent and more established. While it was a hub for some of the Irish living in and around Lexington, particularly those working in Kentucky's horse industry, it was also a destination for people who felt an association with Ireland, whether through ancestry or through other experiences. McCarthy's has since expanded, and people who worked there at the start set up other Irish-themed businesses in Lexington. I went there from time to time, but I was more likely to go to another pub called Lynagh's. It also described itself as 'Irish', but was set up long before Irish pubs went global, and so had a less standardised and more eclectic feel. It was less likely to be frequented by Irish migrants in Lexington, most of whom preferred the atmosphere of McCarthy's. Yet, both I and the McCarthy's regulars were involved in defining and performing 'authenticity', a process that Cliona O'Carroll also noted in Berlin in the 1990s (O'Carroll 2005). Our presence was making the pubs more 'Irish'.

Though on one level McCarthy's represents the new, commodified global Irish pub culture, it also falls within a more established tradition, where the Irish pub plays an important economic and social role for the Irish migrant community. Mary Tilki writes about this in the context of Britain, when she discusses Irish men who migrated during the 1950s and 1960s and worked in the shadow economy of the construction sector. For these men, the pub was 'the place where contractors recruited men, where they were picked up, dropped off, and paid their wages after a day of casual labour' (Tilki 2006: 251). Yet, this was not the end – they were often expected to remain in the pub when work had ended, socialising with other workers. Those who did not were treated with suspicion, and risked not being offered work again. Irish pubs in Britain thus served as economic hubs: places to get and keep work. But they were also social spaces, providing an escape from more general social isolation, though at the same time facilitating a heavy drinking culture among Irish construction workers (Cowley 2001; Tilki 2006: 252–3). The play *The Kings of the Kilburn High Road* is mostly set inside a pub: it is where a group of Irish men gather to mark the death of their friend and to reflect on the different directions their lives have taken. So, while the setting of the pub represents community and closeness and, indeed, refuge, it also symbolises the destructive role of alcohol in the stories of some of the men. Writers on the Irish experience in the US have also highlighted the role of bars. Grantham suggests that 'saloons lay at the heart of Irish political organization, and were therefore distrusted by those who lay outside the Irish political machine' (Grantham 2009: 264).

These accounts of the role of Irish pubs for Irish migrants present the pub as a highly gendered space and migrants as predominantly male. This is despite the fact that Irish women are as likely as Irish men to migrate. Louise Ryan has observed that the overarching stereotype of Irish migrants is the 'Mick or Paddy', even though more women than men migrated from Ireland to Britain for most of the twentieth century (Ryan 2004: 353). Instead, the dancehall is more likely to be mentioned as a place of leisure for Irish women in Britain, particularly in the period from the 1930s on. Indeed, Louise Ryan comments that in her interviews with Irish women who had migrated to Britain, just one mentioned entering a pub, and insisted that it was to buy cigarettes for her friend (Ryan 2003: 79). Irish women in the US, such as Kitty Leyden who moved from Clare to New York in the 1930s, also felt this sense of exclusion. Leyden described the night she heard Irish music coming from a bar, when 'she stopped outside to listen "with the tears streaming down", but could not enter' (O'Shea 2008a: 57). In this way, the Irish pub – for all that it was central to discourses of community for Irish migrants – was an exclusionary space. Contemporary studies of migrant lives in Ireland reach similar conclusions, though for different reasons. There is some evidence of migrants in Ireland, particularly from racial or ethnic minorities, being refused access to 'public' houses (Russell et al. 2010: 24, 36). The cost of spending time in pubs is also seen as prohibitive for some migrants (Coakley and Mac Éinrí 2007: 16). Qualitative studies highlight the extent to which some migrants in Ireland feel uncomfortable and out of place in pubs, or find the centrality of pubs to social life in Ireland troubling (Ugba 2009). In our interviews, male migrants were much more likely to comment favourably on pubs in Ireland. Even though we interviewed many more women, when they mentioned pubs they were often ambivalent. For example, an Australian woman told us she was not 'a huge pub person and I know it is a huge part of Irish culture' (2007OZ01): she thought this was one of the reasons it was difficult for her to meet people. Meanwhile, a Canadian woman who described pub culture as 'interesting in a different way' also expressed concern that children were admitted to pubs. 'You just don't bring a kid to a pub', she said (2007CAN02). In contrast, a Canadian man said, both times we interviewed him, that pubs are 'really nice' and 'special' (2007CAN01). Though he did not often go to pubs, he said 'even if I don't go it is nice to see the people enjoying that. That is the one thing that I think is fine, it is interesting, it is diverse, it is something that you don't have elsewhere' (2007CAN01b). The diversity of Irish pubs also changed during the Celtic Tiger era, when they were increasingly staffed by immigrants. The staff of a family-owned pub in rural Ireland, on St Patrick's Day 2006, is described as follows: 'The two bartenders are Lithuanians, and the tables are waited on by two Poles. The kitchen staff is entirely Latvian' (Bodvarsson and Van den Berg 2009: 1). According to Census 2011, 11.2 per cent of the total number of people employed in 'Accommodation and Food Services' (which includes work in pubs and restaurants) were Polish, 11.2 per cent were from the rest of the EU-12, and 9.7 per cent were from outside the EU. Just 61.9 per cent of all workers in this sector had an Irish nationality (CSO 2012i: Table CD309). Irish pubs outside Ireland rely on Irish staff to create a particular atmosphere and ambience (McGovern 2002: 91), while Irish pubs in Ireland depend on staff from outside Ireland for their continued survival.

All landscapes are cultural. They are created, changed, contested and given meaning by people, and these processes of contestation and change are both material and symbolic. These three different examples offer important ways of thinking about the relationship between cultural landscapes and migration. Glick Schiller and Çağlar (2009) insisted on understanding this as a two-way relationship. Too often, they argue, the emphasis is on just one aspect of the relationship, and on what is clearly visible. The example of Dublin streets offers one way of thinking about this complex relationship. Both the presence of migrants and migrant-run businesses on Moore Street and Parnell Street and the absence of migrant-run businesses on O'Connell Street provide important insights into how migrants shape cities and how cities in turn shape the experiences of migrants. They also show how the less visible or invisible matters, because it highlights who is perceived to belong in/to a particular place and whose presence is discouraged. In considering the relationship between religious landscapes and migration, the emphasis is often on the visible markers of difference. Yet, it is through the symbolic landscapes of belonging and exclusion that religion is of most importance for migrants. Irish pubs offer perhaps the most complex representation of the relationship between migration and cultural landscapes. Both in and outside Ireland, they are a symbolic marker of Irishness and Irish identity and sites of community formation, but they are also replete with practices of exploitation and exclusion. Geographer Peirce Lewis said that we need to learn to look at and read ordinary landscapes (Lewis 1979). In understanding the relationship between migration and cultural landscapes, the challenge is to be alert to the ordinary, less obvious landscapes that show how migrants influence cultural landscapes, and how those landscapes in turn influence migrant experiences.

Migration and sport

As the economic crisis developed and levels of migration from Ireland began to increase, media reports on the difficulties faced by GAA clubs started to appear. These reports paid particular attention to rural clubs: they were published in local and national newspapers, and were aired as features on radio and TV programmes, in Ireland and further afield. The reports focused on individual clubs and their difficulties in fielding teams because of recent emigration, and used these experiences to make broader points about the crisis of emigration from contemporary Ireland. The descriptions and images of empty training fields and rapidly aging communities were evocative and emotive, and the extent to which these stories were picked up and circulated demonstrated their symbolic power.

The GAA is a particularly important institution in Ireland. It is primarily understood as cultural, though it also has social, political and economic significance. The history of the organisation is important for understanding its significance: it was founded in 1884 in order to promote a particular version of Irish cultural nationalism. Since its foundation, therefore, the GAA has been concerned with Irish independence from Britain. This has been expressed in a variety of ways, for example through the insistence on organising the GAA on an all-Ireland basis; through the ban on GAA players also playing 'foreign' games such as soccer and rugby; and through the refusal to allow those foreign games to be played on GAA grounds. From the start, the GAA has been international as well as national in scope. Like the Irish nationalist movement in general, it made extensive use of international and diasporic networks. It used international tours as a way of raising money, but those tours also had the secondary effect of raising interest in the organisation. This, in turn, helped the establishment of GAA football and hurling teams around the world. The GAA of America was founded in 1891 (Darby 2007: 353). Today, there are GAA clubs across the world, from Britain, France, Finland, the US and Canada to Kuwait, China and Australia.

The international reach of the GAA means that it has close connections with Irish migrants. Darby and Hassan, in their review of the role of sport for the Irish diaspora, argue that sport in general 'opened doors to the Irish in terms of acquiring work, accommodation and friends' (Darby and Hassan 2007: 336). The GAA played a very specific role in this. The specialised nature of the sports promoted by the GAA, particularly Gaelic football and hurling, meant that GAA clubs outside Ireland initially attracted people who had been born or grew up in Ireland, and who had learned to play the games there. The clubs were less likely to attract other migrants, for whom the games – particularly hurling – were unfamiliar. In contrast to other types of sports, therefore, GAA clubs were often more ethnically exclusive, allowing Irish migrants to 'mix with "their own"' (Darby 2007: 358). As clubs became more established, their participant base expanded. Second- and later-generation migrants joined the first-generation migrants who set up the clubs and, in some instances, the clubs also attracted people who were not ethnically Irish, but had a connection to or interest in Ireland and/or Gaelic Games. Hassan suggests that the GAA in Europe has been particularly active in facilitating or promoting the involvement of other nationals (Hassan 2007). However, in Europe, as in other parts of the world, the GAA also 'fulfils an invaluable role in allowing the establishment of a mutually dependent network of émigré amid unfamiliar surroundings' (Hassan 2007: 397). A recent report by the National Youth Council of Ireland shows the continuing relevance of the GAA, as recent migrants to London and Toronto mentioned the important support it provides to Irish people in both those cities (McAleer 2013).

The fact that GAA clubs in Ireland were describing a crisis of emigration and clubs outside Ireland were reporting an influx of new players meant that the claims were taken seriously. I became interested in these stories, in part because I thought they might provide an immediate insight into contemporary emigration from Ireland. As I outlined in Chapter 2, statistics on emigration from Ireland are patchy and incomplete, and it seemed that information from GAA clubs could give some more depth and a sense of regional variation in rates of emigration. By chance, I discovered that the GAA had published information on the transfer of players between clubs since 2003. The level of detail provided was remarkable: dates, player names and the clubs they left and joined. It was possible, from these online statistics, to track the mobility of individual players as well as the extent to which particular clubs were affected by migration. There were thousands of individual transfers, stretching back over ten years. I downloaded the details and, working with a colleague at Maynooth University, we tried to identify general patterns of mobility.[1]

As we worked through the records, and as we asked questions about what they did and did not include, we began to identify the ways in which they are incomplete. To explain, GAA players must be registered to play with just one GAA club, and these clubs are organised at a variety of scales. Each of the over 2,300 GAA clubs comes under the authority of a county board: there are thirty-two county boards in Ireland, but there are also international county boards: for example seven in the United Kingdom, two in North America and one covering Asia (stretching from Qatar in the West to Japan in the East). These county boards are in turn organised into provinces. In general, the records show only transfers between counties in different provinces. Inter-county or inter-provincial transfers are usually not shown. The records also show only permanent transfers (defined as transfers for a period of at least a year). Transfers for shorter periods, such as a student working in the US for the summer, are described as 'sanctions' and counted separately. There have also been changes, over time, in how counties and provinces are organised, and in how moves to Australia in particular have been counted. The records use non-standardised spellings, are occasionally provided in Irish and their format changes within and across years. As a data source, they come with warnings. That said, they also provide a timely insight into changing patterns of migration that have emerged over a ten-year period that covers the height of the Celtic Tiger, economic collapse and the persistent recession in Ireland.

Media reports about the loss of GAA players gathered momentum from 2011 onwards. The loss of players was described as a haemorrhage, with particularly devastating effects for small and rural communities around Ireland. To some extent, this concern is borne out by the change in transfer statistics between 2004 and 2013. Total recorded transfers by origin and destination for these years are shown in Table 5.1. From 2011 onwards, the figures show a sharp increase, with over 2,700 transfers in 2011 and 2013, and over 2,200 transfers in 2012. However, these raw numbers tell just part of the story of player mobility within the GAA. Table 5.2 provides a breakdown by origin and destination, showing the broad changes in the regions that people are transferring to and from. Since 2010, there has been a marked increase in the number of transfers to clubs in Britain and North America. There were 1,015 transfers to clubs in Britain in 2011, and almost 900 in both 2012 and 2013. In 2011, 601 people transferred to clubs in North America, while 380 transferred to North American clubs in 2012 and 524 in

Table 5.1 Player transfers between GAA clubs by year and destination, 2004–13

	2004	2005	2006	2007	2008	2009	2010	2011	2012	2013
Ireland	928	991	952	1,036	835	823	855	942	918	988
Britain	470	438	488	352	558	437	672	1,015	896	899
North America	389	129	141	108	120	139	89	601	380	524
Australasia	436	538	583	407	11	110	166	176	12	298
Europe	0	0	0	6	1	1	4	30	38	27
Total	2,223	2,096	2,164	1,909	1,525	1,510	1,786	2,764	2,244	2,736

Source: Adapted from GAA 2014.

Table 5.2 Total player transfers between GAA clubs by origin and by destination, 2004–13

Origin		Destination								
		Ireland				Britain	North America	Australasia	Europe	Total
		Ulster	Munster	Leinster	Connacht					
Ireland	Ulster	29	126	636	124	1,815	695	583	17	4,025
	Munster	149	22	1,515	227	1,680	684	756	25	5,058
	Leinster	440	1,099	76	471	1,300	713	871	35	5,005
	Connacht	123	251	786	43	1,212	423	373	23	3,234
Britain		528	482	393	290	61	54	93	4	1,905
North America		210	178	178	95	70	38	30	1	800
Australasia		183	258	196	98	52	10	17	1	815
Europe		5	6	19	5	6	2	2	0	45
Total		1,667	2,422	3,799	1,353	6,196	2,619	2,725	106	20,887

Source: Adapted from GAA 2014.

2013. While Britain and North America have become more important as transfer destinations, another equally important point to note is the extent to which many of the destinations for transfers are clubs in Ireland, both in the Republic and in the North. There are two sources for these transfers. The most important source is the transfer of players *within* Ireland. Throughout the period covered by the transfer records, the number of players transferring clubs within Ireland has remained significant. This suggests that internal migration, particularly from more rural and less wealthy parts of Ireland to its urban centres, is an important factor in the loss of membership experienced by small clubs. This is likely to be exacerbated by changes in the patterns of transfers from clubs outside Ireland, the second source. These types of transfers have fallen in number in recent years, suggesting that migration from Ireland may now extend over a longer period than previously. So, while clubs were losing players during the Celtic Tiger era, returning players were taking their place. This is no longer happening at the same rate.

On one level, then, the GAA transfer records provide an interesting insight into the patterns of movement of young men. Through these records, we get a sense of where players move to and from, and we also get a sense of both established and new destinations for players as migrants. These records corroborate the changing patterns of migration from Ireland identified by the CSO, but also provide more local and regional information. It is not unusual, for example, to see clusters of players transferring from the same small club in rural Ireland to the same club in urban Britain or North America, at the same time. Movements like these help to give rise to the stories of crisis at local level, which are then translated to the national scale. Yet, the reasons for international migration are varied. For example, McAnallen et al. have highlighted the increase in the numbers of Irish people attending British universities from the 1970s onwards. This included students from Northern Ireland, who moved to Britain for a variety of reasons. They describe these migrants as a 'temporary diaspora' (McAnallen et al. 2007: 402), a phrase similar to that used by Hassan. He suggested that Irish migrants in Europe are 'temporary emigrants. … [M]ost are well paid, mobile professionals working in the banking, finance, IT and recruitment sectors' (Hassan 2007: 393). Equally, the transfer statistics also show a consistent international movement of people from clubs outside Ireland to clubs in Ireland. In 2013, for example, over 300 players transferred from clubs in Britain, the vast majority moving to clubs in Ireland. While players do not necessarily transfer back to their original club, they do return to the country, though not at the same rate that was evident during the Celtic Tiger era.

The focus on rural clubs and international migration masks the other important stories that are highlighted by the transfer statistics. The first is the internal migration of players, and the extent to which clubs in rural areas have consistently been losing players to clubs in urban areas. For example, while Dublin clubs recorded a net gain from transfers each year, clubs in other counties, e.g. Kerry and Mayo, but also counties in the North of Ireland such as Tyrone, Down and Armagh, were recording growing net losses. The second is the extent to which the records show migration from Northern Ireland, particularly to Britain. While this may be understood as a form of internal migration, the specific issues faced by people from Northern Ireland living in Britain mean that it is not an unproblematic movement (Ní Laoire 2002). Yet, its classification as internal migration means that it receives limited attention. The third is the level of return migration: in many ways, it is the fall in return migration rather than the rise in the overall levels of migration that is the most significant change as a consequence of the recession. In addition, there are also important absences in these statistics that, in turn, raise questions about the relationship between migration, place and identity. The first relates to gender, and the second relates to diversity.

The GAA is masculinist. The structure of the GAA prioritises sports played by men, and games for women – Ladies Football and Camogie[2]– have separate structures within the organisation. The games played by men receive most funding, most sponsorship and most official, media and other attention. Women's teams, in contrast, receive significantly less support. The transfer records cover only the movement of men. The Ladies Gaelic Football Association of Ireland keeps a separate record of women who transfer, but the numbers are very small (less than forty in total in 2010). A leading (male) official in GAA headquarters hinted this was because the 'Ladies' are at an earlier stage of development than their male counterparts. However, the consequence is that GAA transfer records only provide insights into the migration of men, and of particular kinds of men – those who are young and active in sports. So, when media and other reports about the crisis of emigration surfaced, they were really concerned with male migration. The crisis of migration, then, was that young heroic men were leaving Ireland, and would perhaps not return. That women were also leaving, in similar numbers, did not appear to be constructed as a crisis in quite the same way.

In relation to diversity, the GAA offers a particular and relatively narrow version of Irish identity. Accounts of the history of the GAA outside Ireland, particularly in the US, the UK and Australia, emphasise its nationalist tendencies. This persists today. McCarthy describes the

presence of the Irish flag and the playing of the Irish national anthem at
GAA games in Western Australia (McCarthy 2007: 374), and notes the
rendition of 'On the one road' – a contemporary and populist nationalist song – as a victory song for the team he studied (McCarthy 2007:
378). In Philip O'Connor's account of the establishment of a GAA club
in Stockholm, Sweden, getting a version of the Irish national anthem
to play at the Stockholm Gaels' first match was of crucial importance
(O'Connor 2011: 54). While accounts of the GAA in Europe suggest
the clubs are open to people who are not Irish getting involved, this is
often for pragmatic reasons (Hassan 2007). O'Connor's book illustrates
these tensions well. On the one hand, he recognises that local involvement is necessary if the team is to develop and grow. On the other hand,
his narrative consistently highlights the problems caused by non-Irish
players who have not been adequately acculturated to Gaelic Games,
in this way enforcing an Irish/not-Irish divide. The nationalist associations of the GAA also led to claims that it excluded Irish people who
were not Catholic, such as Northern Ireland Protestants (Cronin et al.
2008). Beyond this, many Irish migrants and their descendants turned
to other sports in order to express Irish identity. Soccer is particularly
important as a marker of Irish cultural identity in Scotland, with Celtic
Football Club receiving widespread support from across Scotland and
beyond (Boyle 2011; Bradley 2007). Meanwhile, the Irish international
soccer team is well supported among second- and later-generation Irish
in Britain, despite challenges to their right to do so (Arrowsmith 2004;
Free 2007). It is equally common for other Irish migrants to play more
locally popular sports in order to create connections in their new homes
(Cronin 2013; Cronin et al. 2008; Darby and Hassan 2007), or to not
play sport at all.

   However, all these discussions of the relationship between the GAA
and migration pay limited attention to contemporary Irish society. In
particular, there is an apparent silence on the relationship between the
GAA and recent immigrants to Ireland. The GAA has a section on its
website entitled 'Inclusion and Integration', though 'Integration' has a
different meaning here to its general use in the context of migration. For
the GAA, integration means bringing different GAA groups together
within the same parish. There is a strategy for inclusion and integration,
the organisation has appointed an inclusion officer, and there are plans
and targets for inclusion initiatives at club, provincial and national
levels (GAA 2013). Cronin et al. argue that the GAA 'has been at the
forefront of work to welcome and include new immigrant groups in its
activities', though evidence for this claim is slight, such as a 'non nationals fun day' in Dungannon, a small grant to a club in Dublin to help

it expand the involvement of ethnic minority children in the club, and plans for 'Have-a-go' days for immigrants (Cronin et al. 2008: 1025–6; see also Cronin 2013). Yet, Sport Against Racism Ireland (SARI) reports regular racist abuse of children playing GAA and other sports, and there are also frequent accounts of racist abuse directed towards adult players (Breheny 2012; Furlong 2012; SARI 2013). While the GAA Congress agreed to make racism a specific offence in 2014, earlier efforts to tackle racism were not supported by officials. For example, a 2013 proposal for a six-month ban for any GAA player found guilty of racial abuse was ruled out of order by GAA management (O'Kane 2013). It was replaced by a new rule that affirms the GAA's 'anti-sectarian and anti-racist' stance, and that suggests a minimum ban of eight weeks (*Irish Examiner* 2013). In short, while there appear to be some moves towards considering how to make children and adults from racial and ethnic minority groups welcome in the GAA in Ireland, these are as yet limited in ambition, scope and effect. For the GAA, as for other organisations in Ireland, emigration rather than immigration is now receiving most attention.

The GAA is important for understanding the relationship between sport and migration in the context of Ireland. It facilitates internal migration within Ireland, and provides support for international migrants from Ireland living in other parts of the world. In doing so, it asserts a particular understanding of Irish identity, often organised around the ritual performance of Irishness. It provides support for migrants that goes well beyond the playing field, usually on a voluntary basis. However, it also creates its own exclusions, claiming authority over the expression of an authentic Irish identity that is highly gendered and racially and ethnically exclusive. The broader implications of this for contemporary Ireland are clear. A video prepared for the Council of Europe included vox pops with immigrants in Ireland. Asked what GAA stands for, one young man said 'that thing that they play, that funny game' (Near TV 2012). In our research with sixty recent migrants, not one mentioned the GAA in their discussions of Ireland.

Cultural representations

Music travels. Scholars who study global music point to the mobility of musical instruments, influences and styles, and find musical links between parts of the world that seem quite distant and remote. Most genres of music have emerged in a particular form because of mobility and migration, whether temporary or permanent. As examples, hip hop is linked to Jamaican migration to the US; reggae is linked to migration between

Africa and the Caribbean; bluegrass and country music are connected to Irish and Scottish migration to the US; and blues and jazz developed as a consequence of slavery and its abolition, as well as the influence of movement between the US and Europe. Traditional Irish music has similar international connections. Migrants from Ireland to the US in the early twentieth century, such as fiddle players Michael Coleman and Paddy Killoran, were among the first to have their music and style of playing recorded (Spencer 2010). Those recordings preserved particular forms of traditional Irish music that, in turn, were copied in Ireland and elsewhere. For example, Scott Spencer suggests that since most of the early recorded fiddlers were from Sligo, the Sligo style has now become dominant around the world (Spencer 2010: 446). A similar phenomenon is evident in the recent success of *Riverdance*. Michael Flatley and Jean Butler, the first lead dancers in the show, are Irish-American, and their reinterpretation of Irish dancing has led to its growing global popularity (Casey 2002). The global and local reach of Irish traditional music and dance has thus been enabled by ongoing migration, whether to the US or to Britain, where 'a vibrant musical scene' developed in Irish bars in London and other cities (O'Shea 2008a: 57). Irish migrants have helped to reshape Irish traditional music, and they have also influenced other musical genres. For example, there is a growing awareness of the influence of second-generation Irish on popular music in England (Campbell 2010). Key figures include John Lennon and Paul McCartney from the Beatles, John Lydon, Kevin Rowland from Dexy's Midnight Runners, Boy George, The Smiths and The Pogues. While The Pogues and Dexy's Midnight Runners sought to fuse Irish music with other forms, such as punk or soul, performers like The Smiths or Boy George 'eschew[ed] Irish sounds and styles' (Campbell 2010: 44). The diversity of musical practices and influences evident among Irish migrant communities demonstrate a form of 'in-between-ness' or 'ambivalence' (Campbell 2010: 44; Leonard 2005: 526) that, in turn, challenges boundaries between traditional and other musical forms (Scahill 2009).

Despite the diversity of musical forms associated with Irish migration, music that expressly addresses the topic of Irish migration is more limited in its focus. Colleagues in University College Cork have assembled a database of music connected to Irish migration (*Emigré* 2013). Much of this is historical: it includes laments by people who remained behind and lyrics of loss and loneliness by those who moved, many dating to the nineteenth century and beyond. Even more contemporary music, such as that of London-Irish band The Pogues, highlights the hardships of migration. While there is an extensive sense of migration as a historical occurrence in Irish music, there are fewer attempts to make sense of contemporary migration. The most recent popular anthem of emigration from Ireland is 'N17' by the Sawdoctors. A song from the late 1980s, its lament for the N17 road in Galway – 'I wish I was on the N17, stone walls and the grass is green' – both mirrors and expands previous migrant expressions of desire and loss. Beyond 'N17', the musical expression of contemporary migration to and from Ireland is limited. There are some exceptions. The Pogues' 'Fairytale of New York', a ballad of faded and failed dreams, represents the downside of migration, while Morrissey's 'Irish Blood English Heart' shows the conflicting allegiances of the second-generation. In Ireland, meanwhile, there are few lyrical attempts to represent migration to the country. A notable exception is Jinx Lennon, whose 'Stop Giving Out About Nigerians' targets insidious and overt racism and xenophobia.

The relationship of migration to literature is similarly complex. On one level, there is an apparent association between Irish writers, migration and representations of Ireland. Some of the most famous Irish writers, writing on Ireland, were writers in exile. James Joyce, who wrote Dublin into literary history through *Ulysses*, did so from Paris and Trieste, while Samuel Beckett wrote from his home in Paris. W.B. Yeats moved between Ireland and Britain, but one of his most famous early poems, 'The Lake Isle of Inishfree', is a lament for a faraway place: 'As I stand on the roadway, or on the pavement grey, I hear it in my deep heart's core'. Other well-known writers, like Kate O'Brien and Patrick Kavanagh, wrote about 'home' from some distance. There is also a recurrent strain in Irish literature that focuses on the disruptions caused by the returning emigrant. Coming back to his homeplace from time spent on the African missions, Father Jack causes social and cultural turmoil in *Dancing at Lughnasa* (Friel 1990), while the suggested return of his brother from England deeply troubles Jamsie, one of the main characters in John McGahern's final novel, *That They May Face the Rising Sun* (Gilmartin 2013b). This literature provides a particular perspective on the relationship between Ireland and migration: where migration offers the possibility of seeing 'home' in a new way, rather than necessarily the opportunity to make a new home. This perspective is also present in popular memoirs about Ireland and migration, most notably *Angela's Ashes* by Frank McCourt (McCourt 1996).[3]

While Irish migrant writers have constructed a lasting body of creative literature about Ireland as home, work that deals with the experiences of Irish people as migrants is less prominent. There is, as Liam Harte points out, a strong tradition of autobiography and biography among Irish migrants to Britain, though primarily among Irish men (Harte 2009). Domhnaill Mac Amhlaigh's *Dialann Deoraí*, first published in

Irish in 1960 and later translated to English as *Diary of an Irish Navvy*, is a good example.[4] Mac Amhlaigh describes his spontaneous decision to emigrate, his experiences of working on construction sites across Britain, other people he met and his frequent return trips to Ireland (Mac Amhlaigh 2003). In contrast, the fictional representation of Irish migration to Britain is sparse. While many novels deal with the experiences of other immigrant groups in Britain, most recently the work of Andrea Levy on Caribbean first- and second-generation migrants (Levy 1996, 2004), Monica Ali on migrants from India and Pakistan (Ali 2003), Marina Lewyzka on migrants from Ukraine (Lewyzka 2006) and Zadie Smith on multicultural migrant London (Smith 2000), finding a comparable literature that deals with Irish migration is difficult. In his survey of London Irish literature, Tony Murray comments on the limited literary accounts by second-generation Irish in that city, in contrast to that of other ethnic groups. As he observes, 'the experience of growing up in London of Irish parents has historically been recounted more often in memoir than in fiction' (Murray 2012: 151). Bronwen Walter, a keen chronicler of Irish migration to Britain, discusses *So Many Ways to Begin*, a novel by Jon McGregor that features an English man who discovers, in his twenties, that his birth mother is Irish (Walter 2013b). Yet, the main protagonist is a man who identifies as English, uncovering his connections to Ireland. In this way, the novel is more concerned with investigating Englishness than Irishness, evoking McGregor's view of England as a place 'full of people arriving from elsewhere, or leaving, or hankering after a life they've left behind, an England which keeps changing as it always has done' (quoted in Walter 2013b: 13).

Because of these silences, a recent novel by Maggie O'Farrell is worth noting. First published in 2013, *Instructions for a Heatwave* is mostly set in London, and has first- and second-generation Irish as its main characters. The novel centres on a couple, Gretta and Robert Riordan, and their three adult children: Monica, Michael and Aoife. Robert, who has recently retired from his job in a bank, leaves his home one morning, and doesn't return. The search for Robert draws the three siblings back to the family home, in the process uncovering family secrets about their parents and each other. On one level, O'Farrell's novel is about families and how they are held together by a web of tentative truths and half-truths that emerge at times of crisis. For me, though, the book is just as interesting because of how it portrays the Irish community in Britain and its relationship with Ireland at another time of crisis. The book is set in July 1976, during the heatwave of the title, but it also takes place after a string of IRA bombings in England, and a series of convictions of Irish people living in London for their involvement in bombings.[5] It was a difficult time to be Irish in Britain, and the novel makes oblique reference to this when it describes an encounter between Michael, the London-born son of Gretta and Robert, and his girlfriend Claire's father:

> 'Michael's parents are Irish', Claire said, and was it his imagination or was there a hint of warning in her voice, a slight wrinkle in the atmosphere?
> 'Really?' Her father turned his eyes on him, as if searching for some physical manifestation of this. He was seized with an urge to recite a Hail Mary, just to see what they would do....
> 'Yes', he said instead. ...
> 'Ah but you're not IRA, are you?'
> His hand, carrying food to his mouth, stopped. (O'Farrell 2013: 26–7)

In this moment, Michael is marked as (troublingly) Irish, even though he has spent much of his life trying to create a distance between himself and his parents, particularly his mother, whom he was always embarrassed by, wishing she was like other mothers (O'Farrell 2013: 128). Meanwhile, his mother wishes her children were more 'Irish'. The opening chapter, which focuses on Gretta, lists the ways she tried 'to keep Ireland alive' in them: soda bread, Irish dancing, Mass, communion, summer holidays in Ireland (O'Farrell 2013: 7–8). She couldn't have done any more, she thinks, and yet her son 'has given his children the most English of English names' (O'Farrell 2013: 8). Despite how Gretta's children attempt to distance themselves from her and from Ireland, they remain connected. Aoife's name is one connection – her mother is 'the only one who can properly pronounce her name' (O'Farrell 2013: 124). But more directly, they are held together by their experiences of being different in England. As Gretta reflects on how difficult it is, now and in the past, to be Irish in England, she unwittingly shows the ways in which her children were also affected:

> These children of hers think they had it bad, people calling them names at school, telling those wearisome jokes in front of them, certain neighbourhood kids who said their parents didn't want them to play with dirty Catholics. But they have no inkling what it was like to be Irish in England then, a long time ago ... (O'Farrell 2013: 258).

The book is organised into three parts, each corresponding to a day. The first part is made of sections that locate the book and its main characters: Highbury, London; Stoke Newington, London; Gloucestershire; New York. The second part brings all the characters together in one section, entitled 'Home'. Home is the house in London where the family lived together, and it is also the place where the various family secrets begin to emerge. The third part is also made up of one section, entitled

'Ireland'. It recounts the trip that Gretta, her children, daughter-in-law and grandchildren make to Ireland in search of Robert, having been alerted to his possible presence by an early-morning phone call from relatives in Ireland. The trip to Ireland – the ferry to Cork, the drive to Gretta's cottage on Omey Island – repeats the familiar rhythm of previous, happy family holidays. Each of the family members leaves the cottage: Michael with his wife; later Aoife; and later again Monica. That act of leaving, against the backdrop of a magical, beautiful landscape, allows each of the siblings to come to terms with their own half-truths.

O'Farrell's novel looks at family from the perspective of an Irish immigrant family in London, and uses Ireland as a site where at least some of the family crisis might be resolved. In this way, it echoes discussions of the narratives of Ireland recounted by first- and later-generation migrants in Britain, particularly the sense of Ireland as a place of escape (Boyle 2011; Walter 2013a). This, too, was a common theme in interviews we carried out with UK nationals now living in Ireland, who had Irish parents. As one man told us, his summer holidays in Ireland were a welcome change from his inner-city home. He described the excitement of the ferry trip to Ireland: 'I used to really enjoy the sailing because I would be up at four five o'clock in the morning standing out on the deck waiting for the coast to come into view. So there was something magical about it … I would have really good memories of those sort of times yes' (2004UK02). For Vid Ćosić, the Serbian narrator of Hugo Hamilton's 2010 novel, *Hand in the Fire*, there is a similar sense of freedom associated with the Irish landscape. 'I loved the place right from the moment I arrived – the landscape, the wind, the change of heart in the weather' (Hamilton 2010: 7). The rural landscape – particularly by the sea – is a recurring theme in this novel: it marks an escape from the claustrophobic urban building sites where Vid spends most of his time. And, like *Instructions for a Heatwave*, the novel ends in the west of Ireland, in search of explanations for secrets.

While many recent Irish novels have immigrant characters, *Hand in the Fire* is one of the first to be narrated primarily from an immigrant point of view.[6] Through Vid, we encounter Ireland and a particular Irish family in a new way. Vid is a cautious narrator. He is unsure of his ability to express himself correctly in English, so he recounts his mistakes and errors and the times people laugh at him. But his careful use of language also represents his attempts to become part of Irish society. 'I wanted to belong here', he says (Hamilton 2010: 7). Vid searches for belonging in a variety of ways. He tries to create his own map of Ireland, to visit places so they become part of him. He works hard, and goes to bars with his work colleagues and to look for advice about building.

He reports on customs and norms, and accepts them even when he perceives them as strange. For a while, he has a Moldovan girlfriend called Liuda, but they stay together for just around six months. It seems Vid is ambivalent about being with another immigrant, saying, 'Every time we stared into each other's eyes, we were reminded only of our own inadequacies' (Hamilton 2010: 60). Ultimately, Vid's sense of belonging is both strengthened and undermined by his relationship with an extended Irish family, the Concannons. He tries to act as a mediator between family members, but gets caught up in family feuds and in broader acts of violence, which in turn tie him to the family through bonds of guilt and obligation.

Vid is a migrant, as are many of the other characters in the book. Johnny Concannon, the absent father of the family, is also a migrant, a construction worker in London who has returned to Ireland in an attempt to regain contact with his family. At one stage in the novel, Vid – the immigrant – attempts to imagine what it must be like for Johnny – the returning emigrant: 'I understood exactly how he must have felt, not knowing where to fit in, trying to catch up overnight with all the stories of the children growing up which he had missed over the years' (Hamilton 2010: 119). In trying to help Johnny, Vid opens up a rift with Kevin, his friend and Johnny's son. Through this, Vid realises the vulnerabilities of returning emigrants as similar to his own; as Johnny dies trying to help Vid, their lives as migrants become inexorably and painfully intertwined. A similar intertwining is present in Oona Frawley's *Flight* (2014). In this novel, recounted in the third person, the lives of migrants to and from Ireland are yoked together through the everyday experiences of living, caring and dying, set against the backdrop of the 2004 Citizenship Referendum. The main characters in the novel are Sandrine, a black Zimbabwean migrant living in Ireland, and her employer, Elizabeth, a white Irish woman who has spent most of her adult life living outside the country. Together, they care for Elizabeth's aging and infirm parents and, later, Sandrine's baby daughter. The two women reflect on Ireland from the position of outsiders, holding the place up to critical scrutiny. As outsiders they are also searching for 'home', which proves elusive for both, though for different reasons.

Cultural representations such as music and literature are important for reflecting on the relationship between migration, place and identity. Saunders, in a broad-ranging discussion of literary geographies, suggests that they are 'structured through the blending of the obvious and the less obvious' (Saunders 2010: 448). Obvious representations include the memoirs of migrants, or lyrics of loss or lament about emigration. They describe the experiences of migration in a direct and often affective way. However, looking beyond the obvious highlights the ways in which cultural representations provide complex and entangled commentaries on migration and its broader relationship with place and identity. The mobility of musical practice and styles is important, because of the fusion and cross-fertilisation that occurs from playing music in different places with different people. The example of Irish traditional music illustrates this well (O'Shea 2008b). Literature, too, is involved in a process of re-creating: challenging accepted wisdom and providing alternative perspectives. The themes that connect the three novels discussed above – home, belonging, and the in-between-ness of migrants – draw attention to the ways in which cultural representations complicate our understanding of migration and its impact on places and identities. Literature and music thus highlight both the obvious and the less obvious by focusing on connections as well as differences.

The culture of Irish migration

The culture of migration takes different forms. It is evident in material landscapes that are changed by migrants, such as new landscapes of consumption or belief or practice. It is evident in the ways in which people and places adapt to or resist the influence of migrants, and it is evident in the ways in which migration and migrants are represented in the cultural productions of a particular time or place. Yet, discussions of the culture of migration come with their own blind spots or obsessions. In discussing migration from Ireland, the emphasis is often on traditional cultural practices or artefacts that are transported overseas: Irish pubs, GAA clubs and games, traditional Irish music or dance or food (see, for example, Kneafsey and Cox 2002; Leonard 2005). In discussing migration to Ireland, there is a similar emphasis on cultural practices or artefacts that are in some way 'different' or 'authentic'. For example, a discussion of Sikh migrants in Ireland highlights the importance of 'keeping tradition alive' (Jordan and Singh 2011); an account of Filipino migrants in Ireland emphasises the centrality of shared rituals around celebrations, food and language (Nititham 2011); while imported food is described as a comfort for Polish migrants experiencing dislocation in Ireland (Coakley 2012).

An emphasis on difference haunts discussions of migration and culture. For migrants, cultural differences are rarely constructed as benign. Indeed, the identification of cultural differences acts as a form of disciplining (Gramsci 1971: 12), serving to draw attention to or reinforce what does and does not belong. This is one way of understanding what Raymond Williams means by culture as a 'structure of feeling': the attempts to bound and define culture when faced with difference. This chapter has illustrated a variety of ways in which this might happen, whether through conflicts over landscape change, or assertions of identity linked to participation in particular communal identities, such as sport. The power to associate particular forms of cultural production with place and identity results in processes of marginalisation or exclusion. 'Irish' writing is one such space of potential exclusion. For all that fiction offers a place to engage with change, the bordering of 'Irish' writing often means that migrants and ethnic minorities are not admitted, unless they assimilate into an already existing canon (Feldman and Mulhall 2012). Other, everyday spaces of putative inclusion and potential exclusion include the Irish pub and the local GAA club. Yet, as this chapter has shown, the presence of migrants in particular places also results in new and emergent structures of feeling. A focus on similarities in the experiences of migrants, across different times and places, provides insights into this process. This could include recognition of the ways in which migrants use religious communities or sport for social and/or economic support, or of the common themes – such as home or belonging – that recur in fictional representations of migrants and migration. In considering the culture of Irish migration, therefore, it is important to highlight the ordinary as well as the extraordinary, the less visible as well as the visible, and to show how taken-for-granted cultural productions are simultaneously inclusive and exclusive. Both material and symbolic cultural productions matter: the tangible cultural markers of migration, such as changing cultural landscapes, need to be understood in conjunction with their interpretations and meanings.

Against a backdrop of migration, the relationship between culture, place and identity is often asserted as natural and unchanging. As this chapter has shown, key cultural markers of Irish identity – such as the pub or the GAA club or religion – have been and continue to be sites of both exclusion and inclusion in and beyond Ireland; while 'traditional' practices such as music are as much an outcome of migration as of staying in place. The examples considered here show the contested relationship between culture, place and identity, a contestation that is often made visible and then side-lined as a consequence of migration and migrants. While the chapter has emphasised cultural practices as a means of showing the connections between migrants in and beyond Ireland, it also recognises the power of culture to define difference. Taken-for-granted expressions of cultural identity contribute to a dominant structure of feeling; and that structure of feeling is in turn connected to other forms of belonging or not belonging. These other forms of belonging, whether formally expressed in political or legal terms or informally experienced through feeling at 'home', are discussed in more detail in Chapter 6.

Notes

1 Thanks to Martin Charlton for working his magic with these records.
2 Camogie is the female version of hurling, a field stick and ball sport played by men.
3 McCourt also discusses the new home, in this instance the US. His narrative of upward mobility had a particular resonance for Irish-Americans.
4 The direct translation of *Dialann Deoraí* is 'Diary of an Exile'.
5 Many of these convictions, for example of the Birmingham Six, the Guildford Four and the Maguire Seven, were later overturned.
6 Others include two novels by Marsha Mehran, *Pomegranate Soup* (2006) and *Rosewater and Soda Bread* (2008).

6

Belonging

What does it mean to belong? On one level, belonging is intuitive: it is a feeling of being at ease in a particular place or with a particular group of people, such as at work, or within the family, or at the GAA club. However, this lived (often individual) experience of belonging does not always translate into a clear and unambiguous definition. There are two main reasons for this. The first is the conflict that often emerges between individual and group feelings of belonging. The second is the struggle to make sense of the different scales at which belonging may be experienced. These two reasons – alternately social and spatial – mean that, while belonging may well be felt and experienced, it is difficult to fully understand what it means. This is summed up in the difference between 'place-belongingness' and the 'politics of belonging': the emotional connections that we as individuals have to particular places, and the ways in which people are politically excluded from belonging to those places (Antonsich 2010).

The temptations and complications of belonging become even more evident in association with migration. Moving complicates feelings of belonging, both for those who move and for those who remain. As a consequence, qualitative studies of migration often highlight migrant belonging, whether this is through the homes people create, the practices they maintain or the connections they develop or discard. Yet, these attempts to create migrant belonging may be thwarted by broader obstacles, which include uncertain legal status, lack of access to long-term residency or citizenship, or nationalist discourses that mark particular bodies as out-of-place. As a result, belonging – for migrants – is often discussed in conjunction with non- or not belonging, as 'people cannot be simply defined, in most situations, as either belonging or not belonging' (Yuval-Davis 2011: 200).

The tensions between belonging and not belonging, both for individuals and for groups, are discussed in more detail in this chapter. Questions of belonging and not belonging have surfaced in earlier chapters, such as the experiences of work discussed in Chapter 3, or in the discussions of language in Chapter 4 and cultural landscapes in Chapter 5. These and other examples hint at some of the ways in which people struggle to belong, as well as the obstacles they encounter. Here, I make these struggles and obstacles more explicit, with a particular focus on belonging in the context of Ireland and migration. First, I consider questions of legality and illegality, highlighting the links between laws and migrant status, and what these mean for belonging. Next, I consider citizenship as a formal marker of belonging, and link this to political belonging in the form of voting. In the third section, I discuss home as a fluid and contested site of belonging. Each of these three areas of discussion shows the interplay between belonging and not belonging for migrants, and raises broader questions about the relationship between migration, identity and Ireland as a place.

Il/legality

In August 2012, the High Court in Ireland issued a decision in the case of *Hussein* v *The Labour Court & Anor*. Amjad Hussein owned a restaurant in Dublin, and had employed his second cousin, Mohammed Younis, in the restaurant since 2002. While Mohammed Younis had held a valid work permit between July 2002 and July 2003, the permit was not renewed and after that date he became 'illegal'. He made a complaint against his employer in April 2010, and the Irish Labour Court found in his favour, agreeing that he had been underpaid, had been made to work excessively long hours and had not received his rights and entitlements as a worker in Ireland. It ordered that he be paid €91,134 in compensation. Amjad Hussein appealed this decision to the High Court, and it was overturned. In his judgment, Justice Hogan said that the Labour Court decision 'could not be allowed to stand', because it referred to 'an employment contract which is substantively illegal' (*Hussein v The Labour Court & Anor* 2012). In other words, a person who was not legally employed in Ireland could not be protected by Irish employment legislation. The legal status of a migrant was deemed more important than his employment status, in spite of the clear breaches of the law that had been acknowledged by the Labour Court. Justice Hogan acknowledged that this outcome did not yield 'much satisfaction'. 'If Mr. Younis' account is correct', he said, 'then he has been the victim of the most appalling exploitation in respect of which he has no effective recourse' (*Hussein v The Labour Court & Anor* 2012). In spite of the judge's misgivings, his decision remains, and there has been no attempt to address the effective removal of legal protection from some of the most vulnerable workers in Ireland. This is a clear example of what Kitty Calavita calls the 'perverse consequences' of law (2005: 42).

Just as states create international migration, they also create categories of legal and illegal migrants and migration. These categories are rarely straightforward and never fixed (Luibhéid 2013: 118). Mohammed Younis, for example, started off as a legal migrant in Ireland through the use of a work permit to work in Amjad Hussein's restaurant. When that permit was not renewed – whether through his own or his employer's (in)action – he moved from being legal to illegal overnight, even though he did the same job, under the same conditions, while living in the same place. Indeed, most illegal migrants start off as legal. This is one of the reasons many campaigners prefer to use the term 'undocumented', arguing that it is not people, but rather their actions, that are illegal. The MRCI, who supported Younis in his case, now uses the term undocumented, having previously campaigned on behalf of 'irregular' migrants (MRCI 2007b). It suggests that there are up to 30,000 undocumented migrants living in Ireland, and has been advocating on their behalf for an 'earned regularisation' scheme. In campaign literature, it suggests that many undocumented migrants work in Ireland, and have lived in Ireland for a long time, often with partners and children. Despite this, their undocumented status means that they are 'more vulnerable to mistreatment ... [and] forced to stay in exploitative situations' (MRCI n.d. a).

While not necessarily undocumented, asylum seekers in Ireland are also vulnerable to mistreatment. The numbers of people claiming asylum in Ireland have risen and fallen in dramatic fashion: from 39 in 1992 to a high of 11,634 in 2002, and consistently dropping since then (ORAC 2002: 66). In 2013, just 946 people claimed asylum in Ireland, with the largest numbers coming from Nigeria and Pakistan (ORAC 2013). The rapid increase in the 1990s led to a moral panic about asylum, as the state struggled to cope with both the presence and the meaning of significant numbers of people in search of asylum. In 2000, the Irish state introduced a direct provision system for asylum seekers, similar to that of the UK. Direct provision meant that asylum seekers were provided with accommodation and meals in specially designated 'reception centres', and given a weekly allowance that has remained unchanged since (€19.10 for adults, €9.60 for children). The reception centres are located around the country, in rural as well as urban areas, and vary considerably in terms of location, size and facilities (Conlon 2010). Angèle Smith describes the range of centres, from one with 100 individual mobile homes laid out in a grid pattern of ten streets, each with ten homes, to a former hostel in a small village in the west of Ireland, with less than twenty residents (Smith 2013: 168). Regardless of their layout, however, 'most centres have overcrowded private spaces and limited (and mostly poorly used) public spaces of common rooms' (Smith 2013: 168). As the asylum process in Ireland is often long and protracted, people spend years in reception centres, but they can be moved from one centre to another with little notice. Smith describes her reaction to one such removal in poignant terms: 'many of those being moved had school-aged children, and I wondered how the children would react coming home in their school uniforms and with their school books in tow only to learn that they would not be back to school the next day' (Smith 2013: 174–5). The treatment of people in the asylum process and in direct provision in Ireland has been widely criticised on humanitarian grounds, with suggestions that the human rights of asylum seekers are often ignored (Kinlen 2011). Recent reports on the treatment of children in the asylum system, on people – particularly minors – who go missing while in the asylum system and on deaths of people in direct provision continue to draw attention to these concerns. Yet, these concerns remain largely marginalised. When the Minister for Justice and Equality was asked how many separated children seeking asylum had gone missing from state care between 2005 and 2012, he replied that 'the latest figures are being compiled and will be forwarded ... as soon as possible by my colleague the Minister for Children and Youth Affairs who has overall responsibility in this area' (Shatter 2013b). In other words, the Minister did not know and did not care to find out.

The legal status of asylum seekers in Ireland is precarious: it has been described elsewhere as liminal (Smith 2013; O'Reilly 2013). While people have a legal right to claim asylum, their status while that claim is being judged is uncertain. Their application may be refused, but when this happens there is a right to appeal to the Refugee Appeals Tribunal or, later, to apply for a judicial review. A small number eventually attain refugee status – Ireland has one of the lowest recognition rates in Europe (Kinlen 2011: 32) – but rarely on first application. In 2012, for example, just 67 of the 1,198 asylum applications *assessed* (5.6 per cent) were given refugee status (ORAC 2012: 3). Those who are not awarded refugee status in Ireland may apply for subsidiary protection or for leave to remain, but this can occur only when they have exhausted the asylum process. So, legal uncertainty can be further extended, particularly because subsidiary protection or leave to remain are not indefinite, are often awarded at the discretion of a minister, and may be revoked if circumstances change. They provide more legal certainty, but it remains limited and restricted. The alternative, though, is deportation. The home page of INIS, under 'News and Events', regularly reports on deportations: in early 2013, seven Georgians were deported to Tbilisi on 13 February, ten people to Islamabad and Lagos on 24 April, fifteen Albanians to Tirana on 16 May and six Nigerians to Lagos on 5 June (INIS 2013). Many deportations from Ireland are carried out in collaboration with other European countries, and people who are deported often spend time in prison before they eventually are removed from the country. People who are to be deported are not separated from the general prison population, despite repeated recommendations that this should occur (ADI 2012).

The occasional regularisations that occur in Ireland, such as the IBC/05 Scheme and the Undocumented Workers Scheme, may serve to change the status of people who have become undocumented. Another campaign began in 2011, arguing for 'earned regularisation' for undocumented migrants. The campaign claims are modest and its suggestions for regularisation are quite stringent: people who are undocumented would register, pay a fine, have a probationary residence period of between two and five years and earn points through working, paying taxes, becoming proficient in English and integrating into community life. At the end of that five-year period, people could be granted permanent residence, or else be 'repatriated' (MRCI n.d. b). The advocate of the scheme, the MRCI, draws connections between its campaign and another, more distant campaign, for immigration reform in the United States. In making those links, it is aiming to capitalise on a broader sympathy for the plight of Irish undocumented living in the United States. There are, inevitably, no authoritative statistics on this group. Campaigners now suggest it could be up to 50,000 people (ILIR 2013). In the late 1980s, the Irish Bishops' Commission for Emigration estimated that there were around 136,000 undocumented Irish in the United States, many of whom were visa overstayers who lived in larger cities such as New York, Boston or Chicago (Sadowski-Smith 2008). This number has decreased for many reasons, including regularisation and return migration, but there are concerns that it may again increase because of the economic crisis in Ireland.

The stories of undocumented Irish in the United States often make for difficult listening. When Niall O'Dowd of the Irish Lobby for Immigration Reform (ILIR) testified to the Senate Immigration Hearings on Immigration in 2006, he described the experience of 'Mary, who is 36, whose brother was killed in a car crash a few months ago, and she had to listen to his funeral down a phone line because she cannot go home and grieve with her family' (ILIR 2006). Different versions of the plight of the undocumented are regularly recounted in Irish media reports. In her PhD thesis on the topic of illegality, Elaine Burroughs comments on the large numbers of media reports that focus on the plight of the undocumented Irish in the United States, and that mostly depict them as hard-working and culturally desirable immigrants (Burroughs 2012: 159, 195–6). This is in contrast to the generally negative depiction of other undocumented migrants in the United States, such as people from Mexico, and of undocumented migrants living in Ireland, who are mostly portrayed as a danger and threat in Irish media reports (Burroughs 2012: 194–201). To illustrate this, Burroughs lists the range of criminal activities linked to illegal immigrants in the Irish media:

> petty theft, burglary, violent crime, drug trafficking, human smuggling, money laundering, commodity smuggling, fraud, financial crime, public order offences, benefit fraud, false identity/identity theft, gang members, other fugitives, drug smuggling, violence, drug pushing, and forged and stolen documents. (Burroughs 2012:197)

In her analysis of Irish parliamentary discourses on illegality, Burroughs identifies similar patterns. As she concludes, 'the undocumented Irish are overtly portrayed in a "positive" manner, while illegal immigrants in Ireland are mainly portrayed as having deviant characteristics and as embodying the "other"' (Burroughs 2012: 150). In her discussion of what she described as the reconceptualisation of Ireland as a diaspora nation, Ronit Lentin drew similar parallels (Lentin 2007b). She contrasted the general sympathy for Irish illegals in the United States with the, at times, hostility towards many immigrants in Ireland, particularly those who were not quite/fully legal. Her broader argument about the racialisation of Ireland and Irishness is also of some relevance in the United States. Earlier studies of Irish illegals suggested that they occupied a more privileged position because they were 'white' (Corcoran 1991, 1993; Sadowski-Smith 2008). Currently, campaigners for immigration reform have suggested that Irish-interest groups such as the ILIR are looking for a special deal, and thus not working in collaboration with others (Bernstein 2006).

Broader structural arguments – about race and ethnicity, for example – are important for understanding the ways in which il/legality is shaped in particular times and places. They illustrate Kitty Calavita's compelling point about how legal status is 'temporary and contingent' (2005: 43). She argues that illegality is built into any system of immigration, despite wider claims about integration or assimilation. Her focus is on Spain and Italy, but her conclusions are wide reaching. In most countries, legal and illegal migration are overlapping, and while migrants can easily move from being legal to being quasi-legal or undocumented, their route back to a more legal status is more convoluted and fraught. Eithne

Luibhéid charts this process in the context of contemporary Ireland, showing the centrality of sexuality – for example, pregnancy – to the construction of illegality (2013). Simultaneously, illegal migrants serve an important function for states eager to show their power and strength and, indeed, sovereignty. In the United States, this has taken the form of increased enforcement, with the devolution of immigration control to state and local levels. For example, people who come to the attention of local police for minor incidents such as fighting at school, noise violation or throwing litter out a car window can be detained and deported when their immigration status is checked (Coleman and Kocher 2011). People deported in this way include Irish citizens, many of whom have grown up in the United States and no longer have strong connections, if any, to Ireland. In Ireland, the prominent presence of announcements of recent deportations on the home page of INIS serves a similar purpose, as does the use of prison detention for immigration-related offences (Kelly 2005).

Yet, the consequences of uncertain legal status stretch further and have wider reach. Illegality is not just experienced through state sanctions such as imprisonment and deportation. It infuses the everyday lives of people whose status is uncertain, and affects their ability to participate in the society they are part of. Corcoran's study of Irish illegals in the United States made this point: despite their relationally privileged position, they too were vulnerable to exploitation. As one of the construction workers she interviewed observed:

> the only reason the Irish are employed is because they [the employers] have a hold over them. So on the job there is no double time, no time and a half. They know the score but they are more interested in getting people without papers. It costs less to hire illegals. (In Corcoran 1991: 45)

Reports from Ireland highlight similar experiences of exploitation, describing people working and living under extremely difficult conditions, but feeling powerless because of their status. As Ruth said, 'when you are undocumented … the person who employs you has all the power' (MRCI 2007b: 50), an issue that is also explored in Chapter 3. These and other reports highlight not just the economic and physical exploitation that occurs, but also the fear and psychological stress of being illegal or even quasi-legal. A study of people who received leave to remain in Ireland through the IBC/05 scheme highlights their ongoing and persistent experiences of anxiety and insecurity over their uncertain long-term status (Coakley and Healy 2012: 9–11). Work with asylum seekers in Ireland reiterates this: Zöe O'Reilly contrasts people's desires for freedom with their anxieties and fears over both the present and the future (O'Reilly 2013), while Ryan et al. (2008) suggest that asylum seekers are at high risk of distress. Our two interviews with an asylum seeker, carried out a year apart, charted this. In the first interview, he was relatively upbeat and hopeful. By the time of the second interview, when he was still waiting to see if he could remain in Ireland, he was more distracted and, at times, sad, talking about his distance from his family, his difficulties in making any kind of provision or plans for them and how the length of time he had spent in the asylum process in Ireland was taking its toll on him.[1] Asylum seekers hoping for asylum, undocumented workers, visa overstayers – these all occupy different legal positions, and their positions are socially and spatially contingent and susceptible to change. Whether they live in Ireland, the United States or elsewhere, they share lives that are individually and collectively framed and marked by uncertainty, stress and fear, and legal statuses that serve an important function in the places where they live. The uncertainties of il/legality lead to a fractured sense of belonging.

Citizenship

The accounts of deportations on the INIS home page are sandwiched between announcements of Citizenship Ceremonies. The first citizenship ceremony in Ireland took place in June 2011, in Dublin Castle (Smyth 2011a). Before then, new citizens had to take an oath in front of a District Court judge, and then later received their certificate in the post (Smyth 2011b). The first ceremony, in 2011, was attended by seventy-five people. Over a year later, 2,300 people received Irish citizenship in three separate ceremonies at the National Convention Centre (McGreevy 2012). The ceremonies have become important events in Irish public life: they receive regular media coverage and they supply feel-good images and stories. Alan Shatter introduced the Citizenship Ceremonies when he was Minister for Justice and Equality and, though he came in for sustained criticism for many of his other policies, the ceremonies are broadly praised.

On one level, recent reforms and changes have made it more straightforward – and more celebratory – for *some* people to qualify for Irish citizenship. However, these reforms come at the end of a period of substantial change in Irish citizenship law, marked by the 2004 Citizenship Referendum. The overwhelming acceptance of this Referendum by the Irish electorate changed the basis of Irish citizenship from birth to blood. Prior to 2004, anyone born on the island of Ireland had an automatic right to Irish citizenship. After that, birth was no longer sufficient. Instead, Irish citizenship was granted on the basis of descent, naturalisation or through marriage. The ostensible reason for the Citizenship Referendum was to close a 'loophole' that allowed people to remain in Ireland by virtue of having an Irish-born child: the practice was described as 'citizenship tourism' (see White and Gilmartin 2008). The rapidity of the change in citizenship in Ireland, and the overwhelming support for the change, has led to much soul-searching. Iseult Honohan suggests that the practice in Ireland is beginning to converge with more mainstream practices in Europe (Honohan 2010). She sees the changes to citizenship as nationalist in scope, but agrees that immigration has played a role in the reformulation of citizenship. This is also the position of Mancini and Finlay, who argue that it is migrant workers who will bear the brunt of recent changes (Mancini and Finlay 2008). These various positions contrast with that of Ronit Lentin, who describes the Referendum as racist, and sees it as the clearest manifestation of Ireland as a 'racial state' (Lentin 2007a). She argues that the campaign in favour of the Referendum used a form of 'crisis racism', where structural failures and problems are constructed as being caused by particular racial groups, a position supported and developed by Luibhéid (2013), who also highlights the role of sexuality. In the months leading up to the announcement of the Referendum, Declan Keane spoke on national media about overcrowding in Holles Street, the large Dublin maternity hospital that he ran. I heard one such interview on 16 October 2003, and was so shocked by what I heard that I asked for a recording. This is what he said when asked by the interviewer, Marian Finucane, 'and who's having the babies?'

> *DK:* ...well we were seeing an increase in the indigenous population anyway and I think the Celtic Tiger had a lot to do with that... and that was compounded further in the year 2000 and on with the non-nationals which have really added an extra dimension to our service.
> *MF:* It's as recent as that, is it, 2000?
> *DK:* Yeah, I mean in 1999 the number of non-nationals who delivered in our hospital would have been only about 2 per cent and most of those would have been European EU nationals working in the IFSC and other places like that ...
> *MF:* Right.
> *DK:* And so the dramatic increase in the non-EU non-nationals has been since the year 2000 and they now account for 20 per cent of our deliveries. This year we will be delivering somewhere between 1,800 and 2,000 of those patients.
> *MF:* Are these people who are living here or do they come here specially to have babies?
> *DK:* These are usually people who are coming here to have babies. They are arriving in this country while pregnant. (RTÉ 2003)

He repeated these claims in an interview during the Referendum campaign, saying 'close to 22 per cent of our births are to non-nationals.... [M]ost of these, as I say, are non-EU non-nationals, and 70 per cent of our births currently are to patients from sub-Saharan Africa and the majority of those are from Nigeria' (RTÉ 2004). These interviews and claims, before and during the Referendum campaign, provided authoritative support for the discourse of 'citizenship tourism'. They particularly drew on the problematic figure of the Nigerian woman (a synonym for black in the context of Ireland) to bolster broader calls for 'common-sense citizenship'. Those calls were supported by 79 per cent of the Irish electorate in June 2004. In the aftermath of the Referendum, it appeared that the statistics that had been used to support the change in citizenship were, in fact, misleading (Coulter 2004).

It is difficult to find out exactly how many people have been given Irish citizenship in the period since the Citizenship Referendum was passed, and under what conditions. Between 2012 and 2013, I sent regular requests to the Department for Justice and Equality, asking them to provide me with this breakdown. Each time I sent the request, by email, I got an automated response, and then silence. Parliamentary questions provide some information. For example, in an answer to a question in June 2013, Minister Shatter said there had been 66,600 applications for naturalisation in the four years from 2009 to 2012, and that 48,800 had been approved in the same period (Shatter 2013c).[2] However, figures for citizenship by descent or by marriage are not so readily available, and there is earlier evidence that Ireland has the lowest rate of naturalisation in Europe (ICI 2011: 28). The process for applying for citizenship does appear to have speeded up since 2011, when the ICI found evidence of people waiting three, four and more years for a decision on their application (ICI 2011). It has also become more expensive. Since 10 November 2011, it costs €175 to *apply* for naturalisation, and a further €950 when a certificate of naturalisation is issued. In the five months to May 2013, this means people paid €1,347,500 just to apply for naturalisation in Ireland.[3] These fees are similar to Australia and the UK, for example, but much higher than in other countries, such as the US, Canada and Germany. They result in financial barriers to naturalisation and citizenship in Ireland, in addition to the other barriers that result from a process that is not clearly outlined and defined, and that gives considerable discretionary powers to the Minister for Justice and Equality and her or his officials (ICI 2011: 79–84). However, there are no restrictions on Irish citizens taking up citizenship elsewhere, or holding dual citizenship. There is limited statistical information on this. Media reports suggest that over 1,400 Irish people became Australian citizens in 2012, and around 1,300 in 2011 (*Irish Independent* 2012; Kenny 2013). In her research in Melbourne, Patricia O'Connor found that 60 per cent of eligible research participants had taken up naturalisation, mostly for pragmatic considerations such as ease of travel or access to entitlements, but in a minority of cases because of a stated commitment to Australia (O'Connor 2013: 155). In contrast, Irish migrants in Britain have a very low rate of naturalisation. Just 194 Irish citizens were granted UK citizenship in 2012 (Home Office 2013).

The paradox that marks contemporary Irish citizenship – now easier to access for some, and more difficult to access for others – is not unusual across a range of states. However, it raises specific issues for people in the context of Ireland. Citizenship is important for a range of reasons. As T.H. Marshall suggested, it confers a range of rights, including civil, political and social. Yuval-Davis extends this framework to include economic, cultural and spatial security rights, and identifies different forms of contemporary citizenship, such as active versus activist, consumer, intimate and multicultural (Yuval-Davis 2011: 47–71). The concept of citizenship – or 'nationality' – is used to distinguish migrants in contemporary Irish society, with the regular use of the phrase 'non-national' or, more recently, 'non-Irish national' to identify migrants in media reports and in official government publications. On one level, there are rights that all people living in Ireland are entitled to, regardless of citizenship, which include equality before the law, freedom to travel and freedom of expression. Despite this, there is some evidence of differential treatment of non-EEA citizens who, since 2011, are required to produce identification *on demand* if requested to do so by the Gardaí. There is no such requirement for Irish or EEA citizens. Irish citizens have additional rights, which include the right to carry an Irish passport, and to vote in elections, and to be elected to government. The right to vote is residence based. Irish citizens living outside the country, with a very small number of exceptions, have no entitlement to vote.

The issue of voting rights is important in the context of Ireland. Unusually among European countries, Ireland offers limited voting rights to all residents, and extended voting rights to EU and UK nationals. Even more unusually among European countries, Irish citizens abroad have no voting rights. In relation to voting in Ireland, there is a four-part hierarchy. Irish citizens may vote in local, national, European and presidential elections, as well as in constitutional referenda. UK citizens may vote in local, national and European elections, as part of a reciprocal agreement where Irish citizens have similar rights in the UK (Bauböck 2005: 685). All others may vote in and contest local elections, and additionally EU nationals may choose to vote in European elections.

Residence in Ireland is the key factor for voting in local elections. In contrast, a combination of residence and citizenship is important for other voting rights, similar to the situation in Spain and Portugal (Schönwaldër and Bloemraad 2013). Despite effectively universal franchise for residents of Ireland in local elections, there have been and are barriers to political participation. The first is knowledge about voting rights. In our research we were struck by how few of the people we interviewed either knew of their voting rights or had registered to vote. The attitude of a young Polish woman was quite typical: 'Maybe I should but I never had interest in politics … [E]ven though I feel like home here, I still don't feel I should avail of any help and throw my vote in any matters regarding, which is weird' (2004POL07), while an Italian couple said 'we asked [if we could vote]. They said no' (2007IT03). The relatively low rate of voter registration among migrants in Dublin was also highlighted by Fanning et al. (2009). The second barrier is the process of registering to vote, which is based on residence. If a person moves address, the process of re-registering at a new address can be complicated and, occasionally, may lead to temporary removal from the voting register. As many migrants in Ireland live in short-term rental accommodation, this is a significant barrier to political participation (Gilmartin 2013c, 2014). In addition, there have been other barriers to participation, such as a ban on non-EU citizens becoming members of one political party, the Progressive Democrats (Fanning and Mutwarasibo 2007: 443).[4] A broader issue of concern is the lack of political power at local level in Ireland. While migrants can vote and be elected locally, unless they become Irish citizens they have no opportunity for political participation in national elections or in the national parliament, which has considerably more power and influence. Despite these obstacles, there have been voter-registration campaigns by migrant and other interest groups, as well as interest in the extent and nature of migrant participation in the political process in Ireland. For example, forty-four migrant candidates stood for election in the 2009 local elections, though just four were elected (O'Boyle 2012: 52).[5] Interviews highlighted a sense that political parties were deliberately recruiting migrants as candidates in areas where there was a high immigrant population, as well as a strong sense of localism among the candidates (Fanning et al. 2010). That localism has been explained, for African migrants, as a way of overcoming racial or ethnic barriers: O'Boyle suggests that '*becoming local* is achievable in a way that changing one's ethnic group or escaping from racialisation is not' (2012: 53–4).

However, political participation and rights must not only be equated with the act of voting, as Yuval-Davis points out (2011: 49–51). Her warning is of relevance in the context of Ireland, where there are no clear plans, and no apparent willingness, to extend voting rights in national elections to anyone other than Irish and UK citizens. Since political power is so concentrated at national level in Ireland, this has clear implications for belonging for many migrants living in the country. Yuval-Davis cautions that it is important to 'not underestimate the sense of empowerment, entitlement and belonging that this participation in elections can give to people' (Yuval-Davis 2011: 51). Conversely, not having the right to participate in elections may leave people feeling as if they do not belong. Writing in 2006, Peter J. Spiro described Ireland – together with India, South Africa, Hungary, El Salvador, Nepal and Zimbabwe – as holding a minority position in its ban on non-resident voting (Spiro 2006). Recognition of this minority position, combined with a sense of being excluded from belonging, has underpinned the various campaigns for voting rights for Irish citizens living outside Ireland. Broader arguments in favour of voting rights include a need to recognise the broader Irish diaspora, a recognition of the 'involuntary' nature of migration from Ireland, and the historical and contemporary contributions migrants have made to Irish society (Honohan 2011). These arguments all centre on a sense of belonging to Ireland, whether that belonging is understood through economic commitment, through social and cultural connection or through a sense of interrupted presence that resulted from emigration as exile.

Honohan outlines various political initiatives directed towards voting rights that have emerged in Ireland since the 1990s. For example, in 1991 the Labour Party suggested extending voting rights to non-resident Irish citizens for a limited period, and there was a government proposal for three dedicated Senate seats in the mid-1990s. While the 2002 All-Party Committee on the Constitution said voting should be limited to residents, there was a recommendation that the Taoiseach should appoint senators who had an awareness of emigration matters. In 2009, the Programme for Government suggested addressing the issue of emigrant voting rights for presidential elections (Honohan 2011). A Seanad Reform Bill, introduced in May 2013, proposed Seanad voting rights for Irish emigrants. The 2013 Constitutional Convention discussed voting rights for emigrants, and invited submissions from the broader public. A number of groups and individuals made submissions advocating for this right. Le Chéile, the Irish network for the North East of England, argued for voting rights in presidential, European and national elections, while Votes for Irish Citizens Abroad (VICA), in its written and oral statements, suggested rights to vote in presidential and general elections (The Convention on the Constitution 2013). VICA is based in London, and it joins a range of other groups, both past and present, that have lobbied to change voting laws in Ireland. Important groups in the 1980s and 1990s included Glór an Deoraí (UK), The Irish Emigrant Vote Campaign (US) and Irish Votes Abroad (Australia) (Glór an Deoraí 1997). However, despite initial lobbying successes, their campaign appeared to lose traction as a consequence of Irish economic growth and return migration. As calls for emigrant voting return, in conjunction with growing levels of migration from Ireland, a range of newer lobby groups have emerged, many using social media platforms to create connections and argue their case. These include Global Irish Vote and We're Coming Back, as well as various Facebook and petition campaigns, and they include people who have limited or no voting rights in their new places of residence because of their migrant status. Despite this, there is clear resistance in Ireland to providing voting rights to Irish citizens living outside the country. Arguments against extending the franchise are varied, but often centre on the number of people who might be eligible to vote and the 'swamping' impact this would have on elections; on whether people not living in the country should have influence over its politics; and on whether or not they would have sufficient knowledge of the issues or be more likely to vote for 'unconstitutional' parties (Honohan 2011; Spiro 2006). Most of these are conservative responses, aimed at protecting the political status quo in Ireland. They rest easily with a seemingly liberal attitude to voting rights for residents of Ireland that masks the limited access to political belonging provided by local elections alone. In short, voting rights based on a potent combination of citizenship and residence show the clear limits to political belonging in Ireland, and raise broader questions about the relationship between Ireland and migration in the twenty-first century.

Home

Legality, illegality, citizenship and voting are all formal expressions of belonging. Yet, belonging occurs and is experienced in other, less formal ways. In the study of migration, home has become an important symbol of belonging. At times, home is juxtaposed with mobility or migration: the process of home-making or 'homing' or 're-grounding' becomes the marker of the transition from migrant to resident (Hannam et al. 2006). Some research focuses on home-making as a material and/or symbolic act, while other research looks at how home – like family – gets stretched across space and time (for examples, see Tolia-Kelly 2010; Walsh 2006, 2011). Increasingly, home, for migrants, is described as transnational or translocal, with emphasis on the ways in which people maintain links and connections between multiple homes, such as through practices, communications or travel. Yet, the emphasis on transnational homes has been criticised by Ralph and Staeheli, who insist that home, for migrants, must also be seen as a localised experience (Ralph and Staeheli 2011). These tensions over where exactly home is get played out in migrant lives, in Ireland and far from Ireland.

The materiality of home-making often centres on food. We found that many people who participated in our research project talked about searching for familiar food in order to feel at home. One woman talked about buying treats for her children in a South African store: 'South African sweets and crisps and a couple of chocolates and things, the chips, and ... some of the cereals' (2007SA01), while many Italians made unfavourable comparisons between the quality of food in Ireland and in Italy. Even some people from the UK commented on food, despite the interconnectedness of food supply and sale in Ireland and the UK. The most vocal was a Scottish man who said:

> There are definitely foods that I miss ... A lot of the things I used to eat at home [in Scotland], there are these bread roll things that they make that I can't get here. I can't get haggis. I really struggle to get porridge some-times. I think I might have found a source for it now. You get Irish white puddings but they are nothing like Scottish white puddings, nothing like them at all. Sometimes I even get my son to send them over. Oatcakes, the smoked fish that we eat back home, you can't get that here. (2007UK03)

A detailed study of Polish food culture in Cork (Coakley 2010) high-lights the ways in which Polish shops selling Polish foods, conducting business in the Polish language, provide homely feelings and places of familiarity for migrants. Being able to buy Polish brands creates a sense of continuity for people living in an unfamiliar place, as they seek to maintain habits and ways of doing things (Coakley 2010: 112). Of course, this is often framed in terms of superiority. Just as some Italians we interviewed complained about the quality of food in Ireland, some of the Polish participants in Coakley's research claimed that Polish food was superior to Irish food. Among the items they thought were better were 'mayonnaise, mustard, flour, bread, milk and breadcrumbs' (Coakley 2010: 110). In their study of Irish migrants in Coventry, Kneafsey and Cox also identified a belief in the superiority of some food from their place of origin, such as dairy products or meat, as well as an attachment to familiar and local brands, such as Tayto crisps, red lem-onade and Barry's tea (Kneafsey and Cox 2002: 11–12). They quote a shop owner in Coventry as saying 'they go mad for the Kimberly cakes' (Kneafsey and Cox 2002: 12). In contrast, not having access to familiar foods can disrupt the establishment of a sense of belonging. This is a recurring theme in studies of asylum seekers in Ireland, whose food is prepared for them as part of the system of direct provision. Angèle Smith describes the women she met who were upset that they could not prepare their own food for their children, and who thought their children were becoming ill as a result. Beatrice, for example, said that her son's stomach ached and that he felt terrible. 'But what can I expect, if I cannot feed him the food that he needs to make him well? ... He needs his own kind of food, he needs Nigerian food' (in Smith 2013: 174). Here, as well as in the case of Polish migrants in Cork and Irish migrants in Coventry, the relationship with food is gendered. In most of these instances, it is women rather than men who emphasise the importance of familiar food and food practices. In contrast, as both Coakley and Kneafsey and Cox suggest, the attitudes of men to food are often more functional and less affective (Coakley 2010: 114; Kneafsey and Cox 2002). In fact, in some cases new food becomes a marker of alternative belonging for men, such as Adam, who was disparaging of Polish shops and said he wanted to 'try something new, different or fresh' (Coakley 2010: 114), or the Irish man in Canada, describing eating Kentucky Fried Chicken and watching hockey with his friend, who said he would never go back to Ireland, because you couldn't get 'chicken like this in Clara' (Clary-Lemon 2010: 16).[6]

Nira Yuval-Davis argues for a feminist politics of belonging that is underpinned by emotions of care and love (Yuval-Davis 2011: 177–99). Much of her discussion highlights the politics of transnational care and carers, with parallels to Geraldine Pratt's more extensive treatment of the topic (Pratt 2012). Yet, her emphasis on care has broader relevance to migration and the question of home than perhaps Yuval-Davis acknowledges. The preparation of food for family and friends is an act of care that is intimately connected to belonging, and restrictions on people's ability to make their own food and to nourish those they care about can disrupt their sense of being at home. Similarly, the act of caring for family and friends at a distance can both maintain and undermine people's relationship to home(s). Breda Gray describes this as the politics of (trans)national social reproduction: drawing on her earlier research with Irish women, she suggests that this is gendered in problematic ways (Gray 2013a). For example, she comments that 'perceptions about the ease of mobility made the absence of migrant daughters or sisters in times of family crisis or need in Ireland the individual failure of the migrant' (Gray 2013a: 26). Gray argues for a foregrounding of the work that goes into caring, both locally and transnationally, and for a recognition of how migrants, particularly women, perform this work in often invisible ways. Yet, caring over distances is not just performed by women. We interviewed men who spoke about caring for their parents, such as the Polish man who described daily phone calls to his mother:

> It is like every single day just for a few seconds' exchange like 'hello, how are you'? 'Everything is fine, yes that's great, love you, love you', and she is still treats me as a little boy [laugh]. 'If it is raining, get your umbrella'. [Laugh] (2004POL02)

In contrast, a young Polish woman described the caring work of her sister, who still lived with their parents, and who worked to console their mother, saying 'my sister is always calming her down, "[Ireland] is her home you can't chain her to this small town"' (2004POL07). Meanwhile, Liam Coakley shows that for male African migrants in Ireland, care is often expressed in economic terms (Coakley 2013). Gray's broader point about the gendered nature of social reproduction does seem relevant in the context of migration from Ireland, and is supported by reports of the loss of independence and autonomy experienced by female return migrants (Ní Laoire 2007). Yet, care is important for the making and maintenance of home for men also, and it is necessary to recognise the different ways in which care is expressed and expected.

In the twenty-first century, technology plays a crucial role in keeping people in touch, and in creating translocal connections. The use of technology varies. In the 1980s and 1990s, migrants from Ireland made use of more affordable phone calls, and began to use email. Starting in 1987, Liam Ferrie used email to distribute his weekly news digest, *The Irish Emigrant*, globally. When I moved to Kentucky in 1994, I joined the thousands of people worldwide who anticipated its arrival in my inbox.[7] Then, satellite television channels broadcast the GAA All-Ireland finals to pubs and clubs in the UK, Europe, the US and further afield. Now, a whole range of GAA matches are shown live, through digital channels and over the internet, while landlines have been usurped by mobile phones and instant messaging, and Twitter and Facebook and the wonders of Skype. King O'Riain, in her discussion of transnational families, picked up on the description of Skype as home (King O'Riain 2013). In their study of transnational media networks, Kerr et al. (2013) highlight the use of Polish satellite channels, internet radio and television among Polish migrants in Ireland, but also their use of local radio and newspapers. They suggest 'the experience of transnational multi-positionality enhanced the importance of feelings of mediated togetherness made possible by key media events both "there" and "here"' (Kerr et al. 2013: 104). They contrast this with Chinese migrants, who they claim are 'less integrated into Ireland as a place' (Kerr et al. 2013: 106) as a consequence of their media practices. Yet, for all the proliferation and immediacy of both visual and aural contact, new technologies also highlight distance and separation. Breda Gray highlights the parallel discourses of contemporary migrants and earlier migrants, commenting that in 'Generation Emigration':

> although the amazing affordances of new media in overcoming separation are referred to in nearly all of the accounts, both women and men emigrants described an emotional and practical struggle to keep in touch with family across long distances. (Gray 2013a: 27)

Home, for migrants, is also tied up with finding a place to live. In Chapter 2, I wrote about the differences in housing tenure among different nationality groupings in Ireland, and also about the polarisation of the housing experiences of Irish people in Britain. Many of the people we interviewed commented on how expensive rent was and how difficult it was to find good rental accommodation in Ireland. Often, people had to share accommodation with others they did not know in order to be able to afford to live in an area that was convenient. A Polish man told us about having to call the Gardaí on his housemates (2007POL02), while a Spanish man explained his poor standard accommodation in terms of its cost: 'I have been in several places here and probably this is the worst but it is so cheap that it helps me a lot' (2007SPN01b). Meanwhile, an Italian couple who loved the area they lived in felt compelled to leave it because of the cost of rent:

> how much we pay for the rent is very high, like €1,000 for a small flat, one bedroom and the kitchen is with a living room. It is new, it is very nice but I think now it is enough, [the landlord] he didn't want to go down. (2007IT03)

Many people spoke about wanting more security of tenure, which sometimes meant a desire to purchase their own home. Coakley notes this also in his research with African migrants in Ireland, where he observes that 'home ownership was a common aspiration' (Kerr et al. 2013: 139). However, the significant reduction in mortgage lending as a result of the recession, combined with more precarious employment conditions, is making this dream a more distant reality. In addition, there is evidence that some migrants in Ireland, particularly in the Dublin region, may be more susceptible to homelessness. This happened to one of the people we interviewed, when the job he thought he had arranged prior to moving to Ireland turned out to be an internet fraud. He spent two months sleeping in a hostel for homeless people, before eventually finding work and a place to live (2007POL02). Recent legislative changes in Ireland, specifically the introduction of a 'right to reside' condition, mean that people who do not have a right to reside in Ireland have no entitlements to social assistance, which includes supports to exit homelessness. Beyond the practical difficulties of finding a place to live, migrants also have to deal with home as an exclusionary construct. Before it was abolished, the National Consultative Committee on Racism and Interculturalism (NCCRI) published regular accounts of racist incidents in Ireland. Many of these involved people who were shouted at to 'go home'. Similarly, children in school reported being told to 'get back to Africa' or to 'go home you stupid Lithuanian' (Darmody et al. 2012: 292). Meanwhile, return Irish migrants may be treated as 'outsiders' or as 'different' when they move 'home' (Ní Laoire 2007; Ralph 2012).

Spaces and scales of belonging

Belonging occurs, and is experienced, in a range of spaces and scales, from the informal sense of being at home to the more formal belonging that is expressed through citizenship and legal status and the right to vote. For migrants, it can sometimes be difficult to feel a sense of belonging, and many migrants are conscious of the barriers to belonging that they encounter. Often, these barriers are expressed and experienced in more everyday, banal ways. In interviews, for example, recent migrants to Ireland often spoke about not being invited to the homes of Irish people, and identified this as a sign that they were not fully accepted in Ireland. Over time, as people became more friendly with Irish neighbours and colleagues, we noted how this changed, and the impact this had on belonging. A woman from the UK, when we first met, described the delays in making friends as 'slowly, slowly get to know neighbours and make friends with neighbours'. A year later, this was less of an issue. She told us that 'the neighbours are friendly and I have been in for coffee with a few of them and I think if I made more effort they would become friends but I am so busy with the friends that I have that I haven't bothered' (2007UK02; 2007UK02b). In this way, she had developed a strong sense of place-belongingness. However, the politics of belonging were still relevant, for even though she had more formal rights as a UK citizen, the impact of the economic recession meant that it was likely she and her family would have to leave Ireland sooner than she wanted.

Formal belonging, whether through legal status or citizenship, is important for migrants, because it shapes the conditions under which they may interact with and participate in the places where they live or have lived. Yet, many people who have a quasi-legal or illegal status, or who do not possess formal citizenship of the country where they live, may still experience a sense of belonging, for all that it is contingent and fraught. This happens through being able to find a place to live where they feel at ease, developing meaningful relationships, establishing comfortable and comforting routines in their everyday lives, and maintaining connections with people in other places. While this may be easier for people with formal access to belonging, those with less formal access are not excluded. However, all migrants may experience obstacles to belonging: through everyday or structural racism, through limited opportunities for or restrictions on participation, or from the actions of a settled population unaware of or unwilling to adapt to the specific needs of particular migrants. Restricted access to employment and negative experiences at work, which are discussed in Chapter 3, offer a clear example of obstacles to belonging with both short- and longer-term consequences. Similarly, questions of language or community (Chapter 4) or participation in sport (Chapter 5) may help to develop or hinder a sense of place-belongingness for migrants. As has been shown in this chapter, the issue of voting rights in Ireland is a clear example of an obstacle to belonging. Restrictions on the right to vote exclude migrants living both in and outside Ireland from full political participation, thus ensuring continued political power and dominance for the settled and indigenous population. *The Gathering* represents another example, for in its construction of a homogenous Irishness as part of an Irish diaspora strategy, it fails to acknowledge the multiple ways in which people might belong, both within and across borders (Scully 2012).

Belonging links place and identity together, in an often-complex relationship. When migrants are introduced into this relationship, it is further complicated. Migrant belonging stretches across spaces and scales, from everyday interactions that may lead to a sense of place-belongingness to transnational belonging that stretches across national borders. Yet belonging must be understood in conjunction with not belonging, and migrants are particularly vulnerable to the politics of not belonging, whether through the denial of voting rights to Irish emigrants, changes to citizenship laws in Ireland or the formal lack of legal protection for undocumented migrants at work. Belonging intersects with work, society and culture to raise broader questions about the place of migration in contemporary societies. In Chapter 7, I discuss this in more detail, and show how an expanded place-based approach provides new insights into the relationship between migrants, place and identity.

Notes

1 In contrast to other extracts from this research, I have not used an identifier, in order to ensure anonymity.
2 Many applications had taken 2–3 years to process, so the approval figure also includes a large backlog of 22,000 applications that existed when Minister Shatter was appointed in March 2011.
3 There were 7,700 applications for naturalisation in this period (Shatter 2013c).
4 This ban, once identified, was quickly changed. The Progressive Democrats are no longer in existence.
5 Maguire and Murphy (2012: 37–63) provide an engaging account of the campaigns of two migrant candidates, Benedicta and Yinka. Neither was elected in the 2009 local elections.
6 Clara is a small town in Co. Offaly, in the Irish midlands.
7 Because I was a student, Liam Ferrie sent me the digest for free. I was, and still am, very grateful to him for his generosity. He and his wife, Pauline, retired in 2012, after producing *The Irish Emigrant* for 25 years (Donegal Democrat 2012).

7

Conclusion

At King's Cross, in London, 'the biggest inner city redevelopment in Europe' (Holgersen and Haarstad 2009: 348) is currently taking place. When I walked around the area in summer 2013, I noticed the hoardings that advertised the main building contractor, Murphy. A UK and Irish-based company, it was set up by an Irish migrant to London in 1945, but is now global. As I walked by one of the entrances to the site, it was the end of a work shift, and men in high-visibility jackets were streaming in and out of the gate. As they spoke, I realised from their accents that they were mostly Irish – both younger and middle aged. I had known of Murphy for a while, because my brother had spent a summer working on a Murphy building site in London. What I hadn't realised was that Murphy continued to provide employment for Irish migrants in London, since recent scholarship created the impression that labouring work in the city was increasingly the preserve of migrants from other places, such as Brazil or Poland (Datta and Brickell 2009; Wills et al. 2010). But that was not the only time I encountered Irish accents during a short trip to London. I overheard Irish people talk in a Turkish restaurant in Dalston, in coffee shops and on the street in Bethnal Green and Hackney, and at a public lecture on 'Obama's America'. They were men and women, young and old, and appeared to have a wide variety of backgrounds and experiences. When I flew back to Dublin on a late Thursday evening flight from London City Airport, I met more Irish people on the plane. Many were suited men and women who seemed to be regular travellers, greeting each other and the flight attendants, or positioning themselves in the plane with weary familiarity.[1] The chief executive of the airport is also Irish: Declan Collier took up the post in 2012, having previously managed the Dublin Airport Authority (Sibun 2012).

Each of the people I encountered has their own story – their own reasons for migrating, their own experiences of migration. The book has highlighted this diversity of migrant experiences, ranging from highly skilled to undocumented workers, from new religious communities to separated families, from citizens to asylum seekers. These experiences are linked together through their connections to Ireland as a place: a place that is contingent and negotiated and thrown-together, and that is defined as much by its links and connections as it is by attempts to bound and fix its borders and its meanings. Yet, despite both the diversity of migrant experiences and the messiness of place, our attempts to understand migration as a process often suffer from a tendency to simplification and generalisation. While this impulse is, on one level, understandable, it has social and political consequences for migrants *in* and *across* places. It also has consequences for those places and *all* the people who inhabit them.

In this book, my aim has been to challenge the simplifications that impair our perception of the relationship between Ireland and migration. I have acknowledged the dominant understanding of this relationship: the narratives of migration from Ireland as a form of exile that have such resonance at times of economic crisis; and the uneasy engagement with recent migration to Ireland that focuses primarily on difference. However, I have also challenged and complicated these understandings. Rather than treating migration *to* and *from* Ireland as separate and distinct processes, I have insisted on looking for links and connections, often through a focus on migration as a lived experience. At times these links are explicit, such as in the discussions of medical migration in Chapter 3 or the GAA in Chapter 5. At other times, these links are more tenuous, framed around a shared experience of migration that is differentially grounded in diverse contexts. This is the case in my account of inadvertent workers (Chapter 3). On first glance, international students in Ireland and Working Holiday Visa holders in Australia may appear to have little in common. Yet they share experiences of precarity and marginality, serving useful functions in their respective labour markets and often enduring exploitation in the cause of personal development. My insistence on the importance of these links and connections is not at the expense of acknowledging that their strength and importance and relevance varies. Similarly, highlighting links does not diminish the symbolic and material importance of boundaries and borders. The role of states in enabling and managing migration is repeatedly recognised in this book, most notably in Chapter 2, which discusses both the laws and policies that frame migration and the statistics that represent the translation of the messiness of migration into manageable, quantifiable units. Across the chapters, the tensions between bounded and more fluid understandings of the relationship between place and migration emerge, for example in the discussion of family in Chapter 4 or of cultural landscapes in Chapter 5.

In Chapter 1, I described this book as having a broad concern, which is to rethink the relationship between migration, place and identity. In doing so, I acknowledged two key challenges. One was the predominant emphasis, in studies of migration, on difference *in place*. Chapters 3 to 6 addressed this, showing how migration to, from and (to a lesser extent) within Ireland might be differently understood. The chapters have been organised around cross-cutting themes – work, social connections, culture and belonging – that are central to a broad body of scholarship on migration more generally. They examined these themes both in and across place, showing the similarities and differences that emerge for migrants as they work, forge social connections and develop a sense of belonging in and beyond Ireland. Yet, my efforts to think about migration and Ireland in a more thematic and dynamic way mean that, at times, I have taken refuge in the comfort of methodological and epistemological nationalism. This was the second challenge I identified in Chapter 1, where I suggested that too much attention was paid to states and cities in the study of migration, and that other spatial scales also needed consideration. As a result, there has been a focus on a number of different scales – for example, cultural landscapes in Chapter 5 or 'home' in Chapter 6. Despite this awareness, the state – in particular the Irish state – keeps appearing as a key player in this book. As can be seen in both the broader discussion of legal frameworks in Chapter 2 and in the more specific discussions of il/legality and citizenship in Chapter 6, the state matters. It continues to have power to shape and frame, though not necessarily to determine, the lived experiences of migrants.

In this final chapter, I want to consider the relationship between migration, place and identity in more detail. Drawing from and building upon the example of Ireland, I discuss first the connection between migration and social change, and second the connection between migration, justice and equality. I conclude by advocating for a place-based approach to migration, showing how this focus on Ireland as a specific place adds to our more general knowledge about migration as a process and as a lived experience. This opening out of the discussion allows me to address the limitations I identified earlier: it allows links and connections to intersect with borders and boundaries; it provides for a multi-scalar approach; and it sees migration and migrants as part of, rather than apart from, contemporary societies.

Social change and migration

Migration emerges from, and results in, social change. Stephen Castles acknowledges this when he observes that 'migration has been a normal aspect of social life – and especially of social change – throughout history' (Castles 2010: 1567). In his call for a 'middle-range theory' of migration, Castles argues that we should start with a 'social transformation framework'. By this, he means that the starting point for the study of migration should be social transformation, which he describes as a 'fundamental shift in the way society is organised that goes beyond the continual processes of incremental social change that are always at work' (Castles 2010: 1576). He illustrates his position with reference to new labour market segmentation. Though Castles is at pains to point out how this takes different forms in contexts that range from New York to Berlin to Britain, he ultimately frames these experiences as differentiated consequences of neoliberal globalisation and economic restructuring. As a consequence, his distinction between a 'fundamental shift' and an 'incremental social change' and his articulation of a 'middle-range theory' is less obvious and less convincing than perhaps he intended. Yet, his fundamental argument – that migration must be understood not as a stand-alone process, but rather one that is intimately connected to broader social relations – remains important and valid. A social change perspective shifts our gaze in new directions, helping us to move beyond exceptionalism in our approach to migration.

Despite the clear importance of Castles' call, his understanding of social transformation is restricted. In particular, his distinction between fundamental shift and incremental change leads to limitations in how we might understand migration. A focus on fundamental shifts directs us towards large-scale and visible changes, sometimes in response to a variety of catastrophic events. A clear example of such a fundamental shift is EU enlargement. In 2004, citizens of the ten new EU member countries were given immediate rights to live and work in Ireland, as well as the UK and Sweden. The impact of this decision is obvious in Table 2.2 where, in the three-year period from 2006 to 2008, close to 190,000 people with EU-12 nationality immigrated to Ireland. This movement of people from the EU-10 to Ireland was a response to broader changes at EU level, though the final decision around implementation at local level was made by the Irish state. The EU is also important for understanding attitudes to migration of non-EU nationals. Though Ireland is not part of the Schengen accord, Irish migration policies – particularly in relation to asylum seekers and to labour migrants – have clear parallels with initiatives at the European scale. However, concerns with the impact of EU membership on migration have faded in recent years as people have diverted more attention to the economic crisis in Ireland. This is a clear example of a catastrophic and fundamental shift, where the combined effect of the bank bailout, a burst property bubble and the EU/

European Central Bank/International Monetary Fund financial bailout has resulted in a stagnant economy and intense financial and social hardships for some. Unemployment levels have tripled, social welfare and, in some cases, pay have been cut, and there are growing numbers of homes being repossessed and people in mortgage arrears. At the same time, levels of emigration from Ireland have increased rapidly, from around 36,000 people in 2006, to an estimate of almost 82,000 in 2014 (see Table 2.3). An obvious conclusion is that emigration is a direct consequence of the dramatic effects of neoliberal austerity in Ireland. Yet, emigration did not suddenly begin in 2008 with the bank bailout. People migrated from Ireland throughout the years of economic prosperity, if in smaller numbers. Now, in the midst of an economic crisis, people continue to immigrate to Ireland. As Table 2.2 shows, an estimated 60,600 people migrated to Ireland in 2014, over 49,000 of whom had a nationality other than Irish. This is despite the assumption that immigration to Ireland was short term, expedient and related solely to the availability of jobs. Ongoing immigration, when the unemployment rate remains above 10 per cent, challenges this belief. The suggestion of a direct causal link between austerity and patterns of migration is thus overstated. While austerity explains some of the increase in migration from Ireland, and particularly the relative reduction in the proportion of return Irish migrants, it does not explain migration from Ireland in its entirety. Equally, it does not explain the growing numbers of people migrating to Ireland, a figure that increased by 45 per cent from 2010 to 2014.

This new focus on the Irish economic situation represents a form of the bias identified by Castles. He labels it as a 'receiving country' bias, but what he describes is more accurately represented as neocolonialism, underpinned by an implicit sense of spatial hierarchies. Thus, contemporary migration to Ireland is often characterised as people moving from poorer countries to benefit from higher wages and benefits, while contemporary migration from Ireland is framed as either as a 'lifestyle choice' or as a necessary if unfortunate response to economic difficulties. Such characterisations simplify the diversity and complexity of people's reasons for migrating. As this book has shown, people move to and from Ireland for work and to make money, but they also move for adventure, for romance and for escape. Within any grouping of people who share a common nationality, all of these different reasons will be present. So, just as in London I encountered retired people, students, construction workers and young professionals from Ireland, people living in Ireland who share a nationality or a collective identity differ in their migration decision making. Macro-scale analyses of the relationship between social transformation and migration simplify places, for example characterising Ireland in terms of austerity or Nigeria in terms of poverty. They may also lead to stereotypes of people as migrants based on their nationality and/or occupation: for example, the Irish nurse or builder, the Polish plumber, the Filipina care worker or the Nigerian asylum seeker. These characterisations are sometimes benign, but often belittling. The effects of stereotyping on the everyday lives of migrants were made painfully clear by Heather Merrill in her discussion of African migrants in Turin, where women repeatedly had to cope with their characterisation as sex workers (Merrill 2006). Writing in the Irish context, Maguire and Murphy showed the types of pervasive myths that affected the lives of African migrants, such as fraud and criminality (Maguire and Murphy 2012).

Sudden transformations in the political or economic circumstances of particular places may make migration more likely. However, other forms of change – at a range of scales – also lead to migration. These changes could be experienced at the individual level; they could be connected to social networks or to families as social structures; and they could result from a complex set of intersections of personal, social and structural factors. The ongoing migration from Ireland to Australia through the Working Holiday Visa programme, discussed in Chapter 3, is one such example. This pattern of movement was established during a period of economic prosperity in Ireland, and often involved groups of young people travelling together. It continues today and this, together with evidence from the GAA transfer records provided in Chapter 5, suggests that social networks and relationships remain important for understanding contemporary migration from Ireland. As Chapter 4 showed, families also matter for understanding migration. People may choose to migrate not because of economic hardship, but because of a personal and social imperative: to join other family members, for example, or to develop stronger relationships with grandchildren. This is also important for later decisions in relation to migration, which may be influenced not solely by economic factors, but by family or friends or other considerations. So, while broader economic transformations may be used to explain changing patterns of movement, the evidence from Ireland suggests that these transformations are experienced and reacted to in often quite different ways. This was highlighted by Cairns' recent work with young people in Ireland, where he concluded that it is 'difficult to establish a direct link between economic recession and mobility decision-making', given the importance of other factors such as social connections and family background (Cairns 2014: 246).

Migration also results in social change and social transformation.[2]

Chapter 6, on belonging, outlined some of the ways in which this
happens. The 2004 Citizenship Referendum in Ireland is a clear
example, where the figures of migrants – in this case, pregnant women
described as citizenship tourists – were used to fundamentally alter the
basis for Irish citizenship. This move was instigated by the main political parties in Ireland, and supported by almost 80 per cent of those who
voted. Though a state-enabled initiative, it has very real consequences
for individuals born in Ireland, who no longer have an automatic entitlement to Irish citizenship. Instead, their identity is now derived from the
status of their parent(s). In this way, myths of migration transform
the state as an entity, which in turn changes the status of migrants in
the state. The extension of voting rights to all residents of Ireland also
results in social transformation, through the involvement of migrants
in local elections and local politics, as does the decision to not allow
non-resident Irish citizens to vote. This contrast between more and less
visible forms of social transformation occurs in politics, in workplaces
and in cultural landscapes. Chapters 4 and 5 detailed some of the different ways in which migration transforms material landscapes, such as
through new buildings, new activities or new uses of existing spaces. For
example, migration sometimes results in new types of multi- or pluri-
lingualism, or in new places of worship, or in new shops or restaurants
or other social spaces. These are visible markers of difference, however,
and the tendency is to see them as in some way distinct from other places
that have not changed, or from places where changes are less visible. As
I suggested in Chapter 3, places like Moore and Parnell Streets in the
centre of Dublin city have to be seen in conjunction with neighbouring
streets such as O'Connell Street. That just some of these streets have a
visible and tangible migrant presence is not mere accident, but rather
is an outcome of a complex set of structures that, in turn, affect future
social changes and transformations. The ways in which migration
transforms work and workplaces is also important. In Chapter 3, I discussed broader global trends like sectoral concentration, where migrants
become associated with particular kinds of labour, for example construction work or care work or service work, across a range of contexts.
This concentration is happening in parallel with increasing precarity for
workers, whether migrants or not, though the presence of migrants in a
workplace – particularly when they are undocumented or quasi-legal –
may accelerate the deterioration of working conditions for all workers
in a particular industry.[3] While some migrants work in well-regulated
employment with high levels of union membership (see Chapter 3),
migrants are also targeted or blamed for broader deteriorations in pay
and working conditions. As Goodwin-White shows, a variety of reports

in Ireland showing that immigrants were the first to lose jobs in the recession were insufficient to prevent hostility towards them 'driven by the idea that they had taken jobs from natives, driving wages down and Irish unemployment up' (Goodwin-White 2013: 215).

The relationship between the changes that result *in* and *from* migration is hinted at but not developed to any great extent by Castles (2010). Yet, this is the most important factor in understanding the relationship between social change and migration. Migration patterns are influenced by economic and political transformations. Ireland offers clear evidence of how this might happen, with increases in intra-EU migration to Ireland following EU enlargement, and increases in migration from Ireland following the property crash and bailout. However, these transformations are not sufficient to explain why migration to Ireland continues despite economic difficulties, or why recent migration from Ireland, particularly of Irish nationals, is directed towards the UK or the US, both with high unemployment rates, rather than to more prosperous European countries where there are few restrictions on living and working. There are clearly other factors at work here, and a macro-level explanation is insufficient to fully explain why particular kinds of migration patterns do or do not develop, intensify or change under conditions of broader societal transformation. Allied to this are the changes that emerge from migration. Chapter 5 detailed some of the visible changes that occur as a result of migration *to* particular places, such as the development of new cultural landscapes. While these may result from a desire for community building, they may also represent a response to the limited number of economic opportunities available to some migrants, or recognition of new market opportunities for existing businesses.[4] However, places also change because people leave them – one of the reasons GAA clubs became such a focus of attention is because they came to symbolise depopulated and aging rural areas, as young people moved away. As Chapter 5 showed, a significant amount of that movement away can be explained by internal migration, often to urban areas. Tertiary education is a key reason for this, as third-level institutions in Ireland are highly concentrated in large urban areas. Those rural places can in turn act as a magnet for return migration at a later stage in people's lives. As Farrell et al. discuss, in their study of return migration to rural Ireland, 'a longing to return to the rural region where they originated' is perhaps even stronger than a more generalised dream of return (Farrell et al. 2012: 39). In this way, factors that may have led to the initial decision to migrate in turn are central to later decisions to migrate. Studies of return migration also emphasise the ways in which people change as a consequence of migration. This is a regular theme in research on Ireland, where return migrants comment both favourably on how they have changed and less favourably on the perceived lack of change in others who have remained behind (Conlon 2009; Farrell et al. 2012; Ní Laoire 2007; Ralph 2012). Narratives of personal change are also common among other migrants to Ireland: many of the people we interviewed commented on how moving to and living in Ireland had changed them, and what this meant for their relationship with their place of origin. Both people and places change as a consequence of migration, and contemporary Ireland offers a dynamic illustration of how this occurs.

The broader question remains, though, which is how to connect the changes that result in migration and the changes that emerge from migration. The discussion of migration and health care, in Chapter 3, offered a particularly good illustration of these interconnections. The internationalisation of medical training, which had its roots in the colonial period, has created the conditions that make medical and nursing students and graduates highly mobile. In addition, the growing privatisation of both health care and medical education mean that both have become highly lucrative sectors. These global trends intersect with local contexts: for example, the role of Irish medical schools in the provision of medical training for people in other countries, such as South Africa and Malaysia and Bahrain; the emphasis on migration as a means to (financial and social) capital accumulation in places such as the Philippines and Ireland; or the dominance of religious orders in the provision of hospitals in Ireland allied to the sectoral concentration of Christians in nursing in India. Internal migration within Ireland is also important, as the movement of Irish nationals into and out of employment in rural and urban areas creates labour shortages that have increasingly been filled by migrants. The presence of migrant nurses and doctors has, in turn, led to some social change across Ireland. At work, migrants bring new practices and agitate for changes to existing, problematic patterns. Both the Irish Nurses and Midwives Organisation and the Irish Medical Organisation have responded to a growth in the number of members who are migrants, establishing separate sections within the associations to address the specific needs of migrant workers and, at times, advocating on their behalf to bring about changes to migration policy. At the level of social interaction, the visible presence of migrants in hospitals and nursing homes across Ireland, performing professional and caring roles, demands social encounters that transcend racial, ethnic and class boundaries. Despite this, practices that enforce social and spatial hierarchies in health care in Ireland persist. In many ways, the presence of migrant workers in health care serves to bring already existing exclusionary practices into sharp relief. This is also relevant to the experiences of migrants living in Ireland in their efforts to access health care. Our research suggested that, contrary to broader claims that migrants were a drain on hospital and other health care resources, many preferred to get treatment in their country of origin because of the varied obstacles they experienced in the Irish health care system (Migge and Gilmartin 2011). Health migration, for work, training and treatment, shows the value of focusing on social change and social transformation as a way of understanding the complexity of migration in a more holistic and less fragmented way.

Justice, equality and migration

A second way of addressing the topic of migration is through a focus on justice and equality. In broad terms, it is important to question the extent to which migration emerges from or results in patterns, practices and/or experiences that are (un)just and (un)equal. For some scholars of migration or migrant advocacy groups, the answer to this question is clear. The differentiations in mobility that people experience based on their nationality, class, gender, race, ethnicity and other social attributes mean that migration, as a global phenomenon, is socially and spatially differentiated in an unfair way. The treatment of migrants to Ireland who are not EEA nationals gives an example of this. Most require a visa to visit Ireland for even a short period, and all require special permission to live and/or work in the country for an extended period (Gilmartin 2014). For migrants who are defined as 'skilled', this is a relatively unproblematic process. Other migrants face considerably more difficulties, and may receive restricted or, alternatively, no permission to live or work in Ireland. This is a clear illustration of the socio-spatial hierarchies that underpin migration policies: nationals of certain countries are favoured over others, and people with particular class backgrounds are favoured within nationality groupings. Irish nationals have often benefited from such privileged treatment in the past, such as in the reciprocal arrangement with the UK that has facilitated movement back and forth across borders, or in the various visa lotteries in the US that awarded disproportionate numbers of visas to Irish nationals. However, Ireland is not unique in this regard: many countries have special arrangements with others in relation to migration. Other examples include Australia and New Zealand, or Argentina and Uruguay. The important point is the way in which state or intra-state migration policies draft maps of the world that distinguish nationalities on the basis of migrant desirability. The implications of this illustrate the birthright lottery that Schacar

(2009) named. The possibilities for migration are circumstantially cir-cumscribed, based primarily on accidents of birth.

Individual and groups of states, as well as their citizens, find justifi-cations for the birthright lottery. State-based socio-spatial hierarchies represent one powerful set of justifications. Thus, there is no clear sense that people from the US or Australia who overstay visas or who violate visa conditions are sought out or ultimately deported from Ireland, in contrast to regular deportations of European or African or Asian nation-als (e.g. from Albania, Nigeria or China). A second set of justifications relates to the integrity of the state. In contemporary societies, migra-tion policy is one of the most important ways in which states – either individually or collectively – assert their sovereignty. In the EU, for example, there are attempts to develop a shared migration policy, but this is limited in scope and allied to even more robust efforts to defend the borders of Europe through increased surveillance of both borders and (some) border-crossers. EU migration policy, specifically when it targets people who are not EU citizens, works through the proto-criminalisation of potential migrants from places that are marked as problematic. At the same time, other – significantly smaller – groups of people are marked as privileged and desired, and their movement into and out of the EU is facilitated. In the US, being 'tough' on migration is also a way of asserting state power, particularly in relation to efforts to prevent migration from Latin America. These include building and defending physical borders with Mexico (though not with Canada), and targeting people on the basis of an assumed racial or ethnic profile. The growing association of 'terrorism' with 'migrants', particularly after the attack on the Twin Towers in New York in September 2001, gives added moral authority to efforts to target particular migrants – for example, 'Muslims' and 'Arabs' – as likely threats to national security and integ-rity. This suspicion of migrants has gained traction in other contexts, for example in the increased surveillance of international students in the UK and the US (King and Raghuram 2013). While Ireland has not yet signed up to the EU common policy on migration, it opts in to certain aspects of the policy, mostly related to issues of security. However, in general Irish migration policy is independent of the EU, though not of the UK. In common with other EU countries, Ireland defines its own routes to citizenship and its own understanding of integration, informed though not determined by the Common Basic Principles on Integration. As this suggests, the rhetoric around sovereignty and migration policy, in Ireland and elsewhere, is often more convincing than the practice, as states compete in the global marketplace for skilled and business migrants, follow each other's lead in securing borders against less desirable migrants and ultimately enable illegal migration as part of any system of immigration. These contradictions are discussed in more detail in Chapter 6.

The limits to (legal) mobility that are imposed by migration policies are one illustration of injustice and inequality, though this characterisation is contested by states that represent their actions as just because they are concerned with protecting both citizens and territory. However, a question that moves beyond the ways in which states define and secure borders relates to the treatment and experiences of migrants within states. These are people who, to a large extent, have formal permission to move to and live in their new home. Yet, there is striking evidence, from Ireland and elsewhere, that migrants often experience different treatment because they are migrants. This is evident in Ireland in terms of how the state treats migrants from outside the EEA, who are subject to different restrictions and controls than their EEA co-residents. This includes having to pay to live in Ireland, having to regularly renew their permission to live in Ireland, having fewer rights to live with family members and having to produce identification to police officers on demand. These restrictions are implicit as well as explicit – research across a range of domains suggests that a lack of transparency in how things work in Ireland is a significant obstacle for migrants, regardless of their nationality (Farrell et al. 2012; Gilmartin and Migge 2013; Ledwith and Reilly 2013a, 2013b; Migge and Gilmartin 2011). However, migrancy also intersects with other aspects of people's identities, such as race. For example, in the US the association of Irishness with whiteness may well result in a form of racial and ethnic privileging, whereas the formal refusal to acknowledge a black Irish identity in the recent Censuses means that being black in Ireland carries with it assumptions of migrant status.[5] In a context where a growing number of Irish nationals express resistance or hostility to migrants, this association of race with migration may have unjust outcomes.

Qualitative studies, in Ireland and elsewhere, often highlight migrants' experiences of unjust treatment. Numerous studies provide individual accounts of discrimination that are often harrowing. The experience of Mohammed Younis, highlighted in Chapter 6, shows how discrimination at work can be enabled by legal status: in the end, Younis's exploitation at work resulted in no sanction for his employer because the laws of the state could not be applied to someone who was not legally resident in Ireland. But injustice is not just the experience of people whose legal status is uncertain. Research with asylum seekers, who are legally resident in Ireland while their claim for asylum is being assessed, highlights the social and spatial exclusion and, at times, degradation they endure

(Conlon 2010; O'Reilly 2013). Similarly, having legal permission to work in Ireland does not necessarily lead to fair or appropriate treatment, as qualitative research carried out by the MRCI shows (MRCI 2006, 2007a, 2007b, 2008, 2012. See also Chapter 3). These experiences are not unique to Ireland. Qualitative studies in a range of other national contexts highlight the scope for exploitation of migrants: these include disturbing stories of maid abuse in Singapore and Saudi Arabia (Huang and Yeoh 2007; Silvey 2004), as well as the hazardous and dangerous working conditions experienced by Latino migrants in the US. These individual stories are emotional, at times heart-wrenching, and evoke compassion. On their own, though, they are perhaps less successful in showing broader patterns and practices of inequality and injustice, since many can be explained away as the actions of unscrupulous individuals. As a consequence, larger-scale studies are also necessary. In Ireland, a number of studies by the Economic and Social Research Institute (ESRI) perform this role. Some deal explicitly with experiences of discrimination, such as reports on immigrants at work, in public places and in relation to access to institutions and services (McGinnity et al. 2006; O'Connell and McGinnity 2008). Others provide evidence of inequality, such as reports on the attitudes of employers or on wage premiums or wage gaps (Barrett and Kelly 2010; Barrett et al. 2013). In general, these reports operate at quite a coarse spatial scale, highlighting only broad nationality groupings and paying limited attention to possible spatial variations. They also pay most attention to work, with an underlying assumption that experiences of work are the best guide to integration and, as a consequence, equality. Goodwin-White (2013) challenges this approach, suggesting that it pays insufficient attention to already existing social inequalities. As she argues, economic and social integration and inequality need to be addressed in tandem rather than separately: 'issues of segregated labour markets, immigrant vulnerability in the labour market and the education of immigrant children are all connected' (Goodwin-White 2013: 223).

While states create the category of international migrant, and create hierarchies of migrants within states, they also provide a means to identify broader patterns of inequality and injustice for migrants living within their borders. Chapter 2 showed some of the ways in which this might happen. When 'Irish' was finally accepted as a separate ethnic category in the UK, the census that followed clearly showed the level and extent of social polarisation and also drew attention to potential health issues within the self-reported Irish community. In Ireland, broad-scale analyses of issues such as place of residence, housing tenure and employment point to similar areas of concern. In particular, the results from the 2006 and 2011 Censuses show important differences in places of residence (Figures 2.2 and 2.3), housing tenure (Table 2.9) and employment sector (Table 2.10) by broad nationality grouping. State-sponsored data collection allows us to identify these issues, and provides a starting point for investigating the processes and structures that give rise to these particular outcomes. It also provides us with evidence for asking questions about the extent to which migrants living in Ireland experience formal and informal barriers to participation in Irish society. In the process of making migrants visible, the Irish state also makes certain aspects of their lives in Ireland – such as potential experiences of inequality – visible.

Inequality and injustice are not just experienced by migrants, who move from and to societies that are already unequal. Similarly, the experience of migration is not always framed by inequality. Many migrants report a greater sense of personal freedom and possibility as a consequence of migration. This was true, for example, for some of the young women we interviewed in Ireland, who suggested that their lives would have been more circumscribed had they remained in their country of origin; and for others who felt they could not openly express their sexuality prior to migration. Migrants also regularly highlight how migration has given them new skills, provided them with new opportunities or given them more confidence. Yet, these narratives of personal growth and development intersect with broader structural obstacles: the impacts of economic transformation; wider hostility towards migrants; limits to formal recognition of qualifications and experience; or the unwritten and invisible rules that govern how societies are regulated. The challenge here is to identify the ways in which migrants experience inequality as migrants; how they experience inequality as residents of a particular place; and the ways in which personal experiences and structural imperatives intersect in these particular places.

Place and migration

Focusing on social change or on equality and justice, in the context of migration, highlights some of the challenges faced by migration studies more generally. Migration studies is marked by dichotomous thinking: between individuals and groups; between local and global; between internal and international; between quantitative and qualitative approaches (King 2012). Despite regular calls to develop more synthetic approaches to the study of migration and migrants, research – and findings – are often fragmented, isolated and reductively policy driven (Castles 2010).

A place-based approach to migration offers us a way of identifying and challenging dichotomous thinking. In Chapter 1, I suggested what a place-based approach might mean. My understanding of place is not primarily shaped by borders and boundaries, but rather by networks and links and connections. Those networks stretch across borders, in the process remaking both the borders and the places they connect. This understanding of place, which draws from the work of Doreen Massey (1991), does not seek to assert that borders and boundaries do not exist. Rather, while acknowledging their existence, it also asserts that they are socially constructed and, for this reason, never quite fixed. The work that goes into border maintenance matters, but so do the ways in which those borders are reconstructed and transgressed. Migration, as a process and as an experience, is simultaneously a site of border maintenance and a route to border transgression. Visa requirements, passport controls and deportations are all means to enforcing a border. Remittances, instant messaging and plurilinguality all render a border more porous and less stable. Cindi Katz describes these connections as a 'countertopography': for her, this involves identifying contours, or lines of connection, between apparently disparate social and geographical locations (Katz 2001). While Katz is most concerned with using countertopography to explore and challenge global capitalism, her idea is sufficiently robust and evocative to be of use in a range of contexts. Deirdre Conlon uses it to underpin an examination of the experiences of migrant women in Ireland, arguing that those experiences need to be understood in a global context that fosters insecurity, flexibility and a desire for relentless 'progress' and expansion (Conlon 2013). This book extends the site of analysis beyond the borders of women and Ireland, highlighting the countertopographies of migration to and from Ireland, where Ireland as a place and as an identity is repeatedly centred and decentred.

Through the various chapters, I have insisted on showing the connections between the experiences of migration and migrants both in and beyond Ireland. These contours cross borders and scales, linking together local and localised sites, such as Irish pubs or GAA clubs, in loose maps of similarity. Just as a contour map links these sites of similarity together, it also shows different local contexts, identified both by the cartographic representation of the terrain over which the contour lines cross and by the distance or proximity between them. In this way, the metaphor of countertopographies also recognises difference. For example, Irish pubs and GAA clubs have a collective and indeed global role, but they also differ, depending on their local context. An Irish pub in Lexington, Kentucky may serve as a common space for some recent Irish migrants, in contrast to the Irish pub I visited in Göttingen, Germany, where all the staff were German and the drinks menu advertised a 'Black and Tan' special.[6] A GAA club in Stockholm may be welcoming to people interested in participating, regardless of nationality or ethnicity, while a GAA club in Ireland may be a hostile environment for some recent immigrants. The countertopographies I have identified illustrate a variety of commonalities. These include the definitional power of the state in relation to migration, as outlined in Chapter 2. States decide who can legally move to and reside in their territories, even though these decisions are contingent and always liable to change and challenge. However, the importance of migration and migrants means that states often pay close attention to movement and settlement, which permits the identification of difficulties faced by migrants in terms of residence, housing and employment. Other commonalities move beyond the state to focus on migrant experiences. The discussion of work, in Chapter 3, highlighted experiences of deskilling, marginalisation and precarity that affect some migrants as well as some non-migrants. Chapter 4 identified social connections around language, family and community that offer possibilities for both encounter and distance, and that show how personal experiences may intersect with broader structures in a range of contexts, but with different outcomes. In Chapter 5, the relationship between culture and migration was discussed. I highlighted cultural landscapes that represent and forge connections and communities, such as sport or religion or pubs or music, and cultural representations that reflect on social change, such as contemporary fiction. Meanwhile, Chapter 6 focused on belonging, at scales that range from the individual and the home to the state. The ways in which migration complicates feelings and experiences of belonging are highlighted, as individual aspirations to belong come into conflict with state and other efforts to make belonging more difficult.

As I outlined in Chapter 1, the overarching concern of this book is to better understand the relationship between migration, place and identity. In addressing this relationship from a perspective grounded in the earlier chapters, one central concept has emerged, which is that of *inclusion* and *exclusion*. This is a concept that is both spatial and social, both individual and collective, and that operates at scales that range from the local to the global. In short, this study of migration may be characterised as an investigation of the interplay between processes and practices of inclusion and exclusion. I contend that this interplay is best understood by focusing on place. This is for two key reasons. The first is that place is intimately connected to constructions of identity. A place-based focus thus allows us to address questions of identity, and to see the ways in which identity is mobilised by appeals to place, whether this is the protection of Irish identity through changes to citizenship laws and increased deportations (Chapter 6), or through the construction of communities that highlight shared geographical origins and destinations (Chapter 4). Inclusion and exclusion are inherent to such place-based identities: for example, Irish citizenship, or indeed Irish identity, is defined as much by what it is not as by what it is. The second reason is that migration as a process disrupts taken-for-granted understandings of the relationship between place and identity. This is well illustrated by the example of New York parades to celebrate the national holiday of Ireland. In Chapter 1, I wrote about the conflicts over who could define Irishness for the purposes of marching in the parade, suggesting that a more established understanding of what it means to be Irish, held by earlier Irish migrants and their descendants, had come into conflict with more expansive understandings of Irishness as expressed by more recent migrants. In Chapter 4, I highlighted the St Pat's for All parade, which, in its effort to reach out to excluded LGBT marchers and other migrant groups in Queen's, created a sense of exclusion for more traditional Irish Americans. Processes of inclusion and exclusion are also evident in Ireland, for example through sectoral employment concentration that means particular jobs become associated with particular nationalities, as discussed in Chapter 3, or through the legal judgments that exclude people living in Ireland from the protection of labour law, as shown in Chapter 6. Meanwhile, the creation of new communities in place by migrants – whether GAA clubs in England or language schools in Ireland – serves a dual purpose of countering perceived exclusion in their own homes and asserting their right to be included in their place of origin. This is often resisted, as in the refusal to grant voting rights to non-resident Irish citizens, detailed in Chapter 6. In this way, we see how migration affects the understanding of place and identity not just for those who move, but also for those who remain in place. Across both of these examples, we can see how migration may be used to reify existing and dominant understandings of place and identity, in the process formalising processes of exclusion. This often occurs simultaneously with efforts to foster inclusion that range from local community initiatives to integration policies at the level of the state.

In an uncertain world, migration and migrants have the potential to become the scapegoats for all kinds of changes and insecurities (Pred 2000). In such a context, the state often assumes a definitional power in relation to migration. The tendency, then, is to frame migration in relation to dominant state concerns, such as (il)legality, criminality or potential threats to security, well-being or sovereignty. While recognising the power of the state in facilitating processes of inclusion and exclusion, it is important not to over-emphasise its importance and relevance to a place-based study. A focus on the state helps us to understand issues as diverse as the limited employment of EU-12 nationals in the Irish public sector, family separation, voting and citizenship. However, it is less useful in helping us to think about other, more symbolic issues, such as home or belonging or cultural representations. In his call for a focus on social transformation, Stephen Castles insisted on the need to consider migration as 'an all-embracing human experience' (Castles 2010: 1582). This call is equally perceptive and relevant for a discussion of place, which is multiscalar, dynamic, and experienced and re-made in a variety of – at times contradictory – ways. Migration, as an integral component of place, brings its thrown-togetherness and its complexity into sharp focus.

Throughout this book, the complexity of Ireland as a place is brought to light. Ireland is, on one level, a bounded state, with its borders policed and maintained by legislation, policy and the day-to-day practices of police and army and navy. Yet, those borders are porous, as evidenced by the demilitarised land border with Northern Ireland and its uncertain position within definitions of Irishness. Within that bounded state, the US government operates its own immigration controls – little pieces of the US on Irish territory. Multinational corporations have branches and plants and head offices that channel global flows of capital, temporarily grounded in Ireland for taxation purposes. People who are citizens or subjects of other countries call Ireland their home. But Ireland also extends beyond these borders, for example through the actions of the Irish state or through the bodies of Irish nationals in other parts of the world. Ireland also exists beyond its borders, through cultural representations or landscapes or as individual or collective imaginaries. This complex understanding of Ireland as a place creates the conditions for an equally complex understanding of migration. As can be seen throughout this book, migration to and from Ireland results in a complicated set of outcomes for both people and the sites they move to and from. Identifying the commonalities of those experiences and outcomes, while not stripping migration of its complexity, is a timely challenge. It is a challenge that has motivated this book.

Ireland as a place is shaped by its contemporary and historic experiences of migration, in ways that are both material and symbolic. In Summer 2013, posters for *The Gathering* were festooned around the country; and the National Library in Dublin, where some of this book was written, welcomed people from around the world searching for clues to their family histories and the places their ancestors had left. But the National Library is also used by people living in Ireland, who are looking for a quiet place to work, away from streets filled with tourists. These are shared spaces of everyday encounter, where people negotiate the dynamic and changing relationship between migration, place and identity on an ongoing basis, sometimes successfully, sometimes less so. Ireland as a place is replete with these shared spaces, whether these are pubs or streetscapes, homes or communities, hospitals or parades. These shared spaces show both the ordinariness and complexity of migration, and also underline the importance of place-based studies of migration that move beyond restrictive borders. From a graveyard in Lexington, Kentucky to Leitrim farmers and Dublin commuter trains, Ireland – expansively understood – provides us with an opportunity to unbound migration studies.

Notes

1 See Ralph (2014) for a discussion of the phenomenon of the 'Euro-commuter', a person who lives in one European country and commutes to another for work.
2 In a wide-ranging and timely body of work, Fanning (2002, 2007, 2009, 2011) discusses the relationship between immigration and transformation in contemporary Ireland from a variety of perspectives, including racism, social change, social cohesion and nationalism.
3 This relationship is not always clear, and economists and social scientists differ on whether precarity emerges from or attracts migrant workers (Castles 2010: 1580).
4 Examples in Ireland include the growing presence of Polish food products in supermarket chains, or banks producing advertising material in a wider range of languages.
5 The 2006 and 2011 Censuses in Ireland carried a question on 'Ethnic and Cultural Identity'. While people could identify as 'White Irish' without any further spatial qualifier, people who identified as 'Black Irish' were asked to say if their background was 'Caribbean' or 'African' (King O'Riain 2007).
6 'Black and Tan' was the name given to an auxiliary police force in Ireland during the Civil War in the 1920s. A lasting folk memory of the atrocities of the Black and Tans mean that the name is unlikely to be used in an Irish pub, but it is regularly used outside Ireland to describe a drink that mixes lager or beer and stout.

References

ADI [Anti Deportation Ireland] (2012) *Preliminary report on deportation in Ireland: the human and economic costs of deportation.* Available online from http://antideportationireland.blogspot.de/p/adi-report-publication.html [Accessed 18 June 2013].

Agnew, J. (1996) 'Mapping politics: how context counts in electoral geography', *Political Geography*, 15:2, 129–46.

Ali, M. (2003) *Brick Lane.* London and New York: Doubleday.

Allon, F. (2004) 'Backpacker heaven: the consumption and construction of tourism spaces and landscapes in Sydney', *Space and Culture*, 7:1, 49–63.

Allon, F. and Anderson, K. (2010) 'Intimate encounters: the embodied transnationalism of backpackers and independent travellers', *Population, Space and Place*, 16:1, 11–22.

Allon, F., Anderson, K., and Bushell, R. (2008) 'Mutant mobilities: backpacker tourism in "global" Sydney', *Mobilities*, 3:1, 73–94.

Anderson, B. (2013) *Us and them? The dangerous politics of immigration control.* Oxford: Oxford University Press.

Antonsich, M. (2010) 'Searching for belonging: an analytical framework', *Geography Compass*, 4:6, 644–59.

Appadurai, A. (2006) *Fear of small numbers: an essay on the geography of anger.* Durham, NC and London: Duke University Press.

Arel, D. (2002) 'Demography and politics in the first post-Soviet censuses', *Population*, 57:6, 801–27.

Armen, A. (2008) 'Doctors, migration and the Irish health care system'. Unpublished MLitt thesis, Department of Geography, University College Dublin.

Arrowsmith, A. (2004) 'Plastic paddies vs. master racers: "soccer" and Irish identity', *International Journal of Cultural Studies*, 7:4, 460–79.

Australian Government Department of Immigration and Citizenship (2012a) 'Working Holiday Maker Visa program report 31 December 2012'. Available online from www.immi.gov.au/media/statistics/pdf/working-holiday-report-dec12.pdf [Accessed 5 June 2013].

Australian Government Department of Immigration and Citizenship (2012b) 'Working Holiday Maker Visa program report 30 June 2012'. Available online from www.immi.gov.au/media/statistics/visitor.htm [Accessed 8 May 2013].

Australian Government Department of Immigration and Citizenship (2013a) 'Overseas arrivals and departure statistics 2011–12'. Available online from www.immi.gov.au/media/statistics/statistical-info/oad/#tot [Accessed 5 June 2013].

Australian Government Department of Immigration and Citizenship (2013b) 'Working Holiday Maker Visa program report 31 December 2013'. Available online from www.immi.gov.au/media/statistics/pdf/working-holiday-report-dec13.pdf [Accessed 20 June 2014].

Australian Government Department of Immigration and Citizenship (2013c) 'Working Holiday Maker Visa program report 30 June 2013'. Available online from https://www.immi.gov.au/media/statistics/pdf/working-holiday-report-jun13.pdf [Accessed 16 September 2014].

Australian Government Department of Immigration and Citizenship (2014) 'Overseas arrivals and departure statistics 2012–13'. Available online from www.immi.gov.au/media/statistics/statistical-info/oad/#tot [Accessed 20 June 2014].

Barrett, A. and Kelly, E. (2010) 'The impact of Ireland's recession on the labour market outcomes of its immigrants'. ESRI Working Paper No. 355. Available online from www.esri.ie/UserFiles/publications/WP355/WP355.pdf [Accessed 27 September 2013].

Barrett, A. and Kelly, E. (2012) 'The impact of Ireland's recession on the labour market outcomes of its immigrants', *European Journal of Population*, 28:1, 99–111.

Barrett, A., Bergin, A. and Duffy, D. (2006) 'The labour market characteristics and labour market impacts of immigrants in Ireland', *The Economic and Social Review*, 37:1, 1–26.

Barrett, A., McGuinness, S. and O'Brien, M. (2008) 'The immigrant earnings disadvantage across the earnings and skills distributions: the case of immigrants from the EU's new member states in Ireland'. ESRI Working Paper No. 236. Available online from www.esri.ie/UserFiles/publications/20080501123344/WP236.pdf [Accessed 27 May 2013].

Barrett, A., McGuinness, S., O'Brien, M. and O'Connell, P. (2013) 'Immigrants and employer-provided training', *Journal of Labor Research*, 34:1, 52–78.

Bauböck, R. (2005) 'Expansive citizenship – voting beyond territory and membership', *Political Science & Politics*, 4, 683–7.

Bernstein, N. (2006) 'An Irish face on the cause of citizenship', *New York Times*, 16 March, p. A1.

Bodvarsson, Ö.B. and Van den Berg, H. (2009) *The economics of immigration*. Berlin and Heidelberg: Springer.

Bornat, J., Henry, L. and Raghuram, P. (2011) 'The making of careers, the making of a discipline: luck and chance in migrant careers in geriatric medicine', *Journal of Vocational Behavior*, 78:3, 342–50.

Bowden, N. (2010) 'Photographer seeks "to immortalise what is being lost to our country"'. Available online from www.globalirish.ie/2010/photographer-seeks-to-immortalise-what-is-being-lost-to-our-country/ [Accessed 11 March 2013].

Boyle, M. (2006) 'Culture in the rise of tiger economies: Scottish expatriates in Dublin and the "creative class" thesis', *International Journal of Urban and Regional Research*, 30:2, 403–26.

Boyle, M. (2011) *Metropolitan anxieties: on the meaning of the Irish Catholic adventure in Scotland*. Farnham: Ashgate.

Boyle, M., Kitchin, R. and Ancien, D. (2013) 'Ireland's diaspora strategy: diaspora for development?', in M. Gilmartin and A. White (eds) *Migrations: Ireland in a global world*. Manchester: Manchester University Press, pp. 80–97.

Bradley, J.M. (2007) 'Gaelic sport, soccer and Irishness in Scotland', *Sport in Society: Cultures, Commerce, Media, Society*, 10:3, 439–56.

Breen, C. (2008) 'The policy of direct provision in Ireland: a violation of asylum seekers' right to an adequate standard of housing', *International Journal of Refugee Law*, 20:4, 611–36.

Breheny, M. (2012) 'Racism accusations fly as GAA star claims opponents used N-word on pitch', *Irish Independent*, 3 December.

Burroughs, E. (2012) 'Irish institutional discourses of illegal immigration: a critical discourse analysis'. Unpublished PhD thesis, National University of Ireland Maynooth.

Byrne, D., McGinnity, F., Smyth, E. and Darmody, M. (2010) 'Immigration and school composition in Ireland', *Irish Educational Studies*, 29:3, 271–88.

Cairns, D. (2014) '"I wouldn't stay here": economic crisis and youth mobility in Ireland', *International Migration*, 52:3, 236–49.

Calavita, K. (2005) *Immigrants at the margins: law, race, and exclusion in Southern Europe*. Cambridge: Cambridge University Press.

Campbell, S. (1999) 'Beyond "plastic paddy": a re-examination of the second-generation Irish in England', *Immigrants & Minorities*, 18:2–3, 266–88.

Campbell, S. (2010) '"Irish blood, English heart": ambivalence, unease and The Smiths', in S. Campbell and C. Coulter (eds) *Why pamper life's complexities? Essays on the Smiths*. Manchester: Manchester University Press, pp. 43–64.

Carey, S. (2008) 'Gaelscoil parents want to have their cake and eat it', *Irish Times*, 24 December.

Carnevale, N.C. (2013) 'Language and migration: perspectives and experiences', in I. Ness (ed.) *The Encyclopedia of Global Human Migration*. Chichester: Wiley-Blackwell. DOI: 10.1002/9781444351071.wbeghm336 [Accessed 30 June 2014].

Casey, N. (2002) 'Riverdance: the importance of being Irish American', *New Hibernia Review*, 6:4, 9–25.

Castles, S. (1986) 'The guest-worker in western Europe – an obituary', *International Migration Review*, 20:4, 761–78.

Castles, S. (2010) 'Understanding global migration: a social transformation perspective', *Journal of Ethnic and Migration Studies*, 36:10, 1565–86.

Castles, S. and Miller, M.J. (2009) *The age of migration: international population movements in the modern world*. Basingstoke: Palgrave Macmillan.

Chan, K.W. (2010) 'The household registration system and migrant labor in China: notes on a debate', *Population and Development Review*, 36:2, 357–64.

Chan, K.W. (2013) 'China: internal migration', in I. Ness (ed.) *The Encyclopedia of Global Human Migration*. Chichester: Wiley-Blackwell. DOI: 10.1002/9781444351071.wbeghm124 [Accessed 30 June 2014].

Chavez, L. (2013) *The Latino threat: constructing immigrants, citizens, and the nation* (2nd edition). Palo Alto, CA: Stanford University Press.

Cheong, P.H., Edwards, R., Goulbourne, H. and Solomos, J. (2007) 'Immigration, social cohesion and social capital: a critical review', *Critical Social Policy*, 27:1, 24–49.

Clarke, N. (2005) 'Detailing transnational lives of the middle: British working holiday makers in Australia', *Journal of Ethnic and Migration Studies*, 31:2, 307–22.

Clary-Lemon, J. (2010) '"We're not ethnic, we're Irish": oral histories and the discursive construction of immigrant identity', *Discourse & Society*, 21:1, 5–24.

Coakley, L. (2010) 'Exploring the significance of Polish shops within the Irish foodscape', *Irish Geography*, 43(2): 105–17.

Coakley, L. (2012) 'Polish encounters with the Irish foodscape: an examination of the losses and gains of migrant foodways', *Food and Foodways*, 20, 307–25.

Coakley, L. (2013) 'African migrants in Ireland: the negotiation of belonging and family life', in M. Gilmartin and A. White (eds) *Migrations: Ireland in a global world*. Manchester: Manchester University Press, pp. 132–56.

Coakley, L. and Healy, C. (2012) 'Ireland's IBC/05 administrative scheme for immigrant residency, the separation of families and the creation of a transnational familial imaginary', *International Migration*, 50:5, 1–24.

Coakley, L. and Mac Éinrí, P. (2007) *The integration experiences of African families in Ireland*. Dublin: Integrating Ireland. Available online from http://emn.ie/files/p_201211161052282007_The-Integration-Experiences-of-African-Families-in-Ireland.pdf [Accessed 6 May 2013].

Coleman, M. and Kocher, A. (2011) 'Detention, deportation, devolution and immigrant incapacitation in the US, post 9/11', *The Geographical Journal*, 177:3, 228–37.

Conlon, D. (2009) '"Germs" in the heart of the other: emigrant scripts, the Celtic Tiger, and the lived realities of return', *Irish Geography*, 42:1, 101–17.

Conlon, D. (2010) 'Ties that bind: governmentality, the state, and asylum in contemporary Ireland', *Environment and Planning D: Society and Space*, 28:1, 95–111.

Conlon, D. (2013) 'A countertopography of migrant experience in Ireland and beyond', in M. Gilmartin and A. White (eds) *Migrations: Ireland in a global world*. Manchester: Manchester University Press, pp. 183–98.

Connolly, G.N., Carpenter, C.M., Travers, M.J., Cummings, K.M., Hyland, A., Mulcahy, M. and Clancy, L. (2008) 'How smoke-free laws improve air quality: a global study of Irish pubs', *Nicotine & Tobacco Research*, 11:6, 600–5.

Cooke, T.J. (2008) 'Migration in a family way', *Population, Space and Place*, 14:4, 255–65.

Corcoran, M.P. (1991) 'Informalization of metropolitan labour forces: the case of Irish immigrants in the New York construction industry', *Irish Journal of Sociology*, 1, 31–51.

Corcoran, M.P. (1993) *Irish illegals: transients between two societies*. Westport, CO: Greenwood Press.

Corcoran, M.P. (2003) 'Global cosmopolites: issues of self-identity and collective identity among the transnational Irish elite', *Études Irlandaises*, 28:2, 135–50.

Coulter, C. (2004) 'Figures do not identify status of non-national mothers', *Irish Times*, 17 June, p. 7.

Cowley, U. (2001) *The men who built Britain: a history of the Irish navvy*. Dublin: Wolfhound Press.

Crenshaw, K. (1991) 'Mapping the margins: intersectionality, identity politics, and violence against women of color', *Stanford Law Review*, 43:6, 1241–99.

Cronin, M. (2013) 'Integration through sport: the Gaelic Athletic Association and the New Irish', in J.V. Ulin, H. Edwards and S. O'Brien (eds) *Race and immigration in the new Ireland*. Indiana: University of Notre Dame, pp. 157–74.

Cronin, M., Doyle, D. and O'Callaghan, L. (2008) 'Foreign fields and foreigners on the field: Irish sport, inclusion and assimilation', *International Journal of the History of Sport*, 25:8, 1010–30.

CSO (2007) 'Census 2006 Volume 7 – Principal Economic Status and Industries'. Available online from www.cso.ie/en/media/csoie/census/census2006results/volume7/Tables%2029%20to%2036%20Volume%207.pdf [Accessed 23 August 2012].

CSO (2012a) 'This is Ireland – Highlights from Census 2011 Part 1'. Available online from www.cso.ie/en/census/census2011reports/census2011thisisirelandpart1/ [Accessed 26 February 2013].

CSO (2012b) 'Population and migration estimates April 2012'. Available online from www.cso.ie/en/media/csoie/releasespublications/documents/latestheadlinefigures/popmig_2012.pdf [Accessed 27 September 2013].

CSO (2012c) 'International movement of passengers (number) by air and sea'. Available online from www.cso.ie/en/statistics/tourismandtravel/ [Accessed 19 March 2013].

CSO (2012d) 'Census 2011 Profile 1 Town and country – population distribution and movements'. Available online from www.cso.ie/en/census/census2011reports/census2011profile1-townandcountry/ [Accessed 5 June 2013].

CSO (2012e) 'Census 2011 Profile 6 Migration and diversity in Ireland – a profile of diversity in Ireland'. Available online from www.cso.ie/en/media/

csoie/census/documents/census2011profile6/Profile,6,Migration,and,Diversit
y,entire,doc.pdf [Accessed 6 June 2013].

CSO (2012f) 'This is Ireland – Highlights from Census 2011, Part 2'. Available
online from www.cso.ie/en/media/csoie/census/documents/thisisirelandpart-
2census2011/This%20is%20Ireland%20Highlights,%20P2%20Full%20
doc.pdf [Accessed 30 July 2012].

CSO (2012g) 'Census 2011 Profile 9 What we know – a study of education, skills and the Irish language'. Available online from www.cso.ie/en/
census/census2011reports/census2011profile9whatweknow-educationskill
sandtheirishlanguage/ [Accessed 24 May 2013].

CSO (2012h) 'Census 2011 Profile 7 Religion, ethnicity and Irish Travellers –
ethnic and cultural background in Ireland'. Available online from www.cso.
ie/en/media/csoie/census/documents/census2011profile7/Profile,7,Education,
Ethnicity,and,Irish,Traveller,entire,doc.pdf [Accessed 27 September 2013].

CSO (2012i) 'Census 2011 reports. Profile 3 At work – employment, occupa-
tions and industry in Ireland'. Available online from www.cso.ie/en/census/
census2011reports/ [Accessed 8 May 2013].

CSO (2013) 'Population and migration estimates April 2013'. Available online
from www.cso.ie/en/releasesandpublications/er/pme/populationandmigra-
tionestimatesapril2013/#.U6RLJY1dWzA [Accessed 20 June 2014].

CSO (2014) 'Population and migration estimates April 2014'. Available online
from www.cso.ie/en/releasesandpublications/er/pme/populationandmigra-
tionestimatesapril2014/#.VB20Hi5dWzA [Accessed 16 September 2014].

CSO and NISRA (2014) 'Census 2011: Ireland and Northern Ireland'. Available
online from www.cso.ie/en/media/csoie/census/documents/north-south-
spreadsheets/Census,2011,Ireland,and,Northern,Ireland.pdf [Accessed 22
June 2014].

Darby, P. (2007) 'Gaelic games, ethnic identity and Irish nationalism in New
York City c.1880–1917', *Sport in Society: Cultures, Commerce, Media,
Society*, 10:3, 347–67.

Darby, P. and Hassan, D. (2007) 'Introduction: locating sport in the study of
the Irish diaspora', *Sport in Society: Cultures, Commerce, Media, Society*,
10:3, 333–46.

Darmody, M., Smyth, E., Byrne, D. and McGinnity, F. (2012) 'New school,
new system: the experiences of immigrant students in Irish schools', in
Z. Bekerman and T. Geisen (eds) *International handbook of migration,
minorities and education – understanding cultural and social differences in
processes of learning*. Dordrecht and London: Springer, pp. 283–99.

Datta, A. and Brickell, K. (2009) '"We have a little bit more finesse, as a nation":
constructing the Polish worker in London's building sites', *Antipode*, 41:3,
439–64.

de Beer, J., Raymer, J., van der Erf, R. and van Wissen, L. (2010) 'Overcoming
the problems of inconsistent international migration data: a new method
applied to flows in Europe', *European Journal of Population*, 26, 459–81.

Department for Work & Pensions (2013) 'NINo registrations to adult overseas nationals entering the UK'. Available online from https://sw.stat-xplore.dwp.gov.uk/webapi/jsf/tableView/customiseTable.xhtml# [Accessed 27 September 2013].

Department for Work & Pensions (2014) 'NINo registrations to adult overseas nationals entering the UK'. Available online from https://sw.stat-xplore.dwp.gov.uk/webapi/jsf/tableView/customiseTable.xhtml [Accessed 16 September 2014].

Department of Justice and Equality (2009) 'Non-EEA student statistics'. Available online from www.justice.ie/en/JELR/Pages/Ahern%20to%20overhaul%20student%20immigration%20regime [Accessed 22 August 2012].

De Tona, C. and Lentin, R. (2011a) '"Building a platform for our voices to be heard": migrant women's networks as locations of transformation in the Republic of Ireland', *Journal of Ethnic and Migration Studies*, 37:3, 485–502.

De Tona, C. and Lentin, R. (2011b) 'Networking sisterhood, from the informal to the global: AkiDwA, the African and Migrant Women's Network, Ireland', *Global Networks*, 11:2, 242–61.

Devlin-Trew, J. (2010) 'Reluctant diasporas of Northern Ireland: migrant narratives of home, conflict, difference', *Journal of Ethnic and Migration Studies*, 36:4, 541–60.

Devlin-Trew, J. (2013) *Leaving the North: migration and memory, Northern Ireland 1921–2011*. Liverpool: Liverpool University Press.

DJEI (2013) 'Employment permit statistics for 2012'. Available online from www.djei.ie/labour/workpermits/statistics.htm [Accessed 5 June 2013].

Donegal Democrat (2012) 'End of an era for The Irish Emigrant', 11 February. Available online from www.donegaldemocrat.ie/lifestyle/home-and-garden/end-of-an-era-for-the-irish-emigrant-1-3497546 [Accessed 21 June 2013].

Dublin Civic Trust (2011) 'Parnell Street East: a vision for an historic city centre street'. Dublin: Dublin Civic Trust. Available online from http://issuu.com/dctrust/docs/parnell_street_final_dct_version [Accessed 27 September 2013].

Dunn, K. (2005) 'Repetitive and troubling discourses of nationalism in the local politics of mosque development in Sydney, Australia', *Environment and Planning D: Society and Space*, 23:1, 29–50.

Dwyer, M. (2012) 'London: a tale of two cities?', *Irish Times*, 4 July. Available online from www.irishtimes.com/blogs/generationemigration/2012/07/04/london-a-tale-of-two-cities/ [Accessed 16 August 2012].

Ellis, M. (2012) 'Reinventing US internal migration studies in the age of international migration', *Population, Space and Place*, 18:2, 196–208.

Embassy of the United States Dublin, Ireland (n.d.) 'Twelve-Month Intern Work and Travel Pilot Program'. Available online from http://dublin.usembassy.gov/general/twelve-month-intern-work-and-travel-pilot-program.html [Accessed 4 June 2013].

Emigré (2013) 'Songs of Irish migration'. Available online from www.ucc.ie/en/emigre/diaspora/emigrant-songs-1/ [Accessed 8 May 2013].

172 References

Esposito, J. and Kalin, I. (eds) (2011) *Islamophobia*. New York: Oxford University Press.
Faist, T., Fauser, M. and Reisenauer, E. (2013) *Transnational migration*. Cambridge: Polity Press.
Fanning, B. (2002) *Racism and social change in the Republic of Ireland*. Manchester: Manchester University Press.
Fanning, B. (ed.) (2007) *Immigration and social change in the Republic of Ireland*. Manchester: Manchester University Press.
Fanning, B. (2009) *New guests of the Irish nation*. Dublin: Irish Academic Press.
Fanning, B. (2011) *Immigration and social cohesion in the Republic of Ireland*. Manchester: Manchester University Press.
Fanning, B. and Mutwarasibo, F. (2007) 'Nationals/non-nationals: immigration, citizenship and politics in the Republic of Ireland', *Ethnic and Racial Studies*, 30:3, 439–60.
Fanning, B., Howard, K. and O'Boyle, N. (2010) 'Immigrant candidates and politics in the Republic of Ireland: racialization, ethnic nepotism, or localism?', *Nationalism and Ethnic Politics*, 16:3–4, 420–42.
Fanning, B., O'Boyle, N. and Shaw, J. (2009) *New Irish politics: political parties and immigrants in 2009*. Dublin: Migration and Citizenship Research Institute, UCD. Available online from www.ucd.ie/mcri/resources/new_irish_politics_report_final.pdf [Accessed 20 June 2013].
Farrell, M., Mahon, M. and McDonagh, J. (2012) 'The rural as a return migration destination', *European Countryside*, 4:1, 31–44.
Favell, A. (2008a) 'The new face of East–West migration in Europe', *Journal of Ethnic and Migration Studies*, 34:5, 701–16.
Favell, A. (2008b) *Eurostars and Eurocities: free movement and mobility in an integrating Europe*. Malden, MA and Oxford: Blackwell Publishing.
Feldman, A. and Mulhall, A. (2012) 'Towing the line: migrant women writers and the space of Irish writing', *Éire-Ireland*, 47:1–2, 201–20.
FIS [Federation of Irish Societies] (2007) 'England: the Irish dimension. An exploration of 2001 Census data'. London: FIS. Available online from www.irishinbritain.org/policy-details.php?id=8 [Accessed 10 August 2012].
Florida, R. (2007) *The flight of the creative class: the new global competition for talent*. New York: Harper Collins.
Flynn, S. (2012) 'To see real educational apartheid, look no farther than your local Gaelscoil', *Irish Times*, 23 October.
Frawley, O. (2014) *Flight*. Dublin: Tramp Press.
Free, M. (2007) 'Tales from the fifth green field: the psychodynamics of migration, masculinity and national identity amongst Republic of Ireland soccer supporters in England', *Sport in Society: Cultures, Commerce, Media, Society*, 10:3, 476–94.
Friel, B. (1990) *Dancing at Lughnasa*. London: Faber and Faber.
Furlong, B. (2012) 'GAA star Lee Chin speaks out about racist abuse to stop it for younger players', *Irish Independent*, 25 June.

GAA (2013) 'Inclusion and integration'. Available online from www.gaa.ie/clubzone/inclusion-and-integration/ [Accessed 27 September 2013].

GAA (2014) 'Transfers archive'. Available online from www.gaa.ie/clubzone/transfers-and-sanctions/transfers-archive/ [Accessed 3 July 2014].

Garrett, P.M. (2005) 'Irish social workers in Britain and the politics of (mis)recognition', *British Journal of Social Work*, 35, 1357–76.

Gilmartin, M. (2008) 'Dublin: an emerging gateway?', in L. Benton-Short and M. Price (eds) *Migrants to the metropolis: the rise of immigrant gateway cities*. Syracuse, NY: Syracuse University Press, pp. 226–54.

Gilmartin, M. (2012) 'The changing landscape of Irish migration, 2000–2012'. NIRSA Working Paper No.69. Available online from www.nuim.ie/nirsa/research/documents/WP69_The_changing_face_of_Irish_migration_2000_2012.pdf [Accessed 26 February 2013].

Gilmartin, M. (2013a) 'Ireland, modern era migrations', in I. Ness (ed.) *Encyclopedia of Global Human Migrations*. Chichester: Wiley-Blackwell. DOI: 10.1002/9781444351071.wbeghm313 [Accessed 1 July 2014].

Gilmartin, M. (2013b) 'British migrants and Irish anxieties' *Social Identities*, 19:5, 637–52.

Gilmartin, M. (2013c) 'Changing Ireland, 2002–2012: immigration, emigration and inequality', *Irish Geography*, 46:1–2, 91–111.

Gilmartin, M. (2014) 'Immigration and spatial justice in contemporary Ireland', in G. Kearns, D. Meredith and J. Morrissey (eds) *Spatial justice and the Irish crisis*. Dublin: Royal Irish Academy, pp. 161–76.

Gilmartin, M. and Migge, B. (2011) 'Working through a recession', *Translocations: Migration and Social Change*, 7:1. Available online from www.translocations.ie/current_issue.html [Accessed 8 May 2013].

Gilmartin, M. and Migge, B. (2013) 'European migrants in Ireland: pathways to integration', *European Urban and Regional Studies*. DOI: 10.1177.0969776412474583.

Gilmartin, M. and Mills, G. (2008) 'Mapping migrants in Ireland: the limits of cartography', *Translocations*, 4:1, 21–34. Available online from www.translocations.ie/v04i01.html [Accessed 26 September 2014].

Gilmartin, M., O'Connell, J.A. and Migge, B. (2008) 'Lithuanians in Ireland', *Oikos: Lithuanian Migration and Diaspora Studies*, 5:1, 49–62.

Glick Schiller, N. and Çağlar, A. (2009) 'Towards a comparative theory of locality in migration studies: migrant incorporation and city scale', *Journal of Ethnic and Migration Studies*, 35:2, 177–202.

Glick Schiller, N. and Salazar, N.B. (2013) 'Regimes of mobility across the globe', *Journal of Ethnic and Migration Studies*, 39:2, 183–200.

Glór an Deoraí (1997) 'The story so far'. Available online from http://ireland.iol.ie/~gad/gadstor.htm [Accessed 21 June 2013].

Glynn, I., Kelly, T. and MacÉinrí, P. (2013) *Irish emigration in an age of austerity*. Available online from www.ucc.ie/en/media/research/emigre/Emigration_in_an_Age_of_Austerity_Final.pdf [Accessed 15 April 2014].

Goodwin-White, J. (2013) 'Context, scale, and generation: the constructions of belonging', in M. Gilmartin and A. White (eds) *Migrations: Ireland in a global world*. Manchester: Manchester University Press, pp. 213–27.

Gramsci, A. (1971) 'The intellectuals', in G. Nowell Smith and Q. Hoare (eds, trans) *Antonio Gramsci: selections from the Prison Notebooks*. London: Lawrence & Wishart, pp. 5–23.

Grantham, B. (2009) 'Craic in a box: commodifying and exporting the Irish pub', *Continuum: Journal of Media & Cultural Studies*, 23:2, 257–67.

Gray, B. (2004) *Women and the Irish diaspora*. London & New York: Routledge.

Gray, B. (2013a) '"Generation emigration": the politics of (trans)national social reproduction in twenty-first-century Ireland', *Irish Studies Review*, 21:1, 20–36.

Gray, B. (2013b) 'Migrant integration and the "network-making power" of the Irish Catholic Church', in M. Gilmartin and A. White (eds) *Migrations: Ireland in a global world*. Manchester: Manchester University Press, pp. 55–79.

Groneman, C. (1978) 'Working-class immigrant women in mid-nineteenth-century New York: the Irish woman's experience', *Journal of Urban History*, 4:3, 255–74.

Grossman, A. and O'Brien, Á. (2010) *Promise and unrest* [documentary film]. Philippines/Ireland.

Hamilton, H. (2010) *Hand in the fire*. London: Fourth Estate.

Hannam, K., Sheller, M. and Urry, J. (2006) 'Editorial: mobilities, immobilities and moorings', *Mobilities*, 1:1, 1–22.

Harte, L. (2009) *The literature of the Irish in Britain: autobiography and memoir, 1725–2001*. Basingstoke: Palgrave.

Hartigan, E. (2012) 'First my uncle left, then my siblings, now my son', *Irish Times*, 7 December. Available online from www.irishtimes.com/blogs/generationemigration/2012/12/07/first-my-uncle-left-then-my-siblings-now-my-son/ [Accessed 29 May 2013].

Hassan, D. (2007) 'The role of Gaelic Games in the lives of the Irish diaspora in Europe', *Sport in Society: Cultures, Commerce, Media, Society*, 10:3, 385–401.

Hethmon, M. (2003) 'Diversity, mass immigration, and national security after 9/11 – an immigration reform movement perspective', *Albany Law Review*, 66, 387–412.

Hickman, M.J. (2011) 'Census ethnic categories and second-generation identities: a study of the Irish in England and Wales', *Journal of Ethnic and Migration Studies*, 37:1, 79–97.

Hochschild, A.R. (2000) 'Global care chains and emotional surplus value', in W. Hutton and A. Giddens (eds) *On the edge: living with global capitalism*. London: Jonathan Cape, pp. 130–46.

Holgersen, S. and Haarstad, H. (2009) 'Communicative planning: urban redevelopment at King's Cross, London', *Antipode*, 41:2, 348–70.

Home Office (2013) 'Immigration Statistics January–March 2013, Table cz_03'. Available online from https://www.gov.uk/government/uploads/ system/uploads/attachment_data/file/200388/citizenship-q1-2013-tabs.ods [Accessed 20 June 2013].

Honohan, I. (2010) 'Citizenship attribution in a new country of immigration: Ireland', *Journal of Ethnic and Racial Studies*, 36:5, 811–27.

Honohan, I. (2011) 'Should Irish emigrants have votes? External voting in Ireland', *Irish Political Studies*, 26:4, 545–61.

hooks, b. (1989) *Talking back: thinking feminist, thinking black*. Boston, MA: South End Press.

Horan, N. (2007) 'Demand soars for all-Irish schools', *Sunday Independent*, 4 March.

Horwath Consulting Ireland Ltd. in association with Rambøll Management and Matrix Knowledge Group (2008) 'Final report to Office of the Minister for Integration and the Department of Education and Science. Development of a national English language policy and framework for legally-resident adult immigrants'. Available online from www.education.ie/en/Publications/ Policy-Reports/horwath_final_report.pdf [Accessed 17 May 2013].

Howard, K. (2006) 'Constructing the Irish of Britain: ethnic recognition and the 2001 UK Censuses', *Ethnic and Racial Studies*, 29:1, 104–23.

Huang, S. and Yeoh, B. (2007) 'Emotional labour and transnational domestic work: the moving geographies of "maid abuse" in Singapore', *Mobilities*, 2:2, 195–217.

Humphries, N., Brugha, R. and McGee, H. (2008) 'Overseas nurse recruitment: Ireland as an illustration of the dynamic nature of nurse migration', *Health Policy*, 87:2, 264–72.

Humphries, N., Brugha, R. and McGee, H. (2009a) 'A profile of migrant nurses in Ireland'. Nurse Migration Project Policy Brief 4. Dublin: Royal College of Surgeons in Ireland. Available online from http://epubs.rcsi.ie/ephmrep/4 [Accessed 22 March 2013].

Humphries, N., Brugha, R. and McGee, H. (2009b) '"I won't be staying here for long": a qualitative study on the retention of migrant nurses in Ireland', *Human Resources for Health*, 7, 68.

Humphries, N., Tyrrell, E., McAleese, S., Bidwell, P., Thomas, S., Normand, C. and Brugha, R. (2013) 'A cycle of brain gain, waste and drain – a qualitative study of non-EU migrant doctors in Ireland', *Human Resources for Health*, 11, 63. DOI:10.1186/1478-4491-11-63.

Hussein v The Labour Court & Anor (2012) IEHC 364. Available online from www.bailii.org/ie/cases/IEHC/2012/H364.html [Accessed 17 June 2013].

ICI [Immigrant Council of Ireland] (2003) *Labour migration into Ireland*. Dublin: Immigrant Council of Ireland. Available online from www.immi-grantcouncil.ie/images/stories/431_labourmigration.pdf [Accessed 5 May 2013].

ICI (2011) *Living in limbo: migrants' experiences of applying for naturalisation in Ireland*. Dublin: Immigrant Council of Ireland.

ICI (2012) *Family reunification: a barrier or facilitator of integration – Ireland country report*. Dublin: Immigrant Council of Ireland. Available online from www.immigrantcouncil.ie/images/stories/Final_online_version_Ireland_country_report.pdf [Accessed 28 May 2013].

ILIR [Irish Lobby for Immigration Reform] (2006) 'ILIR testifies at Senate immigration hearings'. Available online from http://irishlobbyusa.org/ilir-testifies-at-senate-immigration-hearings/ [Accessed 10 July 2014].

ILIR (2013) 'About us'. Available online from http://irishlobbyusa.org/ [Accessed 19 June 2013].

IMO (2013) 'NCHDs – boarding passes at the ready?' Available online from www.imo.ie/specialty/nchd/boarding-passes-at-the-re/index.xml [Accessed 8 May 2013].

INIS (2013) 'News and events'. Available online from www.inis.gov.ie/en/INIS/Pages/News%20and%20Events [Accessed 18 June 2013].

INIS (2014) 'Visa decisions 10/6/14 to 16/6/14'. Available online from www.inis.gov.ie/en/INIS/Visa%20Decisions%2010-06-14%20to%2016-06-14.pdf/Files/Visa%20Decisions%2010-06-14%20to%2016-06-14.pdf [Accessed 22 June 2014].

Integration Centre (2012) *Roadmap to Integration 2012*. Dublin: The Integration Centre. Available online from www.integrationcentre.ie/getattachment/0e6de009-4a53-4049-96b5-5d7cc4222fc9/Roadmap-to-Integration-2012.aspx [Accessed 24 May 2013].

IOM (2013) 'Facts and figures: global estimates and trends'. Available online from www.iom.int/cms/en/sites/iom/home/about-migration/facts--figures-1.html [Accessed 27 February 2013].

Irish Examiner (2013) 'GAA delegates back anti-racism proposals', 23 March.

Irish Independent (2012) 'Australia welcomes over 1,300 new Irish citizens', 26 January.

Irish Times (2009) 'A symbolic landmark', 26 September, p. 17.

Irwin, J., McAreavey, R. and Murphy, N. (2014) *The economic and social mobility of ethnic minority groups in Northern Ireland*. Joseph Rowntree Foundation. Available online from www.jrf.org.uk/sites/files/jrf/ethnic-minorities-northern-ireland-full.pdf [Accessed 25 June 2014].

Jaichand, V. (2010) *Riding along with racism*. Irish Centre for Human Rights, NUI Galway. Available online from www.nuigalway.ie/human_rights/documents/galway_taxi_industry_report__riding_along_with_racism.pdf [Accessed 5 May 2013].

Jandl, M. (2012) 'Methods, approaches and data sources for estimating stocks of irregular migrants', *International Migration*, 49:5, 53–77.

Jordan, G. and Singh, S. (2011) 'On an island without sun: coping strategies of Sikhs in Ireland', *Journal of Intercultural Studies*, 32:4, 407–32.

Joyce, C. (2010) *Annual Policy Report on Migration and Asylum 2009: Ireland*. Available online from http://emn.ie/files/p_201011141041032010_AnnualReportStatisticsIreland2009.pdf [Accessed 4 June 2013].

Joyce, C. (2011) *Annual Policy Report 2010: Ireland*. Dublin: EMN Ireland.

Available online from http://emn.ie/files/p_201205080300452010_Annual%20Policy%20Report_April2012.pdf [Accessed 4 June 2013].

Joyce, C. (2012a) *Annual Policy Report on Migration and Asylum 2011: Ireland*. Dublin: EMN Ireland. Available online from http://emn.ie/files/p_201303261240352011_Annual%20Policy%20Report%20on%20Migration%20and%20Asylum_Mar2013.pdf [Accessed 4 June 2013].

Joyce, C. (2012b) *Misuse of the right to family reunification: Ireland. EMN focussed study*. Dublin: EMN Ireland. Available online from http://emn.ie/files/p_201208201207172012_Misuse%20of%20the%20Right%20to%20Family%20Reunification%20Ireland.pdf [Accessed 31 May 2013].

Kallen, J. (2010) 'Changing landscapes: language, space and policy in the Dublin linguistic landscape', in A. Jaworski and C. Thurlow (eds) *Semiotic landscapes: language, image, space*. London and New York: Continuum, pp. 41–58.

Kathiravelu, L. (2013) 'Friendship and the urban encounter: towards a research agenda'. MMG Working Paper 13-10. Göttingen: Max Planck Institute for the Study of Religious and Ethnic Diversity. Available online from www.mmg.mpg.de/fileadmin/user_upload/documents/wp/WP_13-10_Kathiravelu_Friendship.pdf [Accessed 30 June 2014].

Katz, C. (2001) 'On the grounds of globalization: a topography for feminist political engagement', *Signs*, 26:4, 1213–34.

Keane, J.B. (1976) *The Field: a play in three acts*. Dublin: Mercier Press.

Kelly, M. (2005) 'Immigration related detention in Ireland: a research report for the Irish Refugee Council, the Irish Penal Reform Trust and Immigrant Council of Ireland'. Available online from www.iprt.ie/files/immigrationre-lated_detention_report.pdf [Accessed 19 June 2013].

Kelly, P.F. (2012) 'Labor, movement: migration, mobility and geographies of work', in T.J. Barnes, J. Peck and E. Sheppard (eds) *The Wiley-Blackwell Companion to Economic Geography*. Chichester, West Sussex: Wiley-Blackwell, pp. 431–43.

Kenny, C. (2012a) 'Record high of 87,000 left State in year to April', *Irish Times*, 28 September, p. 11.

Kenny, C. (2012b) 'Emigration: the parents' experience', *Irish Times*, 11 May. Available online from www.irishtimes.com/blogs/generationemigration/2012/05/11/emigration-the-parents-experience/ [Accessed 29 May 2013].

Kenny, C. (2013) 'Destination focus: west is now best in Australia; a cooling economy and new skills shortages have changed the Irish emigrant experience in Australia', *Irish Times*, 17 May, Features p. 13.

Kerr, A., King O'Riain, R. and Titley, G. (2013) 'Transnational media networks and the "migration nation"', in M. Gilmartin and A. White (eds) *Migrations: Ireland in a global world*. Manchester: Manchester University Press, pp. 98–114.

Kilkey, M., Plomien, A. and Perrons, D. (2014) 'Migrant men's fathering narratives, practices and projects in national and transnational spaces: recent Polish male migrants to London', *International Migration*, 52:1, 178–91.

King, R. (2012) 'Geography and migration studies: retrospect and prospect', *Population, Space and Place*, 18:2, 134–53.

King, R. and Raghuram, P. (2013) 'International student migration: mapping the field and new research agendas', *Population, Space and Place*, 19:2, 127–37.

King O'Riain, R. (2007) 'Counting on the Celtic Tiger: adding ethnic census categories in the Republic of Ireland', *Ethnicities*, 7:4, 516–42.

King O'Riain, R. (2013) '"Skype is home!" Transnational families, transconnectivity and emotional streaming'. Unpublished working paper.

Kinlen, L. (2011) 'Welcome to Ireland: seeking protection as an asylum seeker or through resettlement – different avenues, different reception', *Refuge*, 28:2, 31–47.

Kneafsey, M. and Cox, R. (2002) 'Food, gender and Irishness: how Irish women in Coventry make home', *Irish Geography*, 35:1, 6–15.

Kockel, U. (1991) 'Counter-cultural migrants in the west of Ireland', in R. King (ed.) *Contemporary Irish migration*. Dublin: Geographical Society of Ireland, Special Series No. 6, pp. 70–82.

Kofman, E. (2004) 'Family-related migration: a critical review of European Studies', *Journal of Ethnic and Migration Studies*, 30:2, 243–62.

Kofman, E., Kraler, A., Kohli, M. and Schmoll, C. (2013) 'Introduction: issues and debates on family-related migration and the migrant family: a European perspective', in A. Kraler, E. Kofman, M. Kohli and C. Schmoll (eds) *Gender, generations and the family in international migration*. Amsterdam: Amsterdam University Press, pp. 13–54.

Krings, T., Bobek, A., Moriarty, E., Salamonska, J. and Wickham, J. (2009) 'Migration and recession: Polish migrants in post-Celtic Tiger Ireland', *Sociological Research Online*, 14:2. DOI:10.5153/sro.19279.

Krings, T., Bobek, A., Moriarty, E., Salamonska, J. and Wickham, J. (2013a) 'Polish migration to Ireland: "free movers" in the new European mobility space', *Journal of Ethnic and Migration Studies*, 39:1, 87–103.

Krings, T., Moriarty, E., Wickham, J., Bobek, A. and Salamonska, J. (2013b) *New mobilities in Europe: Polish migration to Ireland post-2004*. Manchester: Manchester University Press.

Law, A.O. (2002) 'The diversity visa lottery: a cycle of unintended consequences in United States immigration policy', *Journal of American Ethnic History*, 21:4, 3–29.

Ledwith, V. and Reilly, K. (2013a) 'Two tiers emerging? School choice and educational achievement disparities among young migrants and non-migrants in Galway City and urban fringe', *Population, Space and Place*, 19:1, 46–59.

Ledwith, V. and Reilly, K. (2013b) 'Accommodating all applicants? School choice and the regulation of enrolment in Ireland', *The Canadian Geographer / Le Géographe canadien*, 57:3, 318–26.

Lee, J. (2012) 'US Naturalizations: 2011'. Department of Homeland Security Office of Immigration Statistics. Available online from www.dhs.gov/xlibrary/assets/statistics/publications/natz_fr_2011.pdf [Accessed 1 March 2013].

Lentin, A. and Titley, G. (2011) *The crises of multiculturalism: racism in a neo-liberal age*. London: Zed Books.

Lentin, R. (2007a) 'Ireland: racial state and crisis racism', *Ethnic and Racial Studies*, 30:4, 610–27.

Lentin, R. (2007b) 'Illegal in Ireland, Irish illegals: diaspora nation as racial state', *Irish Political Studies*, 22:4, 433–53.

Lentin, R. and McVeigh, R. (eds) (2002) *Racism and anti-racism in Ireland*. Belfast: Beyond The Pale.

Lentin, R. and McVeigh, R. (2006) *After optimism? Ireland, racism and globalisation*. Dublin: Metro Éireann Publications.

Lentin, R. and Moreo, E. (eds) (2012) *Migrant activism and integration from below in Ireland*. Basingstoke: Palgrave Macmillan.

Leonard, M. (2005) 'Performing identities: music and dance in the Irish communities of Coventry and Liverpool', *Social & Cultural Geography*, 6:4, 515–29.

Levy, A. (1996) *Never far from nowhere*. London: Headline Review.

Levy, A. (2004) *Small island*. London: Headline Review.

Lewis, P. (1979) 'Axioms for reading the landscape', in D. Meinig (ed.) *The interpretation of ordinary landscapes: geographical essays*. New York: Oxford University Press, pp. 11–32.

Lewyzka, M. (2006) *A short history of tractors in Ukrainian*. London: Penguin.

Ley, D. (2010) *Millionaire migrants: trans-Pacific life lines*. Oxford: Wiley-Blackwell.

Loyal, S. (2011) *Understanding immigration in Ireland: state, labour and capital in a global age*. Manchester: Manchester University Press.

Luibhéid, E. (2013) *Pregnant on arrival: making the illegal immigrant*. Minneapolis: University of Minnesota Press.

McAleer, M.-C. (2013) *Time to go? A qualitative research study exploring the experience and impact of emigration on Ireland's youth*. Dublin: National Youth Council of Ireland. Available online from www.youth.ie/sites/youth.ie/files/NYCI_Youth_Emigration_Report.pdf [Accessed 10 May 2013].

Mac Amhlaigh, D. (2003) *An Irish navvy: the diary of an exile* (trans. Valentin Iremonger). Cork: The Collins Press.

McAnallen, D., Mossey, P. and Moore, S. (2007) 'The "temporary diaspora" at play: the development of Gaelic Games in British universities', *Sport in Society: Cultures, Commerce, Media, Society*, 10:3, 402–24.

McCarthy, N. (2007) 'Enacting Irish identity in Western Australia: performances from the dressing room', *Sport in Society: Cultures, Commerce, Media, Society*, 10:3, 368–84.

McCourt, F. (1996) *Angela's ashes*. New York: Scribner's.

McDermott, P. (2012) 'Cohesion, sharing and integration? Migrant languages and cultural spaces in Northern Ireland's urban environment', *Current Issues in Language Planning*, 13:3, 187–205.

McDowell, L. (2009) 'Old and new European economic migrants: whiteness and managed migration policies', *Journal of Ethnic and Migration Studies*, 35:1, 19–36.

McGahern, J. (2002) *That they may face the rising sun*. London: Faber and Faber.

McGinnity, F. and Lunn, P. (2011) 'Measuring discrimination facing ethnic minority job applicants: an Irish experiment', *Work, Employment and Society*, 25:4, 693–708.

McGinnity, F., O'Connell, P.J., Quinn, E. and Williams, J. (2006) *Migrants' experience of racism and discrimination in Ireland: survey report*. Dublin: ESRI.

McGovern, M. (2002) 'The craic market: Irish theme bars and the commodification of Irish identity in contemporary British society', *Irish Journal of Sociology*, 11:2, 77–98.

McGovern, M. (2003) '"The cracked pint glass of the servant": the Irish pub, Irish identity and the tourist eye', in M. Cronin and B. O'Connor (eds) *Irish tourism: image, culture and identity*. Clevedon: Channel View Publications, pp. 83–103.

McGreevy, R. (2012) 'Thousands pledge loyalty in Irish citizenship ceremonies', *Irish Times*, 16 October, p. 7.

McKenzie, D. (2007) 'Paper walls are easier to tear down: passport costs and legal barriers to emigration', *World Development*, 35:11, 2026–39.

Maguire, M. and Murphy, F. (2012) *Integration in Ireland: the everyday lives of African migrants*. Manchester: Manchester University Press.

Maguire, M. and Murphy, F. (2013) 'Neoliberalism, securitization and racialization in the Irish taxi industry', *European Journal of Cultural Studies*, 17:3, 282–97.

Mancini, J. and Finlay, G. (2008) '"Citizenship matters": lessons from the Irish Citizenship Referendum', *American Quarterly*, 60:3, 575–99.

Marrow, H. (2013) 'In Ireland "Latin Americans are kind of cool": evaluating a national context of reception with a transnational lens', *Ethnicities*, 13:5, 645–66.

Marston, S. (2002) 'Making difference: conflict over Irish identity in the New York City St. Patrick's Day parade', *Political Geography*, 21:3, 373–92.

Massey, D. (1991) 'A global sense of place', *Marxism Today*, 38, 24–9.

Massey, D. (2005) *For space*. London: Sage.

MCRI [Migration and Citizenship Research Initiative] (2008) *Getting on: from migration to integration – Chinese, Indian, Lithuanian and Nigerian migrants' experiences in Ireland*. Dublin: Immigrant Council of Ireland.

Medical Council (2004) *Review of medical schools in Ireland, 2003*. Dublin: Medical Council. Available online from www.medicalcouncil.ie/News-and-Publications/Publications/Education-Training/Review-of-Medical-Schools-in-Ireland-2003.pdf [Accessed 8 May 2013].

Mehran, M. (2006) *Pomegranate soup*. New York: Random House.

Mehran, M. (2008) *Rosewater and soda bread*. London, New York, Sydney and Auckland: Fourth Estate.

Merrill, H. (2006) *An alliance of women: immigration and the politics of race.* Minneapolis: University of Minnesota Press.

Migge, B. (2012) 'Irish English and recent immigrants to Ireland', in B. Migge and M. Ní Chiosáin (eds) *New perspectives on Irish English.* Amsterdam: John Benjamins, pp. 311–26.

Migge, B. and Gilmartin, M. (2011) 'Migrants and healthcare: investigating patient mobility among migrants in Ireland', *Health & Place*, 17:5, 1144–9.

Migge, B. and Gilmartin, M. (2013) 'Unbounding migration studies: the intersections of language, space and time', in M. Gilmartin and A. White (eds) *Migrations: Ireland in a global world.* Manchester: Manchester University Press, pp. 199–212.

Migge, B. and Ní Chiosáin, M. (eds) (2012) *New perspectives on Irish English.* Amsterdam: John Benjamins.

Miller, K. (1985) *Emigrants and exiles: Ireland and the Irish exodus to North America.* New York: Oxford University Press.

MIPEX (2010) 'Countries: Ireland'. Available online from www.mipex.eu/ireland [Accessed 19 May 2013].

Monahan, D. (2010) *Leaving Dublin.* Available online from http://thelilliputtion.blogspot.ie/search/label/Claire%20Weir [Accessed 28 March 2013].

Monmonier, M. (2005) 'Lying with maps', *Statistical Science*, 20:3, 215–22.

MRCI [Migrant Rights Centre Ireland] (2006) *Harvesting justice: mushroom workers call for change.* Dublin: MRCI. Available online from www.mrci.ie/publications/index.htm [Accessed October 2010].

MRCI (2007a) *Realising integration: migrant workers undertaking essential low paid work in Dublin City.* Dublin: MRCI. Available online from http://mrci.ie/wp-content/uploads/2012/10/Realising-Integration_Migrant-Workers-Undertaking-Essential-Low-Paid-Work-in-Dublin-City.pdf [Accessed 5 May 2013].

MRCI (2007b) *Life in the shadows: an exploration of irregular migration in Ireland.* Dublin: MRCI. Available online from http://mrci.ie/wp-content/uploads/2012/09/Life-in-the-Shadows-Exploration-of-Irregular-Migration-in-Ireland.pdf [Accessed 17 June 2013].

MRCI (2008) *Exploitation in Ireland's restaurant industry.* Dublin: MRCI. Available online from http://mrci.ie/wp-content/uploads/2012/10/Exploitation-in-Ireland%E2%80%99s-dECEMBER-2008.pdf [Accessed 26 September 2014].

MRCI (2012) *Who cares? The experience of migrant care workers in Ireland.* Dublin: MRCI. Available online from www.mrci.ie/wp-content/uploads/2012/12/Who-Cares-The-experience-of-Migrant-Care-Workers-in-Ireland-Nov-2012.pdf [Accessed 5 May 2013].

MRCI (n.d. a) 'Justice for the undocumented: living here. Working here. Belong here'. Available online from http://mrci.ie/wp-content/uploads/2012/09/Justice-for-the-Undocumented1.pdf [Accessed 17 June 2013].

MRCI (n.d. b) 'Earned regularisation scheme: how would it work?' Available online from http://mrci.ie/wp-content/uploads/2012/09/How-Earned-Regu larisation-would-Work.pdf [Accessed 19 June 2013].

Mullally, S. (2011) 'Citizen children, "impossible subjects," and the limits of migrant family rights in Ireland', *European Human Rights Law Review*, 1, 43–54. Available online from http://papers.ssrn.com/sol3/papers. cfm?abstract_id=1689591 [Accessed 28 May 2013].

Mulligan, A. (2008) 'Countering exclusion: the "St Pats for All" parade', *Gender, Place & Culture*, 15:2, 153–67.

Murray, T. (2012) *London Irish fictions: narrative, diaspora and identity.* Liverpool: Liverpool University Press.

NCCRI [National Consultative Committee on Racism and Interculturalism] (2008) 'NCCRI Six Monthly Racist Incidents Reports'. Available online from www.nccri.ie/incidents-reports.html [Accessed 3 May 2013].

Near TV (2012) 'What Gaelic Games mean to us'. Video. Available online from www.youtube.com/watch?v=I9rYYwbPFFI [Accessed 27 September 2013].

Neligan, M. (2009) 'Letter sums up the plight of our medical exiles', *Irish Times*, 6 October, p. A5.

Nestor, N. and Regan, V. (2011) 'The new kid on the block: a case study of young Poles, language and identity', in M. Darmody, N. Tyrrell and S. Song (eds) *The changing faces of Ireland*. Rotterdam: Sense Publishers, pp. 35–52.

Ní Laoire, C. (2001) 'A matter of life and death? Men, masculinities and staying "behind" in rural Ireland', *Sociologia Ruralis*, 41:2, 220–36.

Ní Laoire, C. (2002) 'Discourses of nation among migrants from Northern Ireland: Irishness, Britishness and the spaces in-between', *Scottish Geographical Journal*, 118:3, 183–99.

Ní Laoire, C. (2007) 'The "green green grass of home"? Return migration to rural Ireland', *Journal of Rural Studies*, 23:3, 332–44.

Ní Laoire, C. (2008) '"Settling back"? A biographical and life-course perspective on Ireland's recent return migration', *Irish Geography*, 41:2, 195–210.

Ní Laoire, C., Carpena-Méndez, F., Tyrrell, N. and White, A. (2011) *Childhood and migration in Europe: portraits of mobility, identity and belonging in contemporary Ireland.* Farnham: Ashgate.

Nititham, D.S. (2011) 'Filipinos articulations of community', in B. Fanning and R. Munck (eds) *Globalization, migration and social transformation: Ireland in Europe and the world*. Farnham: Ashgate, pp. 51–64.

Nolan, J.A. (1989) *Ourselves alone: women's emigration from Ireland, 1885–1920.* Lexington: University of Kentucky Press.

NOMIS (2013) 'Country of birth by year of arrival in the UK (regional)'. Available online from www.nomisweb.co.uk/census/2011/DC2804EWr [Accessed 5 June 2013].

Nowlan, E. (2008) 'Underneath the Band-Aid: supporting bilingual students in Irish schools', *Irish Educational Studies*, 27(3): 253–66.

O'Boyle, N. (2012) 'Becoming local: immigrant candidates in Irish politics', *Observatorio*, 6:2, 51–70.

O'Brien, D. (2010) 'The export of our children makes a return', *Irish Times*, 22 September, p. 18.

O'Brien, S. and Long, F. (2012) 'Mathematics as (multi)cultural practices: Irish lessons from the Polish weekend school', *American Journal of Mathematics*, 5:2, 133–56.

O'Carroll, C. (2005) 'Community, belonging and desire in Irish pubs in Berlin', in T.M. Wilson (ed.) *Drinking cultures*. Oxford and New York: Berg, pp. 43–78.

O'Connell, P.J. and McGinnity, F. (2008) *Immigrants at work: ethnicity and nationality in the Irish labour market*. Dublin: Equality Authority/ESRI. Available online from www.esri.ie/publications/search_for_a_publication/search_results/view/index.xml?id=2608 [Accessed 5 May 2013].

O'Connor, P. (2011) *A parish far from home*. Dublin: Gill & Macmillan.

O'Connor, P. (2013) '(Re)negotiating belonging: the Irish in Australia', in M. Gilmartin and A. White (eds) *Migrations: Ireland in a global world*. Manchester: Manchester University Press, pp. 147–63.

O'Donoghue, J. (1999) *Dáil Debates*, Vol. 500, No. 1, 9 February. Available online from http://debates.oireachtas.ie/dail/1999/02/09/00021.asp#N4 [Accessed 27 September 2013].

O'Farrell, M. (2013) *Instructions for a heatwave*. London: Tinder Press.

Office of the Minister for Integration (2008) 'Migration nation: statement on integration strategy and diversity management'. Available online from www.integration.ie/website/omi/omiwebv6.nsf/page/AXBN-7SQDF91044205-en/$File/Migration%20Nation.PDF [Accessed 27 September 2013].

Office for the Promotion of Migrant Integration (2013) 'Learning English'. Available online from www.integration.ie/website/omi/omiwebv6.nsf/page/infoformigrants-learningenglish-en [Accessed 18 May 2013].

O'Kane, K. (2013) 'GAA chiefs pursue own anti-racism motion', *Irish Star*, 31 January.

Olwig, K.F. (2012) 'The care chain, children's mobility and the Caribbean migration tradition', *Journal of Ethnic and Migration Studies*, 38:6, 933–52.

O'Neill, M. (2010) *Asylum, migration and community*. Bristol: Policy Press.

ORAC [Office of the Refugee Applications Commissioner] (2002) 'Annual Report 2002'. Available online from www.orac.ie/website/orac/oracwebsite.nsf/page/CRSE-8XZGEW13172610-en/$File/ORAC-2002.pdf [Accessed 18 June 2013].

ORAC (2010) 'Monthly statistical report, December 2010'. Available online from www.orac.ie/website/orac/oracwebsite.nsf/page/orac-stats-en [Accessed 5 May 2013].

ORAC (2012) 'Monthly statistical report, December 2012'. Available online from www.orac.ie/website/orac/oracwebsite.nsf/page/orac-stats-en [Accessed 5 May 2013].

ORAC (2013) 'Annual statistics 2013'. Available online from www.orac.ie/website/orac/oracwebsite.nsf/page/orac-stats_13-en [Accessed 4 July 2014].

O'Reilly, Z. (2013) '"In between spaces": experiences of asylum seekers in the 'direct provision' system in Ireland'. Unpublished PhD thesis, National University of Ireland Maynooth.

O'Shea, H. (2008a) '"Good man, Mary!" Women musicians and the fraternity of Irish traditional music', *Journal of Gender Studies*, 17:1, 55–70.

O'Shea, H. (2008b) *The making of Irish traditional music*. Cork: Cork University Press.

O'Sullivan, D. (2012) 'A critical analysis of the protection of families under the Irish Constitution of 1937', *Cork Online Law Review*, 11, 1–11. Available online from http://corkonlinelawreview.com/editions/2012/ACriticalAnalysisOfTheProtectionOfFamiliesUnderTheIrishConstitutionOf1937.DonnachaOSullivan.pdf [Accessed 28 May 2013].

Parutis, V. (2014) '"Economic migrants" or "middling transnationals"? East European migrants' experiences of work in the UK', *International Migration*, 52:1, 36–55.

Peel, V. and Steen, A. (2007) 'Victims, hooligans and cash-cows: media representations of the international backpacker in Australia', *Tourism Management*, 28, 1057–67.

Phillips, D. (2006) 'Parallel lives? Challenging discourses of British Muslim self-segregation', *Environment and Planning D*, 24, 25–40.

Pillinger, J. (2007) *The feminisation of migration: experiences and opportunities in Ireland*. Dublin: Immigrant Council of Ireland.

Potter, M. and Hamilton, J. (2014) 'Picking on vulnerable migrants: precarity and the mushroom industry in Northern Ireland', *Work, employment and society*, 28:3, 390–406.

Pratt, G. (2012) *Families apart: migrant mothers and the conflicts of labor and love*. Minneapolis and London: University of Minnesota Press.

Pred, A. (2000) *Even in Sweden: racisms, racialized spaces, and the popular geographical imagination*. Berkeley, Los Angeles and London: University of California Press.

Quinn, E. (2007) *Policy analysis report on asylum and migration: Ireland 2006*. Dublin: ESRI. Available online from http://emn.ie/files/p_20100715113311Policy%20analysis%20report%20on%20Migration%20and%20Asylum%202006.pdf [Accessed 27 September 2013].

Ralph, D. (2009) '"Home is where the heart is": understandings of home among Irish-born return migrants from the United States', *Irish Studies Review*, 17:2, 183–200.

Ralph, D. (2012) 'Managing sameness and difference: the politics of belonging among Irish-born return migrants from the United States', *Social & Cultural Geography*, 13:5, 445–60.

Ralph, D. (2015) '"Always on the move, but going nowhere fast": motivations for "Euro-commuting" between the Republic of Ireland and other EU states', *Journal of Ethnic and Migration Studies*, 41:2, 176–95.

Ralph, D. and Staeheli, L. (2011) 'Home and migration: mobilities, belongings and identities', *Geography Compass*, 5:7, 517–30.

Ravenstein, E.J. (1885) 'The laws of migration', *Journal of the Statistical Society of London*, 48:2, 167–235.

Ravenstein, E.J. (1889) 'The laws of migration', *Journal of the Royal Statistical Society*, 52:2, 241–305.

RTÉ (2003) The Marian Finucane Show. Broadcast on RTÉ Radio 1, 16 October.

RTÉ (2004) Morning Ireland. Broadcast on RTÉ Radio 1, 22 April.

Russell, H., McGinnity, F., Quinn, E. and King-O'Riain, R. (2010) 'The experience of discrimination in Ireland: evidence from self-report data', in L. Bond, F. McGinnity and H. Russell (eds) *Making equality count: Irish and international research measuring equality and discrimination*. Dublin: Liffey Press, pp. 20–47.

Ryan, D., Benson, C.A. and Dooley, B.A. (2008) 'Psychological distress and the asylum process: a longitudinal study of forced migrants in Ireland', *Journal of Nervous and Mental Disease*, 196:1, 37–45.

Ryan, L. (2003) 'Moving spaces and changing places: Irish women's memories of emigration to Britain in the 1930s', *Journal of Ethnic and Migration Studies*, 29:1, 67–82.

Ryan, L. (2004) 'Family matters: (e)migration, familial networks, and Irish women in Britain', *The Sociological Review*, 52:3, 351–70.

Ryan, L. (2007a) 'Migrant women, social networks and motherhood: the experiences of Irish nurses in Britain', *Sociology*, 41:2, 295–312.

Ryan, L. (2007b) 'Who do you think you are? Irish nurses encountering ethnicity and constructing identity in Britain', *Journal of Ethnic and Racial Studies*, 30:3, 416–38.

Ryan, L. (2008) 'Navigating the emotional terrain of families "here" and "there": women, migration and the management of emotions', *Journal of Intercultural Studies*, 29:3, 299–313.

Sadowski-Smith, C. (2008) 'Unskilled labor migration and the illegality spiral: Chinese, European and Mexican indocumentados in the United States, 1882–2007', *American Quarterly*, 60:3, 779–804.

Samers, M. (2010) *Migration*. Abingdon and New York: Routledge.

SARI (2013) 'Media coverage'. Available online from www.sari.ie/media-cover age/ [Accessed 30 May 2014].

Saunders, A. (2010) 'Literary geographies: reforging the connections', *Progress in Human Geography*, 34:4, 436–52.

Scahill, A. (2009) 'Riverdance: representing Irish traditional music', *New Hibernia Review*, 13:2, 70–6.

Schacar, A. (2009) *The birthright lottery: citizenship and global inequality*. Cambridge, MA: Harvard University Press.

Scharbrodt, O. (2012) 'Muslim immigration to the Republic of Ireland: trajectories and dynamics since World War II', *Éire–Ireland*, 47:1–2, 221–43.

Schönwaldër, K. and Bloemraad, I. (2013) 'Extending urban democracy? The immigrant presence in European electoral politics', *European Political Science*, 12, 448–54.

Scully, M. (2009) '"Plastic and proud"? Discourses of authenticity among the second-generation Irish in England', *Psychology & Society*, 2:2, 124–35.

Scully, M. (2012) 'The tyranny of transnational discourse: "authenticity" and Irish diasporic identity in Ireland and England', *Nations and Nationalisms*, 18:2, 191–209.

Scully, M. (2013) 'BIFFOs, jackeens and Dagenham yanks: county identity, "authenticity" and the Irish diaspora', *Irish Studies Review*, 21:2, 143–63.

Share, M. and Kerrins, L. (2009) 'The role of grandparents in childcare in Ireland: towards a research agenda', *Irish Journal of Applied Social Studies*, 9:1, 33–47.

Shatter, A. (2013a) *Dáil Debates* 789(1), Written Answer 474. 22 January. Available online from http://oireachtasdebates.oireachtas.ie/debates%20 authoring/debateswebpack.nsf/takes/dail2013012200074?opendocument [Accessed 18 March 2013].

Shatter, A. (2013b) Parliamentary question: written Answer no. 254. 27 March. Available online from http://oireachtasdebates.oireachtas.ie/debates%20 authoring/debateswebpack.nsf/takes/dail2013032700086?opendocument# WRZ00750 [Accessed 18 June 2013].

Shatter, A. (2013c) Parliamentary question: written Answer no. 49. 13 June. Available online from http://oireachtasdebates.oireachtas.ie/debates%20 authoring/debateswebpack.nsf/takes/dail2013061300046?opendocument# WRE00950 [Accessed 20 June 2013].

Sibun, J. (2012) 'Interview: Declan Collier, chief executive of London City Airport', *The Telegraph*, 10 June.

Silvey, R. (2004) 'Transnational domestication: state power and Indonesian migrant women in Saudi Arabia', *Political Geography*, 23:3, 245–64.

Simpson, L. (2007) 'Ghettos of the mind: the empirical behaviour of indices of segregation and diversity', *Journal of the Royal Statistical Society: series A*, 170, 405–24.

Smith, A. (2013) 'Betwixt, between and belonging: negotiating identity and place in asylum seeker direct provision accommodation centres', in M. Gilmartin and A. White (eds) *Migrations: Ireland in a global world*. Manchester: Manchester University Press, pp. 164–80.

Smith, A. (2014) 'Immediate and short-term housing experiences and situations of Polish newcomers to Dublin, Ireland', *Journal of Housing and the Built Environment*. DOI 10.1007/s10901-014-9399-0.

Smith, Z. (2000) *White teeth*. London: Hamish Hamilton.

Smyth, J. (2011a) 'Government to bring in citizenship ceremony after successful pilot event', *Irish Times*, 25 June, p. 6.

Smyth, J. (2011b) 'New Irish citizens will have to swear oath of fidelity', *Irish Times*, 17 June, p. 9.

Solnit, R. (1998) *A book of migrations: some passages in Ireland*. London and New York: Verso.

Spencer, S. (2010) 'Wheels of the world: how recordings of Irish traditional music bridged the gap between homeland and diaspora', *Journal of the Society for American Music*, 4:4, 437–49.

Spiro, P.J. (2006) 'Perfecting political diaspora', *New York University Law Review*, 81:XXX, 101–25.

Sterne, E.S. (2004) *Ballots and Bibles: ethnic politics and the Catholic Church in Providence*. Ithaca, NY: Cornell University Press.

Sullivan, T. (2012) '"I want to be all I can Irish": the role of performance and performativity in the construction of ethnicity', *Social & Cultural Geography*, 13:5, 429–44.

The Convention on the Constitution (2013) 'Submissions: Voting Rights'. Available online from www.constitution.ie/Submissions.aspx [Accessed 21 June 2013].

The Gathering (2013) 'About The Gathering Ireland 2013'. Available online from www.thegatheringireland.com/About.aspx#.USyGEutFpUs [Accessed 26 February 2013].

Tilki, M. (2006) 'The social contexts of drinking among Irish men in Britain', *Drugs: Education, Prevention and Policy*, 13:3, 247–61.

Titley, G. (2012) 'Getting integration right: media transnationalism and domopolitics in Ireland', *Ethnic and Racial Studies*, 35:5, 817–33.

Tolia-Kelly, D. (2010) *Landscape, race and memory: material ecologies of citizenship*. Farnham: Ashgate.

Toyota, M., Yeoh, B.S.A. and Nguyen, L. (2007) 'Bringing the "left behind" back into view in Asia: a framework for understanding the "migration–left behind nexus"', *Population, Space and Place*, 13:3, 157–61.

Ugba, A. (2009) 'A part of and apart from society? Pentecostal Africans in the "New Ireland"'. *Translocations*, 4:1, 86–101. Available online from: www.translocations.ie/docs/v04i01/Vol_4_Issue_1_Abel_Ugba.pdf [Accessed 3 May 2013].

Ulin, J.V., Edwards, H. and O'Brien, S. (eds) (2013) *Race and immigration in the new Ireland*. Indiana: University of Notre Dame.

Vertovec, S. (2007) 'Super-diversity and its implications', *Ethnic and Racial Studies*, 30:6, 1024–54.

Vossensteyn, H., Beerkens, M., Cremonini, L., Huisman, J., Souto-Otero, M., Bresancon, B., Focken, N., Leurs, B., McCoshan, A., Mozuraityte, N., Pimentel Bótas, P.C. and de Wit, H. (2010) *Improving participation in the Erasmus programme: final report to the European Parliament*. Available online from www.europarl.europa.eu/committees/en/studies.html#studies [Accessed 5 May 2013].

Walls, P. (2005) *Still leaving. Recent vulnerable Irish emigrants to the UK: profile, experiences and pre-departure solutions*. Dublin: Department of Foreign Affairs.

Walsh, K. (2006) 'British expatriate belongings: mobile homes and transnational homing', *Home Cultures*, 3:2, 123–44.

Walsh, K. (2011) 'Migrant masculinities and domestic space: British home-making practices in Dubai', *Transactions of the Institute of British Geographers*, 36:4, 516–29.

Walter, B. (1998) 'Challenging the black/white binary: the need for an Irish category in the 2001 Census', *Patterns of Prejudice*, 32:2, 73–86.

Walter, B. (2001) *Outsiders inside: whiteness, place and Irish women*. London: Routledge.

Walter, B. (2008a) 'From "flood" to "trickle": Irish migration to Britain 1987–2006', *Irish Geography*, 41:2, 181–94.

Walter, B. (2008b) 'Voices in other ears: "accents" and identities of the first- and second-generation Irish in England', in G. Rings and A. Ife (eds) *Neo-colonial mentalities in contemporary Europe? Language and discourse in the construction of identities*. Cambridge: Cambridge Scholars Publishing, pp. 174–82.

Walter, B. (2013a) 'Transnational networks across generations: childhood visits to Ireland by the second-generation in England', in M. Gilmartin and A. White (eds) *Migrations: Ireland in a global world*. Manchester: Manchester University Press, pp. 17–35.

Walter, B. (2013b) 'Personal lives: narrative accounts of Irish women in the diaspora', *Irish Studies Review*, 21:1, 37–54.

Watters, J. (2011) 'Migrant families in Ireland: understanding the cultural landscapes of transnational family life'. Unpublished PhD thesis, National University of Ireland Maynooth.

Whelan, K. (2006) 'Once born for export', *Irish Times*, 23 May, p. B2.

White, A. (2012) '"Every Wednesday I am happy": childhoods in an Irish asylum centre', *Population, Space and Place*, 18:3, 314–26.

White, A. and Gilmartin, M. (2008) 'Critical geographies of citizenship and belonging in Ireland', *Women's Studies International Forum*, 31:5, 390–9.

Williams, R. (1985) *Keywords: a vocabulary of culture and society* (revised edition). New York: Oxford University Press.

Wills, J., Datta, K., Evans, Y., Herbert, J., May, J. and McIlwaine, C. (2010) *Global cities at work: new migrant divisions of labour*. London: Pluto Press.

Wimmer, A. and Glick Schiller, N. (2002) 'Methodological nationalism and beyond: nation-state building, migration and the social sciences', *Global Networks*, 2:4, 301–34.

World Bank (2012) 'Migration and remittances'. Available online from http://go.worldbank.org/RR8SDPEHO0 [Accessed 5 March 2013].

Yeates, N. (2004a) 'Global care chains', *International Feminist Journal of Politics*, 6:3, 369–91.

Yeates, N. (2004b) 'A dialogue with "global care chain" analysis: nurse migration in the Irish context', *Feminist Review*, 77, 79–95.

Yuval-Davis, N. (2011) *The Politics of Belonging*. London: Sage Publications.

Index